INTERNATIONAL LAW IN THE WESTERN HEMISPHERE

INTERNATIONAL LAW IN THE WESTERN HEMISPHERE

Edited by

NIGEL S. RODLEY

C. NEALE RONNING

Prepared under the auspices of New York University Center for International Studies

Springer-Science+Business Media, B.V. 1974

Originally published by Martinus Nijhoff, The Hague, Netherlands

ISBN 978-94-011-8490-8 ISBN 978-94-011-9214-9 (eBook)
DOI 10.1007/978-94-011-9214-9

TABLE OF CONTENTS

PART III

HUMAN RIGHTS

CONTRIBUTORS

Dr. Robert D. Hayton

Associate Dean of Graduate Studies, Hunter College of the City University of New York;

Technical Director, United Nations Panel of Experts on the Legal and Institutional Implications of International Water Resources Development.

Dr. José María Ruda

Under-Secretary of Foreign Relations, Argentina; Member, International Law Commission of the United Nations.

Atwood C. Wolf, Jr.

Of the New York Bar

Dr. Douglas M. Johnston

Professor of Law and Political Economy, University of Toronto.

Dr. F. V. García-Amador

Chief, Department of Legal Affairs, Organisation of American States.

Dr. Thomas M. Franck

Professor of Law and Director, Center for International Studies, New York University.

Dr. Edward Weisband

Assistant Professor of Political Science and Associate Director, Center for International Studies, New York University.

Nigel S. Rodley

Research Fellow, Center for International Studies, New York University; Visiting Lecturer of Political Science, Graduate Faculty, New School for Social Research.

Dr. Arthur W. Rovine

Department of Government, Cornell University.

Detlev F. Vagts
Professor of Law, Harvard University.

Dr. A. J. Thomas, Jr.
Professor of Law, Southern Methodist University.

Dr. Ann Van Wynen Thomas
Assistant Professor of Political Science, Southern Methodist University

Dr. C. Neale Ronning
Professor of Political Science, Graduate Faculty, New School for Social Research.

PREFACE

The essays and commentaries in this collection were presented at a Conference on Problems of International Law in the Western Hemisphere, the Second Conference on Problems of Regional International Law under the joint sponsorship of the American Society of International Law and the Graduate Faculty of the New School for Social Research, April 2 & 3, 1971. Contributors have been given the opportunity to revise their papers since their original presentation.

The editors acknowledge with gratitude the important contributions made by the Chairmen of the respective panels, namely, Professor Louis Henkin of Columbia Law School (Water Resources Panel), Professor Richard B. Lillich of the University of Virginia Law School (Panel on Intervention) and Dr. Egon Schwelb of the United Nations (Human Rights Panel). The assistance of the Graduate Faculty of the New School for Social Research in the organization of the conference and that of the New York University Center for International Studies in the editing of these papers have been indispensable. We wish to make particular mention of the unstinting secretarial support of Ms. Donna Welensky and Ms. Judith Chazen. Certain problems would have been insuperable without the critical (in all senses) aid provided by Lyn Rodley.

The descriptions of contributors are those that obtained at the time of the conference. Since then, Professors Rovine and Rodley have moved to new pastures, the former to the Department of State's Office of the Legal Adviser, the latter to Amnesty International, while Dr. Ruda has been elevated to the bench of the International Court of Justice.

INTRODUCTION

Law and organization are instruments through which weaker units find a measure of protection in ordered domestic societies. By organizing into larger and more powerful groups they are better able to alter the structure of power in these societies and, having done so, they may then alter the legal system in order to serve their interests and objectives.

To a lesser extent the same processes are observable in our less ordered international society. In the Western Hemisphere we may observe these processes on a regional level where Latin American states in particular have attempted to use law and organization as instruments for their protection and in pursuit of national objectives.

Soon after independence many of the Latin American states were threatened by European powers who sought special privileges, the protection of their nationals or the collection of public debts. These conflicts usually had their roots in the political instability of the Latin American states, a situation which affected adversely the interests of European nationals. The European states relied not only on their greater power, but pointed to "generally accepted norms of international law" as well.

In response to this situation the idea of a regional system of law – an American international law, more in keeping with the needs and interests of the new states soon began to take shape. This seems to have been emphasized more in Latin America than in the United States where public and private jurists were more inclined to share views widely held in Western Europe and where political stability and general economic progress helped to avoid conflicts with the European powers.

The closing years of the 19th century found jurists throughout the world greatly concerned with the codification of international law and the establishment of institutions and procedures for international arbitration. The two were, of course, related: it was expected that the codification of international law would clarify and formalize general practice and make it possible to bring more questions within the scope of arbitration. Jurists and statesmen in the Western Hemisphere were very much a part of this worldwide trend and showed renewed interests in the development of regional norms and institutions.

The idea of American international law was at least implicit in the proposed agendas of early 19th century inter-American Congresses, including the Panama Congress of 1826. Although the conventions signed at these conferences failed to receive the necessary ratifications, they were clearly a reflection of a widespread interest in establishing regional norms to meet specific regional problems.

At the Second Inter-American Conference (1901-1902) a treaty was signed authorizing a commission of five American and two European jurists to codify American international law and submit the code to the American governments for their approval. Other bodies were created for this purpose at subsequent inter-American conferences until the idea was permanently institutionalized with the formation of the Inter-American Council of Jurists (originally the Inter-American Neutrality Committee, 1940) and the Inter-American Juridical Committee (1948). In one way or another, "codes of American international law," in the form of drafts of multilateral conventions, have been presented for discussion and signature at each of the general inter-American conferences.

Insofar as legal norms are a means of protection for the weaker members of the international community, the Latin American states, in view of their members, theoretically have it within their power to create norms reflecting their interests as small powers. The fact is, however, that there have been few conventions which might clearly be said to reflect Latin American interests and to be contrary to the interests of the United States and other great powers. There are several reasons for this. First, Latin American diplomats have recognized that "law" which strays too far from the realities of power becomes a mere exercise in futility. Thus, they have been reluctant to use their greater numbers as "juridical equals" to write codes which would not be recognized even formally as law by the most powerful members of the international community. Second, the fact that they have not dictated norms contrary to the interests of the United States is a reflection of the role of power in yet another way. Latin American economic and military dependence on the United States has meant that the latter can use pressure to discourage all but the most determined delegations (and their are fewer of these) from pursuing such a course of action. Finally, the assumption that small powers necessarily have a set of interests distinct from those of the great powers is clearly unjustified. As this collection of essays will show, there are issues in which interests cut across the line between the great and small powers and not because of any pressure on the latter by the former.

Latin American expressions of confidence in regional organization reached a high point in the short period between the Dumbarton Oaks Conference of 1944 and the San Francisco Conference of 1945. At that time, most Latin American diplomats publicly expressed their concern that American regional organizations would be replaced or eclipsed by the proposed United Nations Organization. The principle of universality emphasized in the Dumbarton Oaks documents could also be interpreted as a threat to regional autonomy and, thus, to regional legal systems.

Although the concern expressed was probably unfounded, some changes were made in the Charter in order to preserve the principle of regional organization. Nearly three decades later one could only say that neither the functions of the Organization of American States nor the development of American international law has been obstructed in any way by limitations imposed by the United Nations Charter. The 1950's and the early 1960's saw a great deal of activity directed toward the development of American codes relating to territorial waters, the continental shelf, the control or regulation of fisheries, the protection of human rights and the illusive question of intervention. The problems and issues involved in the development of these codes at the regional and universal levels are dealt with in several of the essays included here.

Of special interest to the student of international law and organization are the efforts of states to work for the development of legal norms at the regional and universal level simultaneously. We have already noted the traditional interest of Western Hemisphere states in the development of regional norms. But in the 1950's Latin American states also showed a growing interest in the United Nations as a forum for the development of codes of law. Important changes in the structure of the United Nations had much to do with this. In the 1950's the United Nations began to take on a new character when a large number of new states, former colonial areas, became members. Their presence became most obvious in the General Assembly which under Article 13 is charged with initiating studies and making recommendations for the purpose of encouraging the progressive development of international law and its codification. As former colonial dependencies, the new states shared many of the complaints of Latin American states with respect to their relations with the more developed part of the world and the legal norms supposedly regulating those relations. Thus, Latin Americans, who for more than a century had been about the only "underdeveloped" members of the community of independent states, now found themselves with many potential allies or sympathizers.

The similarity of interests among Latin American states and the so-called new states is often reflected in areas of agreement on territorial waters, fisheries, the expropriation of private property and intervention, all of which are dealt with in the essays that follow. These are clearly issues that transcend regional boundaries. On the one hand, they transcend regional boundaries in the sense that they involve states outside of a particular region. They also do so in the sense that all states in a given region do not necessarily see these issues in the same way while they might very well share the point of view of other states outside their region. Thus we see some Latin American states resorting to sub-regional efforts at creating law, as illustrated by the Santiago Declaration on Fisheries, at the same time that they pursue similar efforts within the United Nations.

In short, a study of regional international practice shows that: 1) there may be a community of interests in a region, identifiable as separate from other interests shared by states; 2) there may be conflicts of interest between large and small members, the interests of each being more analogous to those of states of comparable power outside the region; and, 3) even within the more homogeneous parts of a region, smaller groupings of states may find their vital interests best served by engaging in sub-regional cooperation. The essays that follow will confirm this.

The areas covered were chosen because they have assumed special significance in either intra- or inter-hemispheric relations. They do not possess an overarching unity, although there are areas of contact among all of them. Thus, a quite different expertise is required in assessing regional practice in international water resources management from that needed to define conflict over the status of foreign property. Similarly, human rights practices and procedures, possessing the special regional tradition that they do, demand yet a different perspective, having their primary focus in the relationship of the individual to his national government. Nevertheless, a concern for the conservation, protection and development of natural, industrial and human resources would find much of relevance in all those areas.

The classifications we have adopted suggest three groups of interests: ecological (Part I – Water Resources), super power hegemony (Part II – Super Power Intervention: Military and Economic), and the rights of individuals (Part III – Human Rights). But it would be well to bear the point of contact in mind. Thus, as Dr. Ruda shows, super power-small state conflicts are clearly present in the problems relating to the exploitation of the continental shelf and the seabed, just as they have been with respect to the development of an inter-American approach to the protection of human rights. Similarly, Professor Rodley suggests that the future development of the law of diplomatic protection of nationals abroad may best be seen in terms, not of the protection of multi-national enterprises (a traditional area of large state – small state friction) but of the international protection of human rights.

In Latin America as elsewhere, international rivers, when they have not merely provided a natural boundary to keep the countries they divide comfortably isolated from each other, have often been the cause of significant inter-state hostility. Professor Hayton, in his paper on *Non-Maritime International Water Resources: Development and Conservation in the Americas,* now shows the need for inter-state cooperation in the development of laws and institutions to permit the most effective and beneficial use of international water systems. Here primordially regional cooperation is a necessity, though perhaps the various mechanisms employed to secure such cooperation would be governed more by geographical than cultural/historical phenomena. Some progress has been made, particularly among the five states of the huge Plata Basin system, but Professor Hayton warns that key projects or programs have little possibility of materializing withing less than a generation: the time required for reconnaisance and testing and community building. The traditional Latin American antipathy to supra-national authority provides a substantial hurdle to be negotiated.

In his study of *The Outer Limit of the Continental Shelf,* Dr. Ruda addresses himself to what is one of the most important legal issues since World War II. The conflicts relate to arrangements for an equitable and rational sharing of the world's resources (with strong developed *versus* developing country undertones), the preservation of national security and the aggrandizement of national sovereignty. In Latin America the problem has become inextricably interwoven with the claims of several of those countries to exercise varying degrees of jurisdiction over their adjacent waters, up to 200 miles from their coasts. But they have conflicting interests among themselves; the Pacific coast states, with virtually no continental shelf, taking markedly different positions from those adopted by their Atlantic coast counterparts that have a huge one. Thus, by combining a 200-mile territorial sea claim with the formula contained in the 1958 Geneva Convention on the Continental Shelf, Argentina and Uruguay lay claim to parts of the seabed beyond 200 miles from their coasts. While Dr. Ruda's suggestion that, in the future, the limit of national jurisdiction should be at the termination of the continental shelf, or even of the continental slope, may be challenged, the issues he raises are of the greatest interest, in terms both of the eventual regime to be established for the exploitation of the seabed and of the nature of Western Hemispheric regional and sub-regional peculiarities.

Mr. Wolf's contribution, *The U.N. Declaration of Principles Governing the Deep Sea-Bed,* is a survey of the U.N.'s attempts to achieve a viable international regime with respect to the exploration and exploitation of the deep sea-bed. Clearly, such attempts will founder, unless some understanding is reached on the limits of national prerogatives. Accordingly, he is skeptical of regional approaches and challenges what he perceives as the attempts of some Western Hemisphere states to extend their authority over the sea, the sea-bed and its sub-soil virtually without limit. Perhaps next year's Caracas Conference will provide some solution. In any event, this paper shows that the Latin American states recognize that they must defend and secure acquiescence in their claims, in the larger world forum. For, unless non-regional states accept the regional assertions of authority, such assertions will remain no more than that.

Part II deals with the one issue where one might expect to find complete Latin American solidarity, namely, that of intervention and non-intervention. But solidarity has existed only with respect to the statement of a general rule or principle – and here, one might add, "law" has strayed farthest from the realities of power. "As naive as it might appear," remarks one student of Latin American affairs, "the main Latin American legal defense against paramount dominance has been through the doctrine of non-intervention – in other words, a frontal attack, outlawing, in effect, paramount dominance." * It must be added, however, that even the paramount power, the United States, has joined the Latin American states in subscribing to the principle of non-intervention. In practice we see a more ambiguous situation. Having outlawed intervention in principle, many Latin American states are no more willing to adhere strictly to a policy of non-intervention than is the United States.

For a variety of reasons, often depending on the nature of the government in power at a particular time, Latin American states have themselves intervened in the domestic affairs of their neighbors and have accepted or even supported United States' intervention for political or ideological reasons. The essay by Professors Franck and Weisband on intervention sheds much light on the contradiction between the doctrine of non-intervention and the political fact of "paramount dominance". The emphasis of this

* Norman A. Bailey, *Latin America in World Politics* 132 (1967).

essay (*Regional Interventionism by the Superpowers: A Study of Words and Acts as Inchoate Law Making*) on extra-hemisphere factors is of particular significance to the theme of regional and universal norms. For they show that in the military/security sphere, the principles adopted by one superpower in the region of its paramountcy may be espoused by the other in its own area of dominance. In other words, reciprocal claims over what the authors have referred to as "ghettos", although couched in terms of regional norms of behavior, are really no more than expressions denoting traditional spheres of influence. The authors are concerned to show that the parameters of such parallel behavior are set not just by acts but also by the verbal formulations adduced to justify them. Arguing in terms both of the United States' national interest and the dictates of morality, they suggest that an awareness of this inter-relationship of words and acts could lead to an easing of the rigors of the "two-ghetto system." If their hopes were to be realized, the traditional inter-American doctrine of non-intervention would be revitalized from its dormant state of being barely more than a cynical profession of piety.

The expropriation of foreign-owned industrial and extractive enterprises has become closely related to another popular issue of the last half of the twentieth century – national development. The Drago Doctrine and the Calvo Clause were examples of early Latin American efforts to set up legal barriers against intervention by the Great Powers to protect the financial and commercial interests of their nationals in Latin American countries. The essay by Professor Rodley on *The Nationalization by Peru of the Holdings of the International Petroleum Company* shows some of the contemporary techniques and legal arguments that have been developed more recently. What appears to some parties to be a flagrant disregard for traditional property rights appears to others to be a key to national development and a better standard of living. He concludes that the Peruvian incident marked the demise of the efficacy of unilateral sanctions by capital-exporting countries to protect the economic interests of their (multi-) nationals within the territory of capital-importing states and that international law has not yet developed an adequate substitute regime to regulate the settlement of disputes between foreign investors and host states.

Being intimately associated with the concept of national development and social revolution (the implicit underlying concern of these papers), the development of political institutions that will assure respect for human rights and democracy is a challenge of greater significance than ever before. The revolutionary genesis of most of the American states took place generally under the banner of just these concepts. Furthermore, the involvement of the Inter-American Commission on Human Rights in the resolution of the United States' intervention in the Dominican Republic, in 1965, vividly demonstrates the connection between the protection of human rights and the problems of strengthening the norms of non-intervention. The exhaustive analytical survey of *Human Rights and the Organization of American States* by the Professors Thomas traces the development in Latin America of international standards of human rights and the institutions charged with their implementation. While pessimistic about the possibility of wide ratification of the American Convention on Human Rights, the authors find encouragement in the activities of the Inter-American Commission on Human Rights, whose short existence has not prevented it from taking important initiatives in the discharge of its mandate.

The editors hope that this collection of case studies of regional international law and organization will be of use, not only to international lawyers and hemispheric specialists, but to all those who share a concern for the peoples of the other America south of the Rio Grande.

C. NEALE RONNING
NIGEL S. RODLEY

Since these essays were written significant developments have taken place in the Western Hemisphere. President Salvador Allende Gossens of Chile, the Hemisphere's first constitutionally elected Marxist Head of State and Government, has been overthrown and gone to his death. The military government in Argentina organised elections that permitted Juan Perón, their old foe, to become President. Meanwhile, in the post-Watergate political re-orientation in the United States, the Congress has put stringent limits on the ability of the Executive to commit the armed forces of that country to hostilities abroad.

These developments will probably not affect the situation regarding the management of non-maritime water resources or the status of competing claims regarding maritime jurisdiction. It is not known how much external involvement there was in the Chilean *golpe*. To the extent that there was any, it would not be unrelated to the economic policies being pursued by the Allende government regarding foreign, particularly mining, economic interests. In the human rights field, the at least temporary amelioriation in Argentina is more than offset by the egregious situation in Chile. The latter may well prove to be a test of the commitment and efficacy of the Inter-American Commission on Human Rights' Certainly, the importance of the topics discussed in this collection will be in no way diminished by these developments.

The editors.

Part I

WATER RESOURCES

NON-MARITIME INTERNATIONAL WATER RESOURCES: DEVELOPMENT AND CONSERVATION IN THE AMERICAS*

by

R. D. HAYTON

I. IMPORTANCE OF OPTIMIZATION OF WATER RESOURCES

The United Nations' XXV General Assembly adopted, on 8 December 1970, a resolution on the "Progressive development and codification of the rules of international law relating to international watercourses." [1] This was the first formal General Assembly action in this field since 1959, when it was resolved that preliminary studies should be made of the legal problems relating to the utilization and use of international rivers.[2] The XXV General Assembly's recent Resolution notes that water "is of growing concern to humanity, that the available fresh water resources of the world are limited and that the preservation and protection of those resources are of great importance to all nations." It goes on to point out that "the use of international rivers and lakes is still based in part on general principles and rules of customary law, despite the great number of bilateral treaties and other regional regulations, as well as the Convention on the Regime of Navigable Waterways of International Concern, signed at Barcelona on 20 April 1921, and the Convention relating to the Development of Hydraulic Power affecting more than one State, signed at Ge-

* Many of the general formulations contained in this paper are the product of the author's work as Technical Director of the United Nations Panel of Experts on the Legal and Institutional Implications of International Water Resources Development and may be found in more extended fashion in the Report of that Panel, in preparation. Acknowledgment is made of the invaluable intellectual stimulation and experience provided the author by each Member of the Panel and by the staff experts of the United Nations. However, the author makes no claim that the views here expressed are those of the Panel or of the Secretariat. Grateful acknowledgment is also made of the invaluable research assistance on this topic over an extended period of time by Miss Ksenia Horoshak.

[1] U.N. Doc. No. A/RES/2669 (XXV), 4 January 1971. See also the Report of the Sixth Committee, U.N. Doc. No. A/8202.

[2] U.N. Doc. No. A/RES/1401 (XIV), 21 November 1959. The result, a report prepared by the Secretariat, was published on 15 April 1963, U.N. Doc. No. A/5409.

neva on 9 December 1923." [3] This felt need for a firmer legal base in the field of international non-maritime water reflects the growing awareness of serious immediate and prospective problems in the supply and regulation of this essential, ubiquitous compound.

Until modern rapid expansion of populations and of efforts to accelerate economic development, the availability of adequate supplies of water could be taken for granted in regions of heavy precipitation, and its non-availability was accepted as a dictate of fate in those regions of water scarcity, limiting or even precluding agriculture and industry and, thus, intense human habitation.

Innumerable studies have made us painfully aware of the massive waste and abuse of this precious resource wrought by our traditional methods of utilization. But technology, in turn, has provided us with the means of conserving, augmenting and managing the supply – including recycling, storing and regulation of flow and even modification of weather. Unfortunately, intensified use of the earth and the atmosphere has already resulted in serious degradation of the quality of water in many areas of the world. Detrimental pollution of the remaining supplies of sweet water is only a matter of time, unless population trends and the practices of agriculture, industry and municipalities can somehow be reversed. Underground aquifers can be permanently polluted. Watershed surfaces can be worked in such a way as to ruin the catchment foundations, virtually forever. Streams can be mismanaged with often permanent damage to many uses, such as fishing, navigation, timber floating and recreation.

The optimal development of water resources has as its aim, therefore, in common with development generally, the enhancement of human well-being, and must become an integral part of the social and economic development programs of all countries.

In the long run, sheer human survival is dependent upon much better management of this critical resource. The future development of all countries will be limited, if not crippled or precluded altogether, wherever rational utilization of water is not achieved. The goals chosen by our American governments for their peoples are, generally speaking, not realizable in the absence of water adequate in quantity and quality.

At the same time, in some regions of the Hemisphere, water is present in such a way and in such quantities as to constitute a distinct nuisance. Permanently flooded land precludes agricultural utilization and renders

[3] The Resolution's main purpose is to stimulate the International Law Commission to undertake without further delay the study of the law of non-navigational uses, with a view to its progressive development and codification.

the construction of vital bridges impractical. Temporary flooding may imperil or destroy homes, factories, crops, roads and railroads, for example. Where soil water does not drain away, the use of the land for crops, animal husbandry or construction is impeded. Standing water is often a breeding-ground for disease-carrying or otherwise undesirable insects; it may turn brackish or evaporate leaving salts that make the land unfit for use. Erosion of valuable farm or industrial sites may take place through the action of strong currents or flooding. Where the presence or action of water causes these or similar harmful effects, there is a need for drainage works and flow regulation. Controls, however, mean water management projects and programs, which, in turn, mean – and an international basin is no exception – the creation of appropriate and adequate legal bases and institutional machinery for the accomplishment of these objectives.

II. INTERNATIONAL ASPECTS OF WATER RESOURCES DEVELOPMENT AND CONSERVATION

A. International Water Resources Systems

When waters drain and flow across the boundaries between man's political divisions, difficult problems may be presented by the occurrence of significant alterations in the characteristics of that flow. For example, upstream erosion may endanger downstream ports, channels or dams and reservoirs in another state by the deposit of siltation. Downstream pollution may harm upstream fishing in another state by diminishing or blocking fish migration to and from the sea. Irrigation upstream may deprive a downstream state of adequate supplies of water for established navigation or municipal, industrial and agricultural uses. Works, or lack of works, downstream may deprive an upstream state of the ability to use the river for navigation or timber floating. Pollution from uses upstream may cause a danger to health or make necessary expensive purification works in downstream states. Even where man has chosen to employ a stream as the permanent frontier feature between countries, water has often acted in such a way as to shift the entire course or main channel of the stream, with attendant difficulty along the line of political demarcation. And water related activities on one side of a boundary stream may interfere with the use of water by nationals of another state on the other side.

Clearly, if these and other detrimental effects of water behavior and use are to be mitigated, if not avoided, the states sharing the resource must work together to establish programs and controls yielding maximum achievable benefit for each interested state.

The territory within a watershed area, or basin, has been found to constitute a most useful physical context for organizing cooperation and collaboration in the field of water resources. It is a naturally delimited area within which water appears and is stored, or is discharged to some common place such as the sea. Count Hartig, the late Austrian authority who pointed up the consequences of the physical interrelationship of water as a flowing resource in a basin and developed from that the legal "principle of coherence," contributed significantly to the progressive development and acceptance among lawyers of this comprehensive approach.[4]

When a drainage area encompasses more than one state's territory, international consequences perforce arise. The Inter-American Bar Association, in its Buenos Aires Resolution of 1957 on the principles of law governing the use of international rivers, applied the included principles to "every watercourse or system of rivers or lakes (non-maritime waters) which may traverse or divide the territory of two or more states." [5] The Institute of International Law formulated its definition of non-maritime international waters in 1961 as comprising "waters which form part of a watercourse or hydrographic basin which extends over the territory of two or more States." [6] The Helsinki Rules of the International Law Association, adopted in 1966, define an international drainage basin as "a geographical area extending over two or more States determined by the watershed limits of the system of waters, including surface and underground waters, flowing into a common terminus." [7]

The sole physical unity within the basin is, however, water. Patterns of land use, climate, fauna and flora are not coincident with the basin, though they may be influenced by it. In important respects, lines of communication and transport usually will not be confined to the basin. Centers of industrial, hydroelectric and agricultural production may lie in one basin, while the markets for these products may lie in another basin or overseas. Raw

[4] See E. Hartig, *Ein neuer Ausgangspunkt für internationale wasserrechtliche Regelungen: das Kohaerenzprinzip,* Wasser- und Energiewirtschaft, 50 : 1-2 (Zurich, 1958).

[5] Inter-American Bar Association, 10th Conference, Buenos Aires, 1957. Resolution adopted, together with papers submitted to the Association (Washington, 1958).

[6] Institute of International Law. Resolutions adopted at the Salzburg Session, September 4-13, 1961 (Geneva, 1962).

[7] International Law Association, Helsinki Rules on the Uses of the Waters of International Rivers, Adopted . . . at the 52nd Conference held in Helsinki on 20th August, 1966 (London, 1967); A. H. Garretson, R. D. Hayton, and C. J. Olmstead, eds., The Law of International Drainage Basins (1967), Appendix A.

materials, component parts, breeding stock or seed may need to be imported into the basin. Power, generated by water, may be sent beyond the basin, or brought into the basin at one or more points.[8]

By means of canals, tunnels or underground aquifer links, the waters in one basin (national or international) may be connected with the waters of another basin (national or international). The result may be planned or natural importation of water into the first basin or loss from the first basin to the second.

Water may go underground with no apparent, that is, surface water connection with an international basin. This same water may flow underground and make its appearance in the territory of another state. As a consequence, these states share an interest in an international water resources system. The traditional riparian concepts would not comprehend the international water resources relationship between them.

The same may be said for atmospheric water. The presence and renewal of fresh water can be augmented or diminished by manipulation of the atmospheric segment of the water cycle. Movement of the air may carry rain clouds from the territory of the state where they are formed across the territory of an intervening state and into the territory of another state where precipitation may occur. Interference, deliberately or otherwise, with the formation, transit or physical condition of such air-borne moisture is interference with an international water resources system. Although man's ability to influence atmospheric moisture is still quite limited, the time has come to begin to incorporate into the thinking of those charged with long-range development plans and agreements, this potentially important aspect of the system. No state can afford to remain aloof from developments in this new field of "weather modification". Water, in the form of rain or snow, may be caused to precipitate at times and at places where it would not do so, at least to the same extent, under natural conditions; by appropriate techniques hail may be inhibited and storms mitigated. Even *climate* modification, involving major and possibly permanent changes in a region's weather, is being studied.

If the man-made precipitation extends to another state's territory, a question of international responsibility arises. For example, crops may be damaged by too much rainfall, or rainfall at an improper time; flooding or hail may occur, with attendant damage. The location of a particular "tar-

[8] See L. A. Teclaff, The River Basin in History and Law (1967); C. B. Bourne, *The Development of International Water Resources: The "Drainage Basin Approach,"* 47 Can. B. Rev. 62 (1969).

get area" for increased precipitation may require the cloud seeding to be effected over the adjacent territory of another state.

Although the requisite techniques are lacking at present, precipitation naturally tending to fall on one state's territory may in the future be made to fall elsewhere. If water is scarce in a particular region, deprivation of the expected rain or snow fall may bring disaster. On the other hand, if precipitation is excessive in that region, reduction of the rain or snow fall might avert floods, reclaim land, salvage crops and reduce erosion; if the same, surplus water can be made to precipitate instead over a water-scarce region in the same or a different country, the benefit could be multiplied.

Unless and until water falls on the land, the basin or watershed is not directly involved; however, atmospheric water that is carried overhead from one state to another is of vital interest to both states. Weather modification activities adversely affecting interests of another state will need to be prevented by international controls or regulated within a larger scheme of development, conservation and use of all available water resources.[9]

A thorough inventory of international fresh water resources must also take into account certain major occurrences or deposits of ice. Glaciers, "continental ice mantles" and polar ice constitute frozen international water resources, if such move across or straddle international frontiers. Most of such ice is "ancient," that is, laid down hundreds or thousands of years ago. These major ice-covered areas influence weather and climate on a grand scale. It may eventually prove feasible to "import" polar icebergs, towing or pushing them to the vicinity of populated areas in order to provide a source of fresh water in water-scarce areas.[10] The systematic acquisition and removal by a state of ice in polar high seas areas, or, for example, from shelf ice occurring in association with polar land bodies, would raise some vexing international legal problems. Any of these vast stores of frozen fresh water may, with increasing demand, be put to use by states capable of developing or applying the necessary technology.

[9] This problem was considered in a paper presented at the International Conference on Water for Peace, Washington, D.C., 23-31 May 1967 (see: R. J. Moses and J. N. Corbridge, Jr., *Legal Structures for International Supervision of Weather Modification Techniques,* 2 Water for Peace 410). See also H. J. Taubenfeld, ed., Controlling the Weather, A Study of Law and Regulatory Processes (1970).

[10] Icebergs as a fresh water source was recently studied by Dr. William Campbell of the Department of Interior's Geological Survey and Dr. Wilford Weeks of the Army's Cold Regions Research and Engineering Laboratory. According to the New York Times of 18 March 1970, the two U.S. scientists estimated that if an iceberg 250-yards thick and 2,700-yards across was towed to Australia [from Antarctica] it would provide 207 billion gallons of water – even though 70 per cent of the iceberg would melt during the trip."

The physical interconnection across state boundaries of water in frozen form creates another international status, because the removal or accelerated melting of such ice by one state could affect the water resources reserves, or the run off, in another state. For example, along the southern portion of the continental divide of the South American continent, a "permanent" ice mantle, including many glaciers, is found. Roughly along this same divide runs the border between Chile and Argentina. The natural melting of this ice feeds a number of streams that begin in one country or the other and flow to the sea without entering the other state's jurisdiction. Yet the principal source for their waters is the continental ice mantle, situated astride the boundary. Are such rivers therefore international? Perhaps not, but a state may not melt or remove the ice on its side of the boundary without regard to the consequences to the neighboring state. Any "wholesale" melting or removal of ice from these polar or sub-polar regions might, moreover, produce a discernible impact on the environment, including weather or climatological change and significant shifts in the water balance. On the assumption that the future needs of man may make inroads on the frozen reserves of fresh water attractive, if not imperative, additional study and appropriate controls should be considered in the interest of preserving friendly relations between neighboring states and to assure efficient use of all available sweet water with minimal harmful side effects. Any international agreement on this subject matter would constitute a pioneering effort instructive to many other states with similar conditions.

In certain cases the development or utilization of a natural resource *other than water* by one basin state in one sector of an international drainage basin may cause an identifiable and substantial impact on the development or utilization of water by another basin state in another sector of the basin, and *vice versa*. For example, a river may have its headwaters in State A and thereafter flow as a contiguous river between State B and State C. The extensive deforestation by the logging off of the headwaters area in State A may lead to land erosion and provoke siltation and significant alteration in the natural timing of flow, affecting thereby State B's and State C's utilization of the water.

Other development efforts involving the basin states, some of them, or other states, will need to be coordinated with water resources plans and undertakings. Conversely, if mining or forestry or agriculture or transportation – to cite only a few examples – are to be fostered and maximized, the water regime cannot be ignored, because of the vital role played by water in such endeavors.[11] Thus, international legal and institutional arrangements for water are indicated whenever regional development or national development is contemplated and an international drainage basin is present.

Occurrences – natural or man-made – affecting the water in one place or segment of the system have the potential of changing the quantity, quality or the achieveable benefit from the water in any other part of the system. International, non-maritime water resources may be defined, then, as all surface water, groundwater and atmospheric water that flow in, stand on, are present within, or pass over the territory of more than one state. International status is a matter of hydrological fact, namely the hydro-interdependence within or between bodies, aquifers or aggregations of water in any form. The states with internationally protected interests in such water resources are those states with territory (including air space) within which water occurs or flows as part of a physically interconnected international system.[12] Where this physically interactive resource is simultaneously or successively within the jurisdiction of more than one state, no one state may ignore the interests of the other state or states in the waters of the same hydrosystem.

Over time, the conventional concept of "international river" has been broadened to "international drainage basin." The commonly accepted conceptual basis needs once more to be amplified or modified in order to encompass atmospheric water and inter-basin linkage where it is intended that these extra-basin occurrences and relationships be comprehended in development agreements, plans or projects. The increased awareness of the relevance of these other elements now causes the operative concept to be reformulated as "international water resources system." [13]

Recognition is also accorded the many interrelationships between and among all resources, natural and human, in a given area such as a drainage basin. The acknowledged modern objective is to achieve optimum utilization of resources while at the same time taking adequate measures to preserve the quality of life. Environmental protection, or conservation,

[11] UN, Dept. of Economic and Social Affairs, Integrated River Basin Development, rev. ed., 1970 (U.N. Doc. No. E/3066/Rev. 1); G. Cano, Legal and Institutional Problems of Multinational Water Development Schemes in Latin America and the Caribbean (working paper prepared for the UNITAR Regional Seminar in International Law, Quito, Ecuador, January 1969).

[12] Article III of the Helsinki Rules defines a basin state as "a state the territory of which includes a portion of an international drainage basin."

[13] The Inter-American Bar Association adopted the system approach in its 1957 Resolution, *supra* note 5, employing the terminology "system of international waters;" "international river system" had often been employed in earlier literature.

considerations will henceforth loom large in all rational schemes for development of an international water resources system. Under the general principle of state responsibility, reflected also in general international law rules with respect to the use of waters of international rivers, an international claim arises when one state so uses its territory as to produce harm in the territory of another state.[14] But beyond the question of responsibility for "misfeasance," failure to provide affirmatively for the rational management of the system will prove to be detrimental to the national interest of each basin state, to the extent that water in the basin, or system, bears a significant relationship to the human welfare and economic development of the states concerned.

B. Water Resources Undertakings Requiring International Collaboration

Cooperation on the part of the interested states is, obviously, a *sine qua non* to the achievement of any rational approach to system-wide study or planning. Nonetheless, many projects – even those in implementation of a master plan for the basin – can be carried out by the individual state within whose territory specific works are called for. Specific projects ordinarily realizable by a single basin state may, however, necessitate active participation in one form or another by some or all of the co-basin states because of the data required or the financial or technical assistance needed to carry out the undertaking. Other projects and programs require more than consultation and cooperation; that is, they require actual collaboration on the part of two or more basin states. Moreover, inadequate technical or financial capability on the part of a particular basin state, or states, may lead to the recognition of the need for international arrangements in order to make available the requisite human and economic resources from more developed states or from international organizations.

Hydraulic works that create a reservoir that backs water into another state is an example of the kind of undertaking that necessitates collaboration – and at an early stage. Though the dam itself might be undertaken by the one or two states within whose territory the construction is to take place, the upstream state, or states, that will experience territorial inundation must become directly involved. General consent to the project is only the first step. Agreement on the extent and timing of the inundation must be reached; any loss of use of land or other detriment to the third state or states must be compared with any benefits conferred, either direct-

[14] See *Trail Smelter Arbitration* (United States-Canada), 1941, 3. U.N. Rep. Int'l Arb. Awards 1905 (1949), 35 Am. J. Int'l L. 684 (1941) and the commentary (unofficial) to Article X of the Helsinki Rules, *supra* note 7.

ly from the inundation (such as improved navigation, recreation or fishing) or indirectly from delivery of power or water. The third state or states must participate in the determinations of these matters, including the fixing of any compensation for damages or contribution for rights to benefits. Moreover, the relocation of any populations, important roads, and rail, power or communication installations must be accomplished. The frontier regime, including the policing of the body of water for various purposes and any new demarcation of the boundary, must be arranged. If the life of the dam-reservoir project is to be prolonged, abatement or prevention of siltation from upstream sources by means of erosion control or reforestation programs must be ensured. All these matters involve agreement, positive action, cost and participation on the part of the several states involved. The legal and institutional implications of these and other types of collaboration need to be thought out by the representatives and planning officers of the co-system states as they design the organizational machinery to initiate and carry on the development, conservation and use of the waters of their international water resources system.

If dams do not meet safety standards and do not possess the necessary structural strength, a great danger to the lives, sources of livelihood and property of downstream riparians is created. Where such risks are involved, safety and security specifications ought not be determined solely by the unilateral actions of the upstream state in which such works may be situated. Thus, from the very outset consultation and cooperation are indispensable where international repercussions are possible – even for projects executed solely within one country – if later conflicts and disasters are to be avoided.

If costly navigation improvements are to be made – for example, the dredging of channels, the construction and operation of by-pass or connecting canals, or the building and operation of locks – collaboration is ordinarily again required in order that costs may be shared, minimum depth observed, and uniform regulations adopted. Collaboration is likewise imperative if international bridges over or tunnels under a boundary stream are to be built and maintained. Fisheries development and conservation can be only partially successful if simple cooperation is not expanded into collaboration. In many regions, increased exploitation of underground aquifers would be disastrous in the absence of collaboration on the part of states that share the aquifers; ground water aquifers in one state can be affected by diversion of surface waters in another. Control of erosion and control of runoff by, for example, bank protection and reforestation, may require collaboration in order that work may be done (and paid for) upstream for downstream benefit.

Although initial decisions with respect to projects and programs may appear to call merely for coordination and consultation, as soon as major undertakings are envisaged, the additional legal and institutional machinery for the facilitation of actual collaboration becomes desirable, if not indispensable. Types of collaboration, clearly, may include technical, educational, economic, financial, administrative and political collaboration. Planning officers will wish to recommend the kind and amount of institutionalization best suited to meet expected needs, setting up consultative and coordinative arrangements in the beginning but allowing gradual and necessary enlargement of the machinery as bilateral or multilateral collaboration becomes critical.

Within each country, creation of an adequate base for cooperation in the interest of international water resources optimization and management calls for the conjoining of three essential requisites. One requisite is the active support and commitment on the part of top-level political representatives; the second is the mobilization of the available geological, meteorological, legal, economic, social, engineering and other data and expertise; the third is a national governmental structure capable of sustained, effective international collaboration. Without such a combination, the actual *international* cooperation or collaboration will have little opportunity to take place and to thrive.

C. The International Water Resources System in the Americas

There has been a long history of concern for international water resources in the Americas. Early emphasis was, understandably, on the questions of free navigation and free trade. But in the twentieth century, awareness developed of the need for principles to govern non-navigational uses of the resource.[15] Only the highlights can be mentioned here.

At the Seventh Inter-American Conference held in Montevideo in 1933, a famous Resolution LXXII was arrived at, on "Industrial and Agricultural Use of International Rivers," known as the Declaration of Monte-

[15] Although tangential to the focus of this paper, it should be noted in this connection that the several Western Hemisphere countries which are organized on the federal principle have had considerable experience with legal regimes for water resources development and administration at the inter-state or inter-provincial level. This experience, including the creation and operation of inter-provincial commissions, should prove useful to them in determining their positions and evaluating alternatives at the international level.

video.[16] The Declaration affirms that, with respect to both contiguous and successive rivers,

"1. In case that, in order to exploit the hydraulic power of international waters for industrial or agricultural purposes, it may be necessary to make studies with a view to their utilization, the States on whose territories the studies are to be carried on, if not willing to make them directly, shall facilitate by all means the making of such studies on their territories by the other interested State and for its account.

2. The States have the exclusive right to exploit, for industrial or agricultural purposes, the margin which is under their jurisdiction of the waters of international rivers. This right, however, is conditioned in its exercise upon the necessity of not injuring the equal right due to the neighboring State on the margin under its jurisdiction.

In consequence, no State may, without the consent of the other riparian State, introduce into watercourses of an international character, for the industrial or agricultural exploitation of their waters, any alteration which may prove injurious to the margin of the other interested State.

3. In the cases of damage referred to in the foregoing article an agreement of the parties shall always be necessary. When damages capable of repair are concerned, the works may only be executed after adjustment of the incident regarding indemnity, reparation (or) compensation of the damages, in accordance with the procedure indicated below.

* * *

7. The works which a State plans to perform in international waters shall be previously announced to the other riparian or co-jurisdictional States. The announcement shall be accompanied by the necessary technical documentation in order that the other interested States may judge the scope of such works, and by the name of the technical expert or experts who are to deal if necessary, with the international side of the matter.

8. The announcement shall be answered within a period of three months, with or without observations. In the former case, the answer shall indicate the name of the technical expert or experts to be charged by the respondent with

[16] Organization of American States (OAS), Textos de documentos sobre el uso comercial de rios y lagos internacionales (Washington, D.C., 1968; OAS/Official Documents, OEA/Ser. 1/IV. 1, CIJ-97), pp. 2-3; text in English in U.N. Doc. No. A/5409, Annex I, pp. 2-3. Free navigation was still recognized as the paramount use of international rivers; works must not interfere with navigation but, on the contrary, should seek to improve it (para. 5 and 6).

The Declaration of Montevideo, as is the case with other resolutions of Inter-American Conferences, is not in binding treaty form; however, both Bolivia and Chile, in their controversy over the Rio Lauca, have taken its provisions to be the law, differing on the interpretation of the requirements. Exceptions to the Declaration were taken, at the time of its adoption, by Venezuela and the United States.

dealing with the technical experts of the applicant, and shall propose the date and place for constituting the Mixed Technical Commission of technical experts from both sides to pass judgment on the case. The Commission shall act within a period of six months, and if within this period no agreement has been reached, the members shall set forth their respective opinions, informing the Governments thereof.

9. In such cases, and if it is not possible to reach an agreement through diplomatic channels, recourse shall be had to such procedure of conciliation as may have been adopted by the parties beforehand or, in the absence thereof, to the procedure of any of the multilateral treaties or conventions in effect in America. The Tribunal shall act within a period of three months, which may be extended, and shall take into account, in the award, the proceedings of the Mixed Technical Commission.

10. The parties shall have a month to state whether they accept the conciliatory award or not. In the latter case and at the request of the interested parties the disagreement shall then be submitted to arbitration, the respective Tribunal being constituted by the procedure provided in the Second Hague Convention for the peaceful solution of international conflicts."

The Tenth Conference of the Inter-American Bar Association, held in 1957, adopted the well-known Resolution previously mentioned, holding that among states having a portion of an international system of waters within their jurisdiction, a duty exists to recognize the rights of co-system states to share the benefits of the resource.[17]

The Inter-American Juridical Committee in 1963 approved a study, including a draft convention, on Industrial and Agricultural Use of International Rivers and Lakes, and submitted it to the Fifth Meeting of the Inter-American Council of Jurists, held in San Salvador in 1965. The draft convention has met with mixed reactions and is still undergoing revision.[18] And, of course, there have been significant bilateral and regional developments, particularly in recent years.[19]

[17] See text and accompanying studies in Inter-American Bar Association, Principles of Law Governing the Uses of International Rivers and Lakes, Washington, D.C., April 1958. At the 1954 Rio de Janeiro sectional meeting of the World Power Conference, the Chilean position stressed, with respect to the development of international water resources, the principle of integrated utilization of the waters for all uses, as distinguished from power development considered in isolation.

[18] See Inter-American Juridical Committee, Industrial and Agricultural Use of International Rivers and Lakes, Revised Report and Draft Convention prepared in accordance with Resolution I of the Fifth Meeting of the Inter-American Council of Jurists (December 1965; OAS/Official Documents, OAE/Ser. I/VI. 2, CIJ-79).

[19] For texts of the documents mentioned and others not mentioned, see OAS, *supra* note 16, pp. 1-55. For a broader but summary presentation, including the texts of various documents, see Pan American Union, Rios y Lagos Internacionales (Utiliza-

In all, in Latin America alone there are forty-nine separate international drainage basins, varying greatly, of course, in size and potential importance.[20] The Amazon and Plata basins are true geographical giants; but the Orinoco also drains in excess of one million square kilometers. Two very large basins, the Colorado and the Rio Grande (or Bravo) make Mexico and the United States co-system states; treaty arrangements are in force governing the international aspects of these water resources.[21] And among the five Plata Basins states, a number of treaties and declarations operate to govern basin state relationships; important recent actions place this basin in the forefront in the Hemisphere, even if implementation of the concerted policies is just beginning and certain to encounter serious financial and political difficulties.

III. ALTERNATIVE REGIMES

Once two or more states have decided in principle to join forces for purposes of developing their common international water resources, the next step is to delineate the extent of their collaboration and to agree upon a regime conducive to the accomplishment of their objectives. Their agreement with respect to the regime can be manifested in a number of ways. No one way will guarantee success or avoid all pitfalls, but for a given international water resources system at a given time, there may be circumstances that commend one approach or preclude another.

A. Basic Approaches to Coordinated Action

Policy and institutions for the international basin or system, including machinery for coordinating existing national and international bodies, will be determined, probably for a considerable span of time, by the content of the initial instrument or instruments utilized to set into motion the desired joint activities.

A formal treaty is not essential to the creation of an international agreement. It is, however, not considered desirable that an international agreement creating long-term relationships with respect to a vital and complex

ción para Fines Agrícolas e Industriales), 3rd ed., August 1967, OAS/Official Documents, OAE/Ser. 1/VI, CIJ-75 Rev.

[20] For a listing of the international basins in the Western Hemisphere see Annex A.

[21] See C. J. Meyers, *The Colorado Basin*, in Garretson, Hayton and Olmstead, *supra* note 7, pp. 486-607, and works cited therein.

subject matter such as international water resources be concluded without a written record of its substance.

In the initial stages at least, and for specified purposes at any time, it has been found possible and sometimes preferable to reach understandings or administrative agreements informally that are sufficient to allow the desired work to proceed and to bear fruit, without all the formality and built-in delays of treaty making. At the outset, one or more of the participating states may not yet feel in a position to accept the long-term commitments of a treaty, or be in a position to accomplish ratification. Some demonstrable progress with tangible benefits may, indeed, be precisely what a state needs to show, in order to generate interest and a national willingness to enter into more formal arrangements and commitments. If the underlying common accord among the parties and the appreciation of the desirability, even necessity, of cooperation are present, results can be achieved and the foundation laid for subsequent formal commitment, when more intense or elaborate collaboration than can be supported informally is deemed necessary.

The five Plata Basin countries, for example, established – prior to the negotiation of a treaty – an intergovernmental body, the Intergovernmental Coordinating Committee, by an accord signed by the foreign ministers at Santa Cruz de la Sierra, Bolivia, on 20 May 1968, which also approved provisionally a Statute, or By-Laws, for the committee. At the same meeting, a list of priority projects to be implemented by the Committee was adopted.[22]

When the participating states find that they are, collectively, sufficiently clear in the delineation of their interests and objectives with respect to the water resources of their international system to commit themselves quite formally to a treaty regime for the basin, this should be done. The requirement for external financing may precipitate the negotiation of formally ratified agreements when costly projects are called for.

An interesting example of a recent agreement in the Americas relating to the general development of an international river basin is the Treaty concerning the Plata Basin which was concluded among the governments of Argentina, Bolivia, Brazil, Paraguay and Uruguay on April 23, 1969, at

[22] *Acta Final*, II Reunión de Cancilleres de los Paises de la Cuenca del Plata, Santa Cruz de la Sierra, Bolivia, Documentos 9, 10, 20 de mayo de 1968, reproduced in OAS, *supra* note 16, pp. 17-32.

One year later, however, the Governments did conclude a treaty which ratified the Statute and the list of projects.

Brasilia. In the Treaty the five Governments acknowlegde that common action on their part would permit balanced development of the Basin and make possible the optimum utilization of its resources. Provision is made for an annual meeting of the Ministers of Foreign Affairs of the five states; the Intergovernmental Coordinating Committee, previously established, is recognized as the permanent institution of consultation.[23]

Also worthy of study in the formal agreement category are the Canada-United States Treaty of 1961 and the Protocol of 1964 settling the international regime for the Columbia River Basin. Canada and the United States each have special "operating entities" to carry out the provisions of the agreement within their respective national territories. A Joint Permanent Engineering Board functions to supervise implementation of the regime, with an "appellate" judicial role preserved for the International Joint Commission, the highly successful Canadian-United States body originally set up under the Boundary Waters Treaty of 1909.[24]

Absent some very advanced, international regime superseding the national or local water regime in all relevant matters, removal of existing legal conflicts and enactment of needed, counterpart provisions in the respective state statutes and regulations is essential to water use optimization and to the promotion of regional development generally. In this regard, those states that share the same legal "inheritance", that is, have their legal systems derived from the same general source, such as Spanish and Roman Law, should find relatively little difficulty in bringing their existing codes and regulations into essential harmony with one another.

Only those general policies and specific provisions that inhibit or obstruct the desired development, conservation and use of the waters in question need be harmonized. The absence of certain needed provisions in one or more states or the existence of conflicting provisions can be identified by a comparative study of all the applicable national rules and regulations, including quotas, preferences, rates, taxes, restrictions, recharge and pollution abatement obligations and the like.[25] It is important, for ex-

[23] For the background leading up to the recent treaty, see R. D. Hayton, *The Plata Basin,* in Garretson, Hayton and Olmstead, *supra* note 7, pp. 298-442, and works cited therein.

[24] Although often cited as a prominent example of successful international river basin development, note should be taken of the unfortunate degree of specificity given to certain aspects. See esp. R. W. Johnson, *The Columbia Basin,* in Garretson, Hayton and Olmstead, *supra* note 7, pp. 167-255, and J. V. Krutilla, The Columbia River Treaty: The Economics of an International River Basin Development (1967).

[25] The United Nations Food and Agricultural Organization has published a comparative study of water laws in South America. FAO, Las leyes de aguas en Sudamérica (Rome, 1956) Agricultural development paper No. 56 (G. Cano, comp.).

ample, to avoid placing any user, whose activities are or will become transnational, in a position that renders his compliance with the several applicable laws and regulations impossible, or even unduly complicated, burdensome or uneconomic. And conservation practices should be fostered or mandated equitably throughout the basin. The Economic Commission for Latin America (ECLA) has favored the harmonization approach.[26] The harmonization of the several national water laws may in fact pave the way for formal international agreement.

If all or most of the participating states are in need of comprehensive or up-dated water codes, or if they decide collectively to adopt new water policies in the light of modern knowledge and their common objectives, the opportunity is presented for the preparation of a uniform law as a model. Each government then agrees to seek enactment of the text by the appropriate national bodies, with whatever minor modifications or additions may be indicated to meet the internal requirements of each state's legal system, including constitutional limitations, the provisions of other related legislation (such as codes governing mining or other resources) and statutes of authority for regulatory commissions. Once formally sanctioned, the result is identical or nearly identical provisions in each basin state's law authorizing and facilitating the program or projects desired and uniformly regulating water use and conservation practices. Even penalties for infractions may be made uniform.

Often cited examples of the effective use of parallel legislation and regulations are found in the Canada-U.S.A. experience, where the concept of parallel legislation was formally recognized in the 1909 Boundary Waters Treaty.[27] The enactment of parallel legislation on the part of Canada (The St. Lawrence Seaway Authority Act of 21 December 1951) and the United States (The St. Lawrence Seaway Act of 13 May 1954), and an exchange of notes dated 17 August 1954 between the Secretary of State for External Affairs of Canada and the United States Embassy in Canada provided the legal basis for the St. Lawrence Seaway and Power Project.[28] A more recent implementation of parallel legislation is the separate promulgation by the Governments of Canada and the United States of Joint Resolutions Respecting the Transit of Vessels on the St. Lawrence Seaway (the "Sea-

[26] CEPAL, Requerimientos jurídicos y administrativos de los proyectos y obras hidraúlicas multinacionales en América Latina, UNITAR/SIL. 1/BP/2 (Quito Regional Seminar on International Law, 1969).

[27] Treaty Between Great Britain and the United States Relating to Boundary Waters, And Questions Arising Between the United States and Canada, Signed at Washington, January 11, 1909 (102 British and Foreign State Papers 137).

[28] R. R. Baxter, ed., Documents on the St. Lawrence Seaway 54 (1960).

way Regulations") which resulted from consultations between the Seaway authorities in the two countries. The Regulations formulated by the St. Lawrence Seaway Authority were approved (1 April 1959) by a Canadian Order in Council. In so far as they are applicable to the United States, the Regulations were also approved by the Administrator of the St. Lawrence Seaway Development Corporation on the same date, pursuant to the St. Lawrence Seaway Act.[29]

Thus it may be appreciated that the American states have at their disposal the technique of parallel legislation as a specific legal tool to coordinate their development, conservation and use of the waters of an international water resources system.

B. Extent of International Collaboration

Co-system states will wish to consider carefully the limits of their common undertakings. To be decided are the range and intensity of the international collaboration. It is generally regarded as inadvisable to proceed initially on too ambitious a scale. Caution is particularly important where there is, as yet, very little systematic knowledge about the system or where the possibilities of technical assistance or financing are limited, as they usually are. Nonetheless, the interested states will wish to accomplish all that is, under the circumstances, practicable.

Although integrated water resources development suggests the inclusion of all matters with any relationship whatever to the water resource, prudence dictates focus upon matters with present or impending major importance for the economies and human welfare of the peoples involved. Determination of priority matters – and the commitment to fund such undertakings – will help assure effective accomplishment rather than token or inadequate results because the participating states' energies and financial resources have been spread too thinly. Long-range objectives may be enunciated for all the matters of present and future common concern, thus declaring the intention eventually to evolve a comprehensive regime for the system, but more specific agreement should be reached as a practical matter on the matters actively to be undertaken at once and in the near future.

Thus, it must be determined whether the arrangements are to cover (a) consultation, (b) data collection, (c) allocation of the resource, (d) regulation of the use of the resource, (e) planning, (f) construction of facilities,

[29] *Ibid.*

(g) operation of facilities, or (h) some combination of two or more of the foregoing aspects. The choice will depend upon circumstances within the area, except that consultation and data collection are, speaking practically, the *sine qua non*. A number of specific projects and programs will, moreover, be in the minds of the governments, even though feasibility and merits as compared with other projects and programs have not yet been determined. The character of these anticipated undertakings have a strong bearing on the decisions regarding institutional machinery.

It is not always a simple task to define the geographic area to be covered by the agreement. This is particularly true when the various potential uses and services, and their effects, have not been clearly established. It is widely accepted that for surface water resources the river basin is a suitable unit for planning and management. For ground water resources it is widely understood that the entire hydrologic system of which the international aquifers are an integral part should be taken into account.[30] Conceptualization in the field of international atmospheric water has just begun. Particularly with respect to pollution, but also with respect to navigation, timber floating, fishing and recreation, among other matters, especially at the mouths of streams or estuaries and along interfaces between sea water and fresh water underground, international water resources collaboration may need to encompass coastal waters because of the important interaction that in fact takes place.[31]

A general rule to follow in defining the geographic area of coverage may be expressed as follows: The arrangement should embrace at least the area within which development and use activities will have a measurable and significant influence upon benefits and costs. If this general rule is followed, there may be instances in which the operative regime will not embrace all water related activities within a hydrologic system, and there may be some instances in which the territorial reach is determined to extend outside of the system.[32] If one or more co-system states are not direct-

[30] The Working Group on Underground Waters of the International Law Association's Committee on International Water Resources Law has taken this position as its point of departure for all appropriate relationships between states, including customary obligations.

[31] The International Law Association's Committee on International Water Resources Law has a Working Group on Pollution of Coastal Areas and Enclosed Seas.

[32] Water is diverted, with extraordinarily valuable hydropower results, from the Plata Basin (the Tieté River valley near São Paulo, Brazil) and dropped down the Great Escarpment to the Atlantic Coast. This particular exportation of water may be treated merely as a small part of Brazil's total entitlement (in the nature of a consumptive use with zero return to the system) or as an extra- basin link in the territorial scope of the total system.

ly involved in the discussions and negotiations, it may be necessary to treat only the portions of the system within the jurisdiction of the collaborating states. Data collection, at least, should be system-wide. On the other hand, a regional economic development scheme may be adopted to include the entire territory of all of the system states, using as a point of departure master planning for their common water resources, or of their total water resources.

After the territorial and subject-matter limits have been considered, it will still be necessary to anticipate how far, at least initially, the international effort is to be carried in any particular field. For example, the problem area of pollution may be placed within the purview of the collaboration. However, joint pollution concern could be limited to studies, be extended to include recommendations, or go so far as to contemplate international programs and regulations, even enforcement. In other matters, similar decisions will need to be taken with regard to the degrees of "intensity" of the collaboration.

Comprehensive subject-matter treatment and all-inclusive territorial reach on an *intensive* basis is obviously not achievable under anything short of the most ideal political, financial and technical conditions.

IV. CHOOSING APPROPRIATE INSTITUTIONS

The specific legal and organizational structure called for will, of course, vary according to the decisions of the participating states with respect to the range of undertakings within the international basin, or system, and the degree of intensity with which these undertakings will be pursued.

There can be only frustration and disappointment, not to mention a squandering of scarce human and financial resources, if extensive prior planning and generous agreement culminate in institutional arrangements that are incapable of sustained action or, on the other hand, if an expensive and elaborate organizational structure is created when the basin states are not in fact prepared to support major undertakings internationally.

The theoretical possibilities for institutions for international water resources development and administration range from very simple, even irregular consultation arrangements to complex, full-time organizations with autonomous authority. Most basin states reaching this stage in recent years have seen fit to choose something in-between – but stronger, generally, than all but a few of the earlier commissions – tailored to their perceived needs and their current willingness to join forces in expectation of the greater results made possible by institutionalized combined effort.

It is now generally not difficult to justify one overall coordinating organ. It may, however, be regarded as more conducive to positive results if separate bodies are created, perhaps for different parts of the international water resources system or of different programs within the system as particular areas or projects are deemed ripe for action.

Experience has taught us, however, that a high-level commission or similarly denominated policy coordinating body is called for (in order that periodic consideration can be given to far reaching questions) and that, in addition, one or more bodies of technical experts is needed (in order that the hydrogeological, practical engineering and ongoing management aspects may be dealt with knowledgeably and in concert).

Recently there has been much discussion of multi-national public corporations for the performance of regional development undertakings. International water resources system development and management are regarded as "natural," or fertile fields for such employment. This alternative, in one form or another, should be given serious consideration.

The principal advantages, perhaps, of the corporate intergovernmental or multi-national authority is the ability to insulate such a body to a considerable extent from the vicissitudes of changing national governments and the placing of the management of long-range, technical undertakings such as international water resources in the hands of a full-time professional team subjected to cost-accounting procedures and other tests of efficiency and performance possible only in the separate enterprise context. Financing for projects might be more readily obtained by such an entity. Ultimate control, including policy guidance, is still exercised by vote of a board of directors representing the member states or other designated political entities. This control could, however, be turned over to a self-perpetuating body of distinguished citizen-experts of participating countries.

In some, small basins it has been found advantageous to base the international arrangements on existing or desired relationships between local *users* in each country. A most interesting agreement on the Táchira, a Colombia-Venezuela boundary stream, was concluded between users and sanctioned by two "frontier entities," el Distrito Bolívar (Venezuela) and la Municipalidad del Rosario (Colombia) for the benefit of the private riparians on both sides of the river.[34]

[33] See, *inter alia,* C. Fligler, Multinational Public Enterprises (International Bank for Reconstruction and Development, 1967).

[34] See United Nations, Economic Commission for Latin America, Los Recursos Hidráulicos de América Latina, II, Venezuela (U.N. Doc. No. E/CN. 12/593/Rev. 1),

The serious implications for participating states of the choice of institutions are many. Simple coordinating institutions may prove too weak and too slow-acting for implementation of an urgently needed program. A more complex or authoritative international agency may meet resistance from oldline national or local agencies and generate friction as a result of its vigorous action. Authorized international collaboration among users may fail to give sufficient weight to the general public interest in environmental protection (including aesthetics) or may not be expected or able to undertake expensive multi-purpose construction or major facilities operation. The ground must be prepared adequately within each state, or the international cooperation and collaboration will be all too easily reduced to ineffectual discussions and positions on paper, or may be effectively thwarted because of bureaucratic and political rivalries or financial inability. Whatever the participating states decide to accomplish with respect to the waters of the particular international system, this collective *will* can be translated into actual achievement only if appropriate international institutions are created *and* if national and local institutions are disposed, if not required, to cooperate.

V. LEGAL AND ADMINISTRATIVE CAPACITY

In order that the states contemplating meaningful commitments to an international body may realistically evaluate the proposed institutions for acceptability, the body's legal composition, main procedures, powers and jurisdiction – and all limitations thereto – as well as its essential organizational form, need to be delineated and scrutinized.

A. Decision Making

The officials and the public of every country should find the proceedings in an international basin agency reasonable, that is, informed and deliberate, but also (if positive results are expected) effective. Procedures that allow capricious or hasty decisions have to be avoided in the interest, of course, of preserving due process but also in order not to provoke member state alienation from the international institution. Procedures that are cum-

p. 52; and Reglamento de aguas del Rio Táchira y sus repartos que la Jefatura Civil del Distrito Bolívar ha expedido con anuencia de las agricultores residentes en él (1931).

bersome or protracted will only diminish accomplishment and be demoralizing to every person involved.

The unpredictable delays and the misunderstandings that are virtually certain in the absence of prior agreement on the manner and requirements for taking decisions will paralyze the intended undertakings with great loss of momentum, resources and good will. In this connection, if an agency is not delegated the final say on some or all of the matters within its purview, an effective procedure for decisions at a higher level is needed. Striking the proper balance between efficiency and due process is a central problem in decision making.

The rules dealing with representation, elections, credentials, meetings, agenda, voting, committees (or working groups), the status of observers and the appointment and dismissal of staff are, in this connection, matters of consequence, not merely procedural details.

B. Specific Authority

The determination to create an institutional instrument and to give it a mission implies, in principle at least, the will to delegate to the organization, or to particular bodies, specific competences to act, within and outside its structure, to accomplish its mission, in accordance with the policy and decision-making limitations imposed. The participating states should consider carefully the particular authority their international water resources agency needs to carry out its assigned responsibilities.

The concern here, then, is with delimitation of the juridical personality and the bundle of specific powers to be conferred upon an entity deliberately created for the purpose of international cooperation and collaboration affecting an international water resources system. A few examples of the power and authority that *may* be needed include:

- the authority to determine rules of procedure;
- the authority to visit and inspect;
- the authority to hold hearings and conduct investigations, with power to compel appearance and the production of records;
- the right to acquire, own and dispose of property;
- the power to contract for services and materials;
- the power to publish findings independently;
- the power to sell (and, perhaps, to purchase) water and power;
- the authority to engage, direct and dismiss personnel, that is, to function as an employer;
- the authority to draw up and, once approved, to administer a budget;

- the power to make rulings allocating water, conferring rights to use, requiring abatement of pollution or siltation, determining compensation or contribution due, setting conservation standards, etc.;
- the authority to license and to set rates; and
- the authority to borrow money and to issue debentures.

C. Enforcement Arrangements

Where the system states do in fact confer rule making and rate setting authority on their water agency, the problem of enforcement is bound to arise. Whether a state-member is an enthusiastic defender of the international body's authority or an apprehensive watchdog of its actions, *direct* enforcement by the agency of its determinations will find no advocates. Not only does enforcement in its own right amount to the clearest claim to supranational status by such a body, but the practicalities are such that indirect enforcement is a necessity short of providing the agency with some kind of executive arm, including para-military personnel of its own. On waters in specified frontier zones, "international" policing arrangements may be feasible, but enforcement generally is another matter.

In other words, few states can be expected to be prepared to share the police power with a regional development institution of limited competence and experience. Still, the efficacy of the joint "enterprise" set in motion at great expense and with high expectations is indubitably dependent upon the ability to obtain compliance with the regulations and requirements of the agreed-upon program. In most circumstances, the states themselves, then, must undertake enforcement measures in defense and support of the international water resources agency.

The participating states may, nonetheless, agree to give the basin, or system, agency status before their own tribunals, empowering the agency to institute proceedings to obtain proper decrees and even to follow up with execution in its own name. An additional step – that of recognition of the final rulings of a joint water resource's tribunal as enforceable by the state's officers without a separate confirming national court order – is a step that may be able to be considered at an advanced stage of development of the water resources institutions.

D. Immunities

An international agency should have certain minimum exemptions and immunities, assuring it of functional independence from control by any single state and to enable it to discharge its responsibilities impartially on behalf of all the system states. Such provisions should deal with tax exemptions, licensing and permit exemptions, freedom of movement of personnel and immunities from suit in national courts.

E. Relationships with Other Agencies

Whatever type of legal and institutional arrangements are contemplated for development and management of an international water resources system, it should be kept in mind that any new entities that are established need to function in harmony with relevant institutions that function *within* the participating nations and with other relevant institutions of an international character. Moreover, the new entities should be in a position to take full advantage of professional and financial assistance available from numerous sources such as the United Nations Development Programme (UNDP). It is similarly important that the other entities, national and international, recognize the existence, mission and special authority of the new international agency.

By way of illustration of the importance of having a body able to work with international assistance agencies, in 1965 a Plan of Operation (that is, a project agreement) for the conduct of surveys leading to the preparation of a comprehensive regional development plan, was entered into between UNDP (Special Fund sector), the Governments of Brazil and Uruguay, and the United Nations Food and Agricultural Organization (as executing agency) covering the basin of the Merim Lake, or Lagoon. The inter-governmental cooperating agency under the agreement was the Brazil-Uruguay Joint Commission for the Development of the Merim Lagoon Basin created in 1963.

In 1967 a Plan of Operation was signed between UNDP, the World Meteorological Organization and the Governments of Costa Rica, El Salvador, Guatemala, Honduras, Nicaragua and Panamá for a project to expand and improve the hydrometeorological and hydrological services in the Central American Isthmus. The Regional Committee for Water Resources in Central America was designated to act on behalf of the Governments as the overall cooperating governmental agency with respect to the project. The Committee is related to the United Nations Economic Commission for Latin America (ECLA).[35] There was also an undertaking by

[35] ECLA established the Economic Cooperation Committee of the Central American Isthmus (CCE) in 1951, with the objective of promoting the economic integration of the region. The Economic Cooperation Committee thereafter established the Cen-

the Governments in the Plan of Operation to give the Regional Committee financial and administrative support. Each Government also agreed to create a national coordinating committee to be responsible for the execution, on behalf of the Government, of the project activities scheduled for that country. The national coordinating committees were composed of representatives of national agencies concerned with meteorological services and water resources. The six chairmen of the national coordinating committees comprised the Regional Committee. The Governments, in consultation with the World Meteorological Organization, appointed a Project Co-Manager, who also functioned as Secretary of the Regional Committee.

The International lending and technical assistance agencies are, it seems, impressed neither with simple agreements to cooperate to develop an international water resources system nor with elaborate agreement about basin potential. Commitments to do something concrete and feasible must be made within a minimally viable institutional framework. The governments themselves have, moreover, had to undertake direct responsibility for indebtedness incurred.

In any arrangement for outside financing to an international water resources agency acting on behalf of the participating states, the lending or underwriting institutions will certainly look for a clear showing of the ability of the basin institution to satisfy the indebtedness out of revenues, earmarked taxation or guaranteed contributions of the participating states, or some combination of these. A mortgage on a public dam, buildings or equipment will not be deemed sufficient, because financing agencies fully appreciate that foreclosure or the threat of foreclosure, even in the event of protracted default, would not be countenanced politically.

F. Dispute Settlement

Long-range benefits accrue to all parties when there are accepted accommodation and disputes settlement procedures. Successful accommodation or early settlement avoids work stoppages, strained relations, and most importantly the hardening of position that inevitably occurs once a difference emerges as a full-fledged dispute.

A government's negative position is often taken in response to sincere but speculative apprehension, that is, fear of what might happen if a certain course of action, not fully understood, is pursued. The collection of all

tral American Sub-Committee for Electrification and Water Resources, which then established the above-named Regional Committee.

relevant data and their dissemination to all concerned may serve to allay the apprehension, or may show the apprehension to be well founded. Objective discussion of the problem, in the presence of the best possible fact demonstration, may move one side or the other to give ground or to make some proposal that will result in an accommodation of the difference.

When full-dress discussion of the problem does not produce agreement or accommodation, at least a marshalling of the data has been accomplished by the people best equipped to formulate and compare the interpretations of the data and to articulate the many legitimate technical considerations involved in the development, conservation and use of the water resources of the particular international system. This record, and the data base, can then be made available to those who must decide, but who are of necessity further removed from operations and less specialized in their knowledge of the import of each facet of any particular problem.

The complexity and volume of water resources activities may at some stage become sufficient to justify consideration of some quite specialized machinery for conflict resolution within the international institutional framework of the basin or system. In a major international system with many different users, the business of dealing with challenges to power rates, conflicts between users of water, or cases of alleged violation of the regulations for navigation, for example, may become quite technical as well as time-consuming. Therefore, separate or semi-autonomous tribunals for purposes of deciding controversies and of issuing rulings (with or without the assistance of hearing examiners) may at that juncture be needed.

If small differences are not handled fairly and effectively within the agency, confidence in the machinery for the accommodation of more important differences cannot grow. For this reason, more than the usual importance attaches to the states' commitment to make conscientious use of the institutionalized procedures for accommodation and to see to it that only highly regarded and experienced persons are placed in those positions that involve accommodation or adjudicatory responsibility.

When those charged with final review are unable to resolve a critical difference by resort to the machinery created for the purpose, they are obliged to turn the matter over to their respective national governments for settlement at the higher level. At this stage it must be admitted that a formal dispute has arisen. "Referral to the Governments" usually signifies that the Governments' hand are now free of earlier obligations to handle the matter within established procedures, and that all the alternative processes of traditional diplomacy for the settlement of disputes are available.[36] Many disputes between nations are in fact settled by such customary means.

At some stage in the growth of a particularly comprehensive regional development institution, proposals are likely to be made for a standing regional international tribunal for the adjudication of formal disputes. Such a basin or regional court, carefully constituted, may provide the forum most conducive to prompt and acceptable settlement of disputes between or among the members of the water resources system community.

In lieu of creating a special tribunal, the basin states may, of course, choose to take advantage of the existing adjudicatory organ of the world community, the International Court of Justice (ICJ) at the Hague.[37] The basin states may choose to provide for settlement of formal disputes by the ICJ in the operative text of their basin agreement.[38] Or, the basin states may create a regional tribunal and employ the ICJ as an appellate tribunal,[39] remembering that before the World Court, including on appeal, only states may be parties.[40]

Since only states may be parties to case before the ICJ it would not be possible for the system agency to appear as a party,[41] nor for private or other persons to appear. If the desired scope of adjudication with respect to basin matters contemplates parties other than sovereign states, the International Court of Justice, as presently governed, would not be adequate as the sole forum for the settlement of basin disputes.

VI. RECENT EXPERIENCE IN THE HEMISPHERE

There remains, of course, much to be done in the Hemisphere in the field of coordinated international water resources development, conservation and use. Indeed, from the point of view of international administration, we have barely scratched the surface, and that in only a few systems. In North America, substantial regimes are operative in the Colorado,[42] the

[36] See chapter 6 of the Helsinki Rules, cited *supra* note 7. A dispute over water resources between states parties to a pre-existing arbitration treaty may, of course, be subjected to the requirements of such a treaty and handled accordingly.

[37] See Article 35 of the Statute of the ICJ; also, Articles 36, para 2, 40 and 53 of the ICJ Statute, and Article 33 of the ICJ's Rules of Court.

[38] Article 36, paragraph 1, ICJ Statute.

[39] See Article 67 of the ICJ Rules of Court.

[40] Article 34, paragraph 1, ICJ Statute.

[41] But see Article 34, paragraphs 2 and 3, ICJ Statute.

[42] See Pan American Union, *supra* note 19, pp. 73-77, 393-435, 446-50.

Rio Grande,[43] the St. Lawrence [44] and the Columbia basins.[45] The legal and institutional experience being accumulated is particularly instructive to officers charged with the elaboration of future international regimes and institutional arrangements.

Modern regimes have begun to take shape in two international basins in South America. But in most of Latin America, there is a yet no clear commitment to rational resources management. But the traditional tenseness over water boundary questions seems to have subsided.[46]

The Governments of Brazil and Uruguay established, as a result of recorded conversations in 1961, a Mixed Commission for the Merim Lagoon, or Patos-Mirim Basin. The Commission has only recommendatory powers concerning the creation of infrastructure and the execution of projects but has authority to carry out its responsibility of coordinating both national and international technical and financial assistance to the basin. The basin is recognized as a geo-economic unit. The immediate objective is the examination, with international organization assistance, of all technical, economic and social problems that limit progress in the basin and the identification of optimum courses of action for its integrated development.[47]

In the Plata Basin, one of the very largest hydraulic systems in the world,[48] there are five system states and a long and complex diplomatic history of friction as well as some notable cooperation. Since at least 1941, integrated basin development has been accepted in principle.

In 1946 two of the countries, Argentina and Uruguay, entered into a convention for the joint development and operation of large-scale hydroelectric facilities at Salto Grande on the Uruguay, one of the chief rivers in the Plata system. A bilateral Mixed Technical Commission was created, which carried out feasibility and engineering studies; a second "inter-state organization" for operation and administration is contemplated once the works are built. The advisability of forming a special multinational public

[43] *Ibid.*

[44] See OAS, cited *supra,* note 16, pp. 56-156; W. R. Willoughby, The St. Lawrence Waterway (1961).

[45] See Pan American Union, *supra* note 19, pp. 63-72, 245-392.

[46] The friction between Bolivia and Chile over the Rio Lauca is the prime example. On the dispute, see Chile, Min. de Relaciones Exteriores, La Cuestión del Rio Lauca (1963); Chinel, La Desviación del Rio Lauca por Chile (La Paz, Bolivia, 1963); Lecaros, *International Rivers: The Lauca Case,* 3 Indian J. Int'l L. 133.

[47] A second inter-ministerial conversation in 1964 served to stimulate the activities of the Commission. See Pan American Union, cited *supra* note 19, pp. 83-84, 484-86.

[48] See Inter-Amer. Development Bank, La Cuenca del Plata (Resumen del Informe Preliminar, 1970).

corporation as the "inter-state organization" has been discussed. Now that certain boundary and jurisdictional problems in the river have finally been settled, only the massive financing required seems to stand in the way of this "mature" project. The Salto Grande plan is in fact multipurpose. The works would, in addition to electric power, yield supplies of irrigation and municipal water and extend navigability.[49] In 1961, it was decided that a comprehensive statute for the Uruguay River would be drawn up to regulate all uses; provisions for the conservation of living resources and avoidance of contamination are to be included.[50]

The major thrust at least since 1967 has been the strengthening of consultation and cooperation on the multi-lateral, five-state basis. A number of important technical studies have been carried out, several internationally assisted projects are active, and the integrated approach has been embraced virtually without qualification, at least outwardly. In fulfillment of the pre-treaty agreements, each of the five states has created a National Commission for the Plata River Basin.

In the Plata Basin Treaty [51] the five states "agree to coordinate their efforts in order to promote the harmonious development and the physical integration" of the basin "and of those areas of direct and considerable influence." Areas of common interest are to be identified; studies, programs and works are to be implemented. Possible special agreements on nine subjects are anticipated, ranging from navigation to education.[52]

The Intergovernmental Coordinating Committee (ICC) is confirmed and continued as "the permanent body for the Basin," along with the governing Statute adopted for it in Santa Cruz, Bolivia, the previous year. The Statute places the ICC in charge of promoting, coordinating and implementing multinational activities that have as their purpose, "the integrated development" of the basin. Under this new regime, the collective action of the parties is, however, to be undertaken without prejudice to those projects and programs that they may decide to carry out within their respective territories, with due respect for international law and in accord with acceptable practice among friendly and neighboring nations.[53] Such

[49] See Pan American Union, *supra* note 19, pp. 87-90, 498-511.

[50] Art. 7, Tratado entre la República Argentina y la República Oriental del Uruguay sobre Límites en el Rio Uruguay (1961), Pan American Union, *supra* note 19, p. 510.

[51] Concluded on April 23, 1969, in Brasilia at the First Extraordinary Meeting of Foreign Ministers of the Countries of the Plata Basin. Several unofficial translations into English have appeared but are not relied upon here. See, e.g., The Review of the River Plate for Apr. 30, 1969, pp. 607-8.

[52] Art. I.

[53] Art. V.

a limitation on the international regime is hardly consonant with the avowed integrated basin approach.

The Intergovernmental Coordinating Committee also may manage any technical and financial assistance it can arrange for, and it is to carry out the decisions of the new organ composed of the Foreign Affairs Ministers.[54]

The Treaty organizes the five Foreign Ministers formally into the supreme basin institution. They are obliged to meet annually for the purpose of drawing up basic policy directives for the attainment of the Treaty's objectives, of evaluating the results obtained, of consulting with respect to the action of their governments within the scope of the integrated, multinational development of the basin, and, in general, to take the concrete steps necessary to performance of the Treaty. Decisions by this new organ require the affirmative vote of all five Ministers.[55]

A salutory proviso is the authority of the Foreign Ministers to revise the ICC's Statute without going through the treaty process all over again. An extraordinary meeting for the purpose is required; all five votes in the affirmative are necessary to adopt the change.[56]

The ICC is also governed by the unanimity rule. It has the authority to invite any person or entity or international agency representative to furnish information applicable to questions in its preview. The Committee has a Secretariat, headed by a professional Secretary.

The most important function of the Committee is to propose multinational "action programs" contributing to the advancement of the region. It has, however, no engineering board, or planning staff that might cause the Committee to become a bona fide center of proposal development and authoritative evaluation instead of a series of "diplomatic conversations."

This particular intergovernmental group, the ICC, because it is small, has the unusual potential of becoming a generator of collaboration. Of course, organs such as this, cannot in the end do much in the face of determined reluctance on the part of political leadership in one or more of the governments; the language of the treaty and the best efforts of the Committee will be as nothing. Whether the five National Commissions will be useful in the public persuasion and political roles remains to be seen.

The Plata Basin Treaty has now been ratified by all five parties. This new international regime is as yet largely untried. Expectations were markedly raised with its signing in Brasilia in 1969. In spite of the forward

[54] Art. III.
[55] Art. II.
[56] Art. III, para 2.

looking, integrationist stance of the treaty generally, adherents of comprehensive basin planning are possibly in for another disappointment. The Plata Basin's institutional arrangements, in the form confirmed in the treaty, are obviously inadequate for the attainment of systematic progress toward integrated development. Hedging in this fashion on a far-reaching substantive treaty commitment, by providing an insufficient and weak international institutional structure, is neither novel nor a cause for shame, even though it may be a cause for regret. Governments quite commonly want to have the desirable result offered by a united "team effort" without being disposed, or able, to pay the "price" for it. Nothing could be more understandable. A user or student of the water resources in question must not allow himself to be enticed into believing that the key projects and programs, so convincingly and progressively formulated, have real probability of materializing within less than a generation.

The preliminary period of reconnaissance and testing and "community building" requires a span of years that truly cannot, with rare exceptions, be dispensed with, given our nation-state system. We can, however, make the most of it. For example, properly designed data collection programs and preliminary planning surveys may be able to be mounted during this "post (treaty) gestation" period. Public education efforts could provide useful understanding when the time came to undertake effective system-wide collaboration.

Governments of "sovereign" states are, moreover, wary for good reason. One of the unavoidable consequences of actual implementation of the integrated regional development approach is a concomitant diminution of the freedom of action of the individual state. Let there be no doubt about that result where collaboration really counts, such as in the field of water resources. If a given country is finally ready to cast its lot rather irretrievably with its co-system states, and its leaders are ready, really, to share some of their power with the leaders of those governments, through an agency not subject to their sole control, then the benefits possible from optimum development and management of an international water resources system can be pursued effectively. Few leaders and, therefore, few states are, at this juncture in time, really "converted."

Thus, in conclusion, it should be noted that, in several important basins in the Hemisphere, there has been promising commitment to integrated water resources development, obviously stemming from an awareness that considerable net benefits are, potentially, to be had, and perhaps also out of a creeping conviction that – cost-benefit calculations and national freedom of action aside – there is no viable alternative, given the threat to our environment and the increased demands for water uses, *but* for states to join forces. The record of performance is, however, throughout the Hemisphere, not yet one to be especially proud of.

As concerns those consequential international water resources systems where *no* progress is thus far being made in development or management: States-members of other systems can, by their example and by sharing their experience, light the way, including the pitfalls, and stand ready to assist.

ANNEX A

INTERNATIONAL DRAINAGE BASINS OF CONSEQUENCE IN THE WESTERN HEMISPHERE

I. South America

A. Over 1,000,000 sq. km. of drainage area

1. Amazon
2. Plata
3. Orinoco

B. Between 100,000 and 1,000,000 sq. km. of drainage area

4. Patos-Mirim
5. Lake Titicaca
6. Essequibo
7. Maroni

C. Less than 100,000 sq. km. of drainage area

8. Chuy
9. Oyapock
10. Courantyne
11. Amacuro
12. Catatumbo
13. Mira
14. Mataje
15. Zarumilla
16. Tumbes
17. Chira
18. Sapaleri
19. Valdivia
20. Puelo
21. Yelcho
22. Palena
23. Aysen
24. Baker
25. Pascua
26. Serrano
27. Gallegos-Chico

28. Cullen
29. San Martín
30. Carmen Silva
31. Rio Grande (in Tiera del Fuego)
32. Lake Fagnano

Sub-total: 32

(14 basins, Nos. 19-32, are along the Chilean-Argentine southern border)

II. Central America and Mexico

A. Between 100,000 and 1,000,000 sq. km. of drainage area

33. Bravo (Rio Grande)
34. Colorado

B. Less than 100,000 sq. km. of drainage area

35. Grijalva-Usumacinta
36. Hondo
37. Suchiate
38. Sarstún
39. Motagua
40. Paz
41. Lempa
42. Goascorán
43. Negro (Nicaragua-Honduras)
44. Coco (Segovia)
45. San Juan
46. Sixaola

Sub-total: 14

III. The Caribbean

A. Less than 100,000 sq. km. of drainage area

47. Massacre (Dajabón)
48. Artibonite
49. Pedernales

Sub-total: 3

IV. Canada-United States

A. Over 1,000,000 sq. km. of drainage area

50. Mississippi
51. St. Lawrence

B. Between 100,000 and 1,000,000 sq. km. of drainage area

52. Columbia
53. Fraser
54. Nelson-Saskatchewan
55. Yukon

C. Less than 100,000 sq. km. of drainage area

56. St. John
57. Stikine

Sub-total: 8

Recapitulation:	Total International Basins	57
	Basins over 1,000,000 sq. km.	5
	Basins between 100,000 and 1,000,000 sq. km.	10
	Basins less than 100,000	42

N.B.:

Basins of tributaries of international rivers and lakes have not been listed separately, even when these are international in their own right (e.g., Uruguay, Paraná, Paraguay, etc., of the Plata; Caquetá, Puntumayo, Madeira, etc., of the Amazon; Meta, etc., of the Orinoco). A number of international tributaries in turn have international tributaries.

THE OUTER LIMIT OF THE CONTINENTAL SHELF*

by

José María Ruda

I. INTRODUCTION

In 1967 Malta took the initiative in proposing that the United Nations General Assembly examine the "[q]uestion of the reservation exclusively for peaceful purposes of the seabed and the ocean floor, and the subsoil thereof, underlying the high seas beyond the limit of present national jurisdiction, and the use of their resources in the interests of mankind." Intense activity then began in the United Nations and in other international and national, public and private, forums to obtain solutions to the problems arising with the start of the technological era of the seabed.

It has been considered indispensable that, before this technology is developed to a higher level, the norms in force for the exploration and exploitation of the seabed should be established with certainty, so that these activities may be carried out with the utmost possible efficacy and economy, consonant with rules of justice that would allow the exploration of submarine resources to be not only for the benefit of those who enjoy a vaster technological capacity, but also for the benefit of mankind in general and particularly of the developing countries, regardless of their maritime, or even non-coastal, position.

To note that the sea occupies two-thirds of the surface of our planet is to show the importance that should be assigned, and is assigned, by countries to these new problems of the seabed, problems that up to now have only been subject to international legislation based on very general principles. The main focus of the law of the sea has been concentrated for centuries on the two main uses of the marine environment: navigation and fishing. Recently, with the Truman Proclamation of 1945 and the begin-

* This essay was written in 1971, before the author was elected member of the International Court of Justice.

ning of offshore oil activities, there was a rapid development of the norms that govern activities in this area.

Various interesting issues have been raised in the discussions which have taken place up to the present. Fundamentally, these can be divided into two: What is the extent of national jurisdiction? And what will be the regime to be applied to the seabed beyond national jurisdiction?

Of the two problems, the former has heretofore been regarded as the more controversial. Some states, particularly those regarded as developed, have shown great interest in defining the limits of national jurisdiction. In this study we shall deal with the questions that arise from the consideration of the limits of national jurisdiction of the seabed. Attention will, however, be paid to the recent claims of several Latin American states to exercise jurisdiction over a 200 mile territorial sea, since these claims would also affect the determination of the limits of national jurisdiction over the seabed, especially in those cases where the 200 mile limit extends far beyond the outer limit of the continental shelf.

We shall begin by analyzing the actual state of the technology with regard to the exploration and exploitation of the bed.

II. PRESENT STATE OF THE TECHNOLOGY

The development of the technology for exploring and exploiting the seabed began in the last two or three decades. Some progress in the exploitation of the mineral resources of the seabed has been made, but we are still at the very initial stages of this new technology. Until now the technology used has been merely an adaptation to the marine environment of that employed on the earth's surface. Everything indicates that we should not nourish more than a cautious optimism regarding the possibility of exploiting economically the mineral wealths of the seabed in the near future. This caveat applies to all minerals except petroleum, which continues to be the only mineral which is now economically exploitable in the seabed.

We shall consider, before entering into the oil problem, the status of the principal mineral resources: the manganese nodules, the phosphorite submarine placers and the metaliferous muds. The report presented to the Economic and Social Council by the Secretary-General in 1969, entitled "Mineral Resources of the Sea." [1] is most informative about these minerals. With regard to manganese nodules, on which so many hopes have been pinned recently, the report pointed out that, although there is no doubt

[1] U.N. Doc. No. E/4680.

"that the potential gross amounts of manganese and associated metal contained in ocean floor nodules are enormous, [t]he possibility of commercial harvesting and processing has however caused controversy, with some experts of the opinion that the copper, nickel, and cobalt contents of the nodules, together with manganese, may warrant their commercial exploitation (Mero, 1967), while most people in the business believe that their economic potential is highly uncertain and is likely to remain so for years, if not for one or two decades." [2] And the problem does not end here. The Secretary-General adds that matters should also be resolved concerning technical designs, operations and procedures for the mining of the materials of these nodules, which seems to be a complex operation, hardly understood from a metallurgical point of view.

With reference to the phosphorite submarine placers, the Secretary-General's conclusions are even clearer. He points out that "up to the present date the phosphorite submarine placers have not been commercially exploited." With regard to the future, he says: "In any event, present recovery costs will favor investigations in less than 50 fathoms of water, at least for the immediate future." [2]

A more optimistic view is to be found with respect to the metalliferous muds. The report states: "although exploitation of the metalliferous mud poses some technical problems, it may prove to be economically feasible in the not too distant future." [4]

The picture presented in regard to manganese, phosphorite and metaliferous muds contrasts with the great breakthroughs achieved in the economic exploitation of oil in the seabed, especially on the continental shelf. Since the first significant discovery of oil, in 1947, eleven miles off the Louisiana shore, 75 countries have started to exploit the continental shelf and 22 are at present exploiting it. The coastal zone has been explored substantially and the potential of many regions, as far as the exploitation of hydrocarbons is concerned, is an already well established fact.

The continental slope and the continental rise (or margin)[5] are not yet

[2] *Id.* at 42.
[3] *Id.* at 27.
[4] *Id.* at 45.
[5] The terminology of this work is similar to the one used by the U.N. Secretary in the Report on "Mineral Resources of the Sea," U.N. Doc. No. ST/ECA/125, p. 1. The report defines the continental shelf, the continental slope, the continental and the ocean floor or abyss as follows:

"*The continental shelf* is defined as that area of the sea or ocean floor between the mean low-water line and that marked change in the inclination of the floor at the upper edge of the continental slope. The change in inclination, from about one eight of 1° to considerably greater angles, occurs at depths usually between sufficiently known, but there are indications that oil may be found in an economically exploitable condition. Naturally, the futher away the oil is from the coast, the costlier will be its exploration and exploitation. The upper part of the continental slope is being considered as the next step for exploration. This is taking place in the North of the Gulf of Mexico, in the Western Atlantic and in the Santa Barbara Channel in California, where the United States has tendered zones located at 183 and 457 metres. Numerous geological studies suggest the very likely presence of hydrocarbons in the continental slope and in the continental margin, due to the existence of sedimentary basins which are evidence of the existence of oil basins.[6] The semi-closed seas can also have certain important sedimentations. Recently, in the Gulf of Mexico, a drilling took place at a water depth of 3572 metres, by the vessel "Glomar Challenger", which found traces of oil in samples taken at a depth of 137 to 144 metres under the floor.

On the other hand, all existing geological information indicates that only thin sedimentary basins exist in the abyssal depth. Nothing can, for the moment, confirm or deny the existence of oil in these zones of the floor. Consequently, the efforts made in the exploration for and drilling of oil are at present primarily directed towards the continental shelf the continental slope and the continental margin.

> about 130 and 200 metres, but exceptionally as shallow as 50 metres or as deep as 500 metres. The width of the shelf ranges from less than one mile to 800 miles."
>
> "*The continental slope*, usually from 10 to 20 miles wide, extends from the outer edge of the Continental shelf to the continental rise. The inclination of the slope varies widely from as little as 3° to over 45°; slopes of 25° are common."
>
> "*The continental rise* is a broad, uniform and smooth-surfaced wedge of clastic sediments, from 100 to 1,000 km wide and up to 10 km thick, which, wherever deep-sea trenches are absent, slopes gently oceanward from the base of the continental slope, usually in 2,000 to 5,000 metres of water."
>
> "*The abyss or ocean floor* appears to be a rolling plain from 3,300 to about 5,500 metres below the surface of the sea: it is scarred by deep gorges called trenches and studded with sea mounts and guyots. The mean depth of the superjacent waters is 3,800 metres. More than 75% of the ocean floor lies at a depth of less than 5,000 metres."

The figures mentioned in the Report by the Secretary-General are not the ones followed by authors. In a recent work there was established for the continental shelf a median distance of 65 kilometres from the coast and the depth of 150 metres; for the continental margin an average of 4000 metres depth, without fixing a distance from the coast. V. E. McKelvey, J. I. Tracey, Jr., G. E. Stoetz and J. G. Velder, *Subsea Mineral Resources and Problems Related to their Development*, 619 Geographical Survey Circular 2 (1969).

[6] National Petroleum Council, Petroleum Resources under the Ocean Floor 24-25 (1969).

With regard to exploration, the oil industry is drilling exploratory wells in waters of 400 metres depth. For scientific purposes and with systems which only allow the use of drilling equipment without re-entry systems, under the JOIDES Programme (Joint Oceanographic Institutions for Deep Earth Sampling), a drilling of 835 metres below the seabed has been achieved, at a water depth of 4973 metres, which totals 5808 metres below sea-level.

As for commercial exploitation, up to now fixed shelves at sea level have been used, having been installed at a depth of 104 metres. New models for drilling at 180 metres are being designed. Work is also being carried out in the development of submarine techniques which will allow exploitation at a depth of 180 metres. In addition, experiments are being made with mobile floatable exploitation systems that have already been successfully tried out at 195 metres of water. Another similar test was carried out at 303 metres, but this had a negative result. Drilling has even been effected at a depth of 396 metres below sea level and at 3667 metres below the sea bed. Everything indicates that in the next 5 years technology will allow exploitation at depths of 457 metres; in 10 years time, depths of probably between 1219 and 1829 metres will be reached.

III. THE LEGAL PROBLEM

The legal problem of the delimitation of national jurisdiction arises from the conflicting interpretations of Article 1 of the Geneva Convention on the Continental Shelf,[7] which defines the continental shelf for the purpose of determining the scope of national jurisdiction over it. It should be remembered that, in the recent judgment of the International Court of Justice in the Continental Shelf Cases,[8] Article 1 of the Convention, together with Articles 2 and 3, has been mentioned as constituting a norm of customary international law. The General Assembly, in its recent Resolution 2574 (XXIV), of 15 December, 1969, considers [9]

[7] Article 1 of the 1958 Convention states:
"For the purpose of these articles, the term "continental shelf" is used as referring (a) to the seabed and subsoil of submarine areas adjacent to the coast but outside the area of the territorial sea, to a depth of 200 metres or, beyond that limit, to where the depth of the superjacent waters admits of the exploitation of the natural resources of the said areas; (b) to the seabed and subsoil of similar submarine areas adjacent to the coasts of islands."

[8] [1970] I.C.J. 70.

[9] This resolution was adopted by 65 votes in favour, 12 against and 30 abstentions.

"that the definition of the continental shelf contained in the Convention on the Continental Shelf of 29 April, 1958, does not define with sufficient precision the limits of the area over which a coastal state exerts sovereign rights for the purpose of exploration and exploitation of natural resources, and that customary international law on the subject is not conclusive."

As can be seen from the previous section, petroleum techniques are close to being capable of exploitation at a depth of around 200 metres and look like exceeding that in a few years time. Consequently, the question has arisen as to the limit to which the sovereign rights of the coastal states extend, if exploitation is effected at considerable depth or at great distances from the coast.

The real problem is that at the time of the formulation of the Geneva Convention of 1958, it was not thought that a technique which would permit the exploitation of mineral resources beyond a depth of 200 metres could be developed so rapidly. It was estimated that it would occur at some distant time. Meanwhile, the definition in the Convention could be applied without inconvenience. Later, if a new technique were to be developed, the treaty revision mechanism, provided for in its Article 13, would come into effect. Thus, after a period of 5 years from its entry into force, any of the parties could request the Secretary-General for a revision of the Convention and it would then fall to the Assembly to take the appropriate measures. The legislative history indicates, to our knowledge, that the idea was to legislate for the then prevailing conditions.

Article 1 of the Geneva Convention originated in Article 67 of the draft prepared by the International Law Commission, during its eighth session, in 1956. The Commission had been working on the continental shelf since its second session in 1950. From that date up to its final draft, the basic focus of the definition of the Commission varied considerably from session to session. In 1950 the Commission stated in its Report:

"The Commission took the view that a littoral state could exercise control and jurisdiction over the seabed and subsoil of the submarine areas situated outside its territorial waters with a view to exploring and exploiting the natural resources there. The area over which such a right of control and jurisdiction might be exercised should be limited; but where the depth of the waters permitted exploitation, it should not necessarily depend on the existence of a continental shelf. The Commission considered that it would be unjust to countries having no continental shelf if the granting of the right in question were made dependent on the existence of such a shelf." [10]

[10] Yearbook of the International Law Commission, 1950, Vol. II, p. 384, para. 198.

The principal thought of the Commission in 1950 was to take into account the criterion of exploitability as the basis for the exercise of rights of "control and jurisdiction," the object being to avoid unjust situations for those countries that did not have a continental shelf.

In the following year, 1951, the Commission, basing itself on the proposal of its Special Rapporteur, Professor François, approved these articles:

"As here used, the term 'continental shelf' refers to the seabed and the subsoil of the submarine areas contiguous to the coast, but outside the areas of marginal seas, where the depth of the superjacent water does not exceed 200 metres." [11]

. . . .

"The rights of control and jurisdiction referred to in the present chapter belong, up to a distance of 20 miles beyond the territorial waters, to all the coastal states which do not possess a continental shelf, as defined in Article 1." [12]

The Commission adopted a dual criterion, according to whether or not the countries had a continental shelf. At the same session, after these two articles were approved, the problem of definition was once again discussed. The new idea put forward omitted all reference to the 200 metre depth line and returned to the criterion of exploitability. The following text of Article 1 was approved:

"As here used, the term 'continental shelf' refers to the seabed and the subsoil of the submarine areas contiguous to the coast, but outside the area of territorial waters, where the depth of the superjacent waters admits of the exploitation of the natural resources of the seabed and subsoil." [13]

The commentary on Article 1, presented in 1951, suggested that the fixed limit of 200 metres had the disadvantage of instability, for it was probable that technology would permit exploitation beyond 200 metres in the near future. Nevertheless, for the time being, that depth was considered sufficient from the practical point of view.

The Commission returned to this position at its fifth session in 1953, adopting the 200 metres standard. It was cognizant of the comments made by various Governments who did not share its ideas, and concluded that its text would bring about controversies and uncertainties. In its commentary, the Commission stated: "On the other hand, the limit of 200 metres – a limit which is at present sufficient for all practical needs – has been

[11] *Id.*, 1951, Vol. I, 113th Meeting, para. 118.
[12] *Id.*, 117th session, para. 65.
[13] *Id.*, Vol. II, p. 141.

fixed because it is at that depth that the continental shelf, in the geological sense, generally comes to an end." It added however, that it did not believe "that the existence of the continental shelf in its geographical configuration as generally understood, is essential for the exercise of the rights of the coastal state as defined in these articles." No doubt the Commission had taken very much into consideration the special situation of the North Sea coast of Norway when arguing that:

"although the depth of two hundred metres as a limit of the continental shelf must be regarded as the general rule, it is a rule which is subject to equitable modifications in special cases in which submerged areas, of a depth less that 200 metres, situated in considerable proximity to the coast are separated by a narrow channel deeper than 200 metres from the part of the continental shelf adjacent to the coast. Such shallow areas must, in these cases, be considered, as contiguous to that part of the shelf." [14]

The approved article of the fifth session, in 1953, read:

"As used in these articles, the term 'continental shelf" refers to the seabed and subsoil of the submarine areas contiguous to the coast, but outside the area of the territorial sea, to a depth of two hundred metres." [15]

During its 1956 (eighth) session, the International Law Commission once again varied its criteria, and the article on the continental shelf, prepared for the Geneva Conference on the Law of the Sea, contained both elements it had previously considered: the 200 metre depth and the exploitability criterion. The definition of the continental shelf was to be:

"For the purposes of these articles, the term 'Continental Shelf' is used as referring to the seabed and the subsoil of the submarine areas adjacent to the coast but outside the area of the territorial sea, to a depth of 200 metres (approximately 100 fathoms), or beyond that limit, to where the depth of the superjacent waters admits of the exploitation of the natural resources of the said areas." [16]

The Commission's commentary to Article 1 called special attention to the results of the Inter-American Specialized Conference on "Conservation of Natural Resources: Continental Shelf and Oceanic Waters," which took place in March, 1956, in the Dominican Republic. The Commission arrived at the conclusion that the right of the coastal state should be extended beyond the limit of 200 metres "to where the depth of the superjacent

[14] *Id.*, 1953, Vol. II, p. 213-114, paras. 64, 65, 66.
[15] *Id.*, p. 212, Article 1.
[16] *Id.*, 1956, Vol. II, p. 296.

waters admits of the exploitation of the natural resources of the seabed and subsoil." Furthermore, the commentary continued:

"Certain members of the Commission ... [w]hile maintaining the limit of 200 metres in this article as the normal limit corresponding to the present needs, ... wished to recognise forthwith the right to exceed that limit if exploitation of the seabed or subsoil at a depth greater than 200 metres proved technically possible. It was therefore proposed that the following words should be added to the article, 'or, beyond that limit, to where the depth of the superjacent waters admits of the exploitation of the natural resources of the said areas." [17]

With regard to the same definition, the Commission gave further explanations in its commentary (paragraphs 5 to 9) which we believe should be quoted fully to facilitate understanding of the draft article:

"5) The sense in which the term 'continental shelf' is used departs to some extent from the geological concept of the term. The varied use of the term by scientists is in itself an obstacle to the adoption of the geological concept as a basis for legal regulation of this problem.
6) There was yet another reason why the Commission decided not to adhere strictly to the geological concept of the continental shelf. The mere fact that the existence of a continental shelf in the geological sense might be questioned in regard to submarine areas where the depth of the sea would nevertheless permit of exploitation of the subsoil in the same way as if there were a continental shelf, could not justify the application of a discriminatory legal regime to these regions.
7) While adopting, to a certain extent, the geographical test for the "continental shelf" as the basis of the juridical definition of the term, the Commission therefore in no way holds that the existence of a continental shelf, in the geographical sense as generally understood, is essential for the exercise of the rights of the coastal state as defined in these articles. Thus, if, as is the case in the Persian Gulf, the submarine areas never reach the depth of 200 metres, that fact is irrelevant for the purposes of the present article. Again, exploitation of a submarine area at a depth exceeding 200 metres is not contrary to the present rules, merely because the area is not a continental shelf in the geological sense.
8) In the special cases in which submerged areas of a depth less than 200 metres, situated fairly close to the coast, are separated from the part of the continental shelf adjacent to the coast by a narrow channel deeper than 200 metres, such shallow areas could be considered as adjacent to that part of the shelf. It would be for the state relying on this exception to the general rule to establish its claim to an equitable modification of the rule. In case of dispute it must be a matter for arbitral determination whether a shallow submarine area falls within the rule as here formulated.
9) Noting that it was departing from the strictly geological concept of the

[17] *Id.*, Commentary, p. 296, para. 4.

term, *inter alia,* in view of the inclusion of exploitable areas beyond the depth of 200 metres, the Commission considered the possibility of adopting a term other than "continental shelf." It considered whether it would not be better, in conformity with the usage employed in certain scientific works and also in some national laws and international instruments, to call these regions "submarine areas". The majority of the Commission decided to retain the term "continental shelf" because it is in current use and because the term "submarine areas" used without further explanation would not give a sufficient indication of the nature of the areas in question. The Commission considered that some departure from the geological meaning of the term "continental shelf" was justified, provided that the meaning of the term for the purpose of these articles was clearly defined. It has stated this meaning of the term in the present article." [18]

The definition adopted in Article 1 by the 1958 Geneva Convention on the Continental Shelf, then, is practically the same as that of the International Law Commission, with the addition of the reference to the seabed and the subsoil of the analogous submarine regions adjacent to the coasts. Article 1 was approved by a considerable majority during the Plenary Sessions. There were 51 votes in favour, 5 against and 10 abstentions. A separate vote was requested for the words "or, beyond that limit, to where the depth of the superjacent waters admits of the exploitation of the natural resources of the said areas." [19]

Various proposals for modification were presented, some restricting and one enlarging the definition formulated by the International Law Commission, but they were all withdrawn or rejected. The proposals were the following:

Panama

"For the purposes of these articles, the common expression 'continental shelf' is used as referring to the seabed, soil and subsoil of the submarine areas adjacent to the coast but outside the area of the territorial sea, including both constituent parts of the continental terrace, namely, the continental shelf proper and the continental slope with its gorges, valleys, depressions and ravines, as far as the further points at which the depth of the superjacent waters admits of the exploitation of the natural resources of the said areas of the continental slope, but excluding the great depths of oceanic basins." [20]

This proposal was rejected by 38 votes to 4, with 26 abstentions.

[18] *Id.*, p. 297.

[19] First United Nations Conference on the Law of the Sea, Official Documents, Vol. II, 8th Plenary Session, para. 44.

[20] U.N. Doc. A/Conf. 13/C.4/L.4.

Argentina

"The term 'continental shelf' refers to the seabed and subsoil of the submarine areas adjacent to the coast but outside the area of the territorial sea."
The sovereignty of a State extends over the submarine shelf contiguous to its sea coast, to a depth of 200 metres." [21]

This proposal was withdrawn.

France

Delete the words:

"or, beyond that limit, to where the depth of the superjacent waters admits of the exploitation of the natural resources of the said areas." [22]

This proposal was rejected by 48 votes to 12, with 7 abstentions.

Yugoslavia

"1. For the purposes of these articles the term 'continental shelf' is used as referring to the seabed and subsoil of the submarine areas adjacent to the coast but outside the area of the territorial sea, to a depth of 200 metres, but only up to a boundary line not extending beyond 100 miles from the outer limit of the territorial sea. Local occurrences of submarine gorges, valleys, depressions and ravines shall not be taken into account in this area of 100 miles, provided they are within the outer limit of the continental shelf as described in the preceding sentence.
2. Where such a depth is greater, the continental shelf stretches only up to a boundary line not extending beyond 50 miles in the direction of the high seas from the outer limit of the territorial sea." [23]

This proposal was verbally amended by its sponsor, replacing the words "200 metres" by "550 metres." The proposal, with the amendment, was rejected by 39 votes to 2, with 21 abstentions. At the Plenary Session the same amendment was rejected by 53 votes to 3, with 11 abstentions.

India

Replace by the following text:

"For the purposes of these articles, the term 'continental shelf' is used as referring to the seabed and subsoil of the submarine areas adjacent to the coast

[21] U.N. Doc. A/Conf. 13/C.4/L.6.
[22] U.N. Doc. A/Conf. 13/C.4/L.7.
[23] U.N. Doc. A/Conf. 13/C.4/L.12.

but outside the area of the territorial sea, extending so far as the seabed is concerned to a depth of 550 metres of the superjacent waters." [24]

This proposal was rejected by 31 votes to 31, with 16 abstentions.

Canada

"For the purposes of these articles, the term 'continental shelf' is used as referring to the seabed and subsoil of the submarine areas adjacent to the coast but outside the area of the territorial sea, to the point where a substantial break in grade occurs leading to abyssal ocean depth or, where there is no such substantial break in grade, to the point at which the depth of the superjacent waters reaches 200 metres." [25]

Canada amended this proposal verbally, replacing the words "200 metres" by "550 metres." The Federal Republic of Germany presented once again the original Canadian proposal, without amendments. This latter proposal was rejected by 45 votes to 4, with 18 abstentions. The amended Canadian proposal was rejected by 39 votes to 16, with 12 abstentions.

Netherlands and United Kingdom of Great Britain and Northern Ireland

"1. The provisions of the following articles shall apply to the seabed and subsoil of submarine areas contiguous to the outer limit of the territorial sea, including the continental shelf, the continental slope, and the submarine areas contiguous to islands.

2. The coastal state exercises over these areas sovereign right for the purpose of exploring and exploiting their natural resources. For this purpose devices working on or in high seas may be used up to a depth of water of 550 metres." [26]

This proposal was withdrawn.

Sweden

"The coastal state exercises over the submarine areas adjacent to its coast but outside the area of the territorial sea, up to a depth of water of 550 metres, control and jurisdiction for the purpose of exploring and exploiting the natural resources of the seabed and subsoil of such areas." [27]

This proposal was withdrawn in favour of India's revised proposal, reproduced *supra*.[28]

It is important to state these proposals because not only do they show

[24] U.N. Doc. A/Conf. 13/C.4/L.29/Rev. 1.
[25] U.N. Doc. A/Conf. 13/C.4/L.30.
[26] U.N. Doc. A/Conf. 13/C.4/L.32.
[27] U.N. Doc. A/Conf. 13/C.4/L.33.
[28] The above proposals are contained in U.N. Doc. A/Conf. 13/42, at p. 127-136.

interesting positions and revive the 550 metre line, but they also reveal the degree to which the Conference might have varied the definition proposed by the International Law Commission. Ultimately they retained the basic draft.

We have made this presentation of the legislative history of Article 1 somewhat detailed, for it reveals that the subject matter requiring regulation by the legislation remains ill-defined. Nobody seemed to question seriously the 200 metre depth line as the outer limit of the continental shelf, but there was not the same assurance on greater depths. On adopting the second part of the definition, regarding the possibility of exploitation, the International Law Commission had in mind, as is shown by the commentary to the final article, the situation of those countries without a continental shelf, geologically speaking, considering it necessary to give them some satisfaction and hope. Clearly, it did not consider it essential to resolve, at that time, the problem of the exploitation of the shelf at more than 200 metres depth. That is why today we are confronted with the controversy on the interpretation of its definition and why there are discussions on modifying it. That is also why, it appears to us, the International Law Commission, in the commentary to Article 27 of its final draft, later to become Article 2 of the Convention on High Seas, stated, as regards the position then:

"The Commission has not made specific mention of the freedom to explore or exploit the subsoil of the high seas. It considered that apart from the case of the exploitation or exploration of the soil or subsoil of the continental shelf – a case dealt with separately in section III below – such exploitation had not yet assumed sufficient practical importance to justify special regulation." [29]

IV. INTERPRETATION OF THE GENEVA CONVENTION

At a time when technology is beginning to create important possibilities for commercial exploitation of the seabed, especially in the realm of petroleum, divergent interpretations of Article 1 of the Geneva Convention have arisen. Indeed, modifications of the norms have been clearly and flatly proposed. Such interpretations are various and include the most extreme positions.

A first theory [30] interprets in a literal way the second part of the defini-

[29] Yearbook of the International Law Commission, 1956, Vol. II, p. 278.

[30] This theory was maintained in the Geneva Conference by Pakistan and the Lebanon. See also S. S. Bernfeld *Developing the Resources of the Sea – Security of Investment.* Int'l Lawyer 67 - 76 (1967).

tion, arguing that if the exploration of the resources of the submarine subsoil is feasible, sovereign rights could be extended up to the point where the exploitation reaches, and that if technology reaches great depths, the seabed should be divided by the median lines between the territories of states, in accordance with the application of Article 6, paragraph 1, of the Convention. Article 6 states that if the continental shelf is adjacent to the territory of two or more states, whose shores are opposite each other, the boundaries will be determined by way of agreements, and in the absence of such, by the median line. Professor Shigeru Oda asserts: "It has been deduced that all the submarine areas of the world have been theoretically divided among the coastal states for this Geneva Convention." [31] This interpretation is based exclusively on the criterion of exploitability.[32] F. P. Christy has prepared a very interesting map dividing the subsoil of the sea, where possession of islands such as Ascension, Santa Helena and Tristan da Cunha by the British, and the Clipperton Islands by the French, will give them extensive seabed territory.[33] The interpretation is not accepted by the majority of writers, nor, in practice, by states. The concept of adjacency, mentioned in the definition, seems to be ignored. Moreover, the legislative history shows that the unexplained expression "submarine regions" was not chosen to replace "continental shelf" and that the International Law Commission did not want to "disregard the geographical phenomenon whatever the term – propinquity, contiguity, geographical continuity, appurtenance or identity – used to define the relationship between the submarine area in question and the adjacent non-submerged land." [34] It should be recalled that on acceding to the Convention, France presented a declaration on the Article, pointing out that "the Government of the French Republic is of the opinion that the expression "adjacent" regions refers to a notion of geophysical, geological and geographical dependence, which excludes *ipso facto* an unlimited extension of the continental shelf." Nobody has objected to this interpretive French declara-

[31] S. Oda, International Control of the Sea Resources 167 (1963).

[32] F. T. Christy, Jr., of the organization Resources for the Future, maintains in a paper entitled *Realities of Ocean Resources* prepared by the Marine Frontiers Conference (University of Rhode Island) in 1967:
"In accordance with the Geneva Convention the resources of the seabed belong to the coastal states up to the depth of 200 metres or beyond that limit up to where the depth of the superjacent waters admits the exploitation of natural resources. The exclusive rights are consequently only limited by the criteria of exploitability and, as has been noticed above, this criteria should have already resulted in an extension of the limits beyond 200 metres."

[33] *Ibid.*

[34] Yearbook of the International Law Commission, 1956, Vol. II, p. 298.

tion and only two parties, Great Britain and the United States, have reserved their positions.[35] It should be remembered that, since 1965, the United Nations Seabed Committee has asserted that:

> "It was generally agreed that there is an area of the seabed and ocean floor which is not subject to national jurisdiction and that this fact, which seemed obvious, needed emphasizing because of the broad interpretation of which article 1 of the Convention on the Continental Shelf was susceptible." [36]

The General Assembly has incorporated this same idea, affirming, in its Resolution 2574 A (XXIV), of 15 December, 1969, "that there exists an area of the seabed and ocean floor of the subsoil thereof beyond the limits of national jurisdiction."

Another avenue of interpretation is based essentially on the concept of contiguity, leading to the conclusion that the exploitation should not be too distant from the shore. The 200 metre isobath would be, for example, a minimum reasonable line of contiguity.[37] Employing primarily the concept of contiguity, Louis Henkin maintains that the criterion of exploitability has ceased to serve as a basis for a definition and that the submarine zones adjacent to the shores, where the coastal states have the exclusive rights over mineral resources, should not take up too much territory of the seabed, nor should it be too distant from the shoreline.[38] This author favours a new definition of the shelf.

The National Petroleum Council (NPC) of the United States has presented to the Department of the Interior, at its request, an extensive study [39] which endorses a broad theory on the continental shelf and has given rise to an intense controversy among jurists of that country. The NPC analyzes four phrases of the Geneva definition. It considers that Article 1, when mentioning the "submarine zones," takes into account not the continental shelf in its strictly geomorphological conception but any submarine zone to be found located offshore, and it reconciles the conditions set forth in the said article. The expression "adjacent to the shores" does not refer to the centre point of the ocean, but to the zones situated in the proximity of the shore. Moreover, it is added that the expression "up to the 200 metre depth line" is unconditionally applied without taking into account the existence

[35] United Nations, Multilateral Treaties in respect of which the Secretary-General performs depositary functions 333 (1968).

[36] Report of the ad hoc Committee to study the peaceful uses of the seabed and the ocean floor beyond the limits of national jurisdiction, p. 48.

[37] This possibility is enunciated, without being supported, by the Polish Professor R. Bierzanek, Towards a Better Use of the Ocean 140 (......).

[38] L. Henkin, Law of the Sea's Natural Resources 24 (1968).

[39] National Petroleum Council, Petroleum Resources under the Ocean Floor (1969).

or not of the capacity of exploiting. Finally, the phrase "or beyond that limit, to where the depth of the superjacent waters admits of the exploitation of the natural resources of the said areas," means that it is allowed to go beyond the 200 metres, in accordance with existing technology, but within the limits of adjacency. That is why it is considered that the definition establishes an elastic limit. In short, the NPC maintains that, up to 200 metres, jurisdiction is unconditional, regardless of exploitability, and that beyond such a depth, it depends on technological advances within the limits of contiguity. As at present everything indicates that any submarine zone may at some time be exploited, only the criterion of contiguity will determine the limits of national jurisdiction. The NPC interpretation is translated in practice to mean that:

> "it can reasonably be concluded that the coastal nations' exclusive jurisdiction over the natural resources of the seabed and subsoil was intended to, and does, encompass in general, the continental mass seaward to where the submerged portion of that mass meets the abyssal ocean floor (including the continental shelf, continental borderland, continental slope, and at least the landward portion of the continental rise overlapping the slope)." [40]

The National Petroleum Council also construes the definition to include the "adjacent" area of the shore, in cases of an abrupt drop of the coast towards the depths, although there does not exist, strictly speaking, a shelf. Moreover, in the case of semi-closed seas, the coastal states can claim jurisdiction up to the median line, even when this line is beyond the exterior border of a typical continental shelf. The National Petroleum Council bases its interpretation of the Convention on extensive arguments which include an analysis of the preparatory works of the International Law Commission and the Geneva Conference, the legislative history, the presentation made by the State Department and the consent thereupon given to this instrument in the American Senate, as well as scholarly writings, the subsequent practice of states and the facts and consequences resulting from the application of the treaty.

A similar interpretation to that of the NPC is offered by the Mineral Resources Committee of the Seabed of the American Branch of the International Law Association. In its Interim Report, published in July 1968, it says:

> "The jurisdiction of coastal states with respect to the natural resources of the seabed and subsoil areas under the high seas is determined by the Geneva Convention on the Continental Shelf.
>
> . . . .

[40] *Id.* at 57.

However, for reasons seldom made explicit, some find difficulty with the boundary definition in the Convention, particularly in terms of the reach of the exploitability criterion in the light of the principle of adjacency.

....

As a general rule, the limit of adjacency may reasonably be regarded as coinciding with the foot of the submerged portion of the continental land mass." [41]

The "House of Delegates" of the American Bar Association in a joint Report by the Natural Resources Section, International and Comparative Law Section and the Peace and Law through the United Nations Section tends to favour the position that the concept of exploitability is limited by that of adjacency and that:

"the exclusive sovereign rights of the coastal nations with respect to the seabed minerals now embrace the submerged land mass of the adjacent continent down to its junction with the deep ocean floor, irrespective of depth." [42]

Another interesting interpretation is the one presented by Professor Jennings of Cambridge, when analyzing the consequences of the recent judgment handed down by the International Court of Justice in the North Sea Continental Shelf cases.[43] Jennings distinguishes between the established regime in the Convention of 1958 and the principles of general international law. With regard to the principles of general international law, the basic norm, according to Jennings, is reflected in what the Court calls "the most fundamental of all rules of law relating to the continental shelf," namely, the following: [44]

"... the rights of the coastal State in respect of the area of the continental shelf that constitutes a natural prolongation of its land territory into and under the sea exist *ipso facto* and *ab initio*, by virtue of its sovereignty over the land, and as an extension of it in an exercise of sovereign rights for the purpose of exploring the seabed and exploiting its natural resources. In short, there is here an inherent right."

Consequently, for this writer, the idea of dependency or prolongation constitutes the basis of the limit and this can only be identified by way of reference to physical fact, whereby geomorphological, and perhaps geological, considerations obtain special significance. In the case of the definition in the Geneva Convention, Jennings' interpretation is that the Convention goes beyond the concept of continental shelf "in the strict sense,"

[41] Committee on Deep Sea Mineral Resources, Interim Report, July 19, 1968 pp. IX-X

[42] Cited in National Petroleum Council, *supra* note 39, at 62.

[43] R. Y. Jennings, *Some Possible Implications of the North Sea Case Judgment, Continental Shelf Jurisdiction* 18 Int'l and Comp. L. Q. 819-32 (1969).

[44] *North Sea Continental Shelf* [1969] I.C.J. 22.

since it refers to the 200 metre depth, adding "or beyond that limit." That is to say, in some way the Convention is limited to the 200 metre area. Since those 200 metres constitute the regular limit of the drop, Jennings concludes that the Geneva Convention also returns us to geography and geology to resolve the question of boundaries. He concludes that in drawing data from these sciences, there is no doubt that the continental slope is as much a prolongation of the continental mass as is the continental shelf, because the rock structure is the same in the shelf and in the slope. As far as the continental margin goes, Jennings believes that here all is not that clear, for the elements of the continent and the ocean floor are intermixed. He considers that, with regard to this, the law does not provide a clear answer, and points out that it will take a long time before this becomes a practical problem.

With Jennings' interesting idea we conclude the enumeration of the main interpretations we know to have been given lately to the definition of the continental shelf. As can be appreciated, they differ considerably on the question of the outer limit of the shelf. This uncertainty has resulted in direct thinking in many circles about revising the 1958 definition.

V. PROPOSALS FOR THE REVISION OF THE GENEVA DEFINITION

The different proposals for revision extend from those that want to limit to a minimum the boundaries of the continental shelf to those that wish to extend them to the very maximum. Some of these proposals tend to simplify the definition, taking as a base only the bathymetric criteria. For example, Professor Oda seems to lean towards the 550 metre depth, if the convention is revised. He points out that:

> "Careful thought must still be given to whether the 200 metres depth is an appropriate criterion for determining the line between the continental shelf under the control of the coastal state and other deep sea areas free from such control. It should be recalled that a 550 metres depth line was proposed by the Netherlands delegation to the Geneva Conference." [45]

Others tend primarily to avoid the bathymetric criterion and set fixed distances from the baselines of the territorial sea. Professor Juraj Andrassy, of the University of Zagreb, argues that a 30-mile horizontal limit would be advisable, as it corresponds to the median breadth of the continental shelf.[46] He considers that 50 miles would be too generous.

[45] S. Oda, Towards a Better Use of the Ocean 198 (1969).
[46] E. Mann Borgese, The Ocean Regime 26 (......).

Another approach would combine the criteria of depth and distance from the shoreline. The Commission to Study the Organization of Peace has recommended that the Convention be revised to establish national rights of exploitation of the resources of the sea floor up to the depth line of 200 metres or 50 nautical miles from the shore, whichever be the greater.[47] It is maintained that this test would be most equitable for states that have narrow continental shelves. The Commission takes the 200 metre depth because it considers it to be the median of the border of the shelf, and 50 miles because it would be the median of the shore breadth. This theory is followed by Professor Aaron Danzig [48] and in the draft treaty, prepared by Elizabeth Mann Borgese [49] for the Centre for the Study of Democratic Institutions, on the international regime for the peaceful uses of the high seas and the seabed beyond national jurisdiction. A group from the Massachusetts Institute of Technology,[50] using the same general criteria, proposes 24 miles or 200 metres depth, whichever is the greater. The distance of 24 miles is adopted to satisfy those nations that do not have an extensive continental shelf; it is a figure recognised as arbitrary and as a starting point for negotiation. United States Senator Claiborne Pell, an influential figure of that organ in matters pertaining to the sea, has prepared a draft on legal principles which would govern the activities of states in the exploration and exploitation of the ocean space. Regarding the limits of the continental shelf, he defines the shelf, for the purposes of his declaration, as referring to the soil and subsoil of the submarine area adjacent to the shore beyond the area of the territorial sea up to a breadth of 550 metres or a distance of 50 miles from the baseline of the territorial sea. whichever be the greater.[51] Senator Pell has varied considerably the criteria he advocated in a previous proposal that was considered in the Senate's Committee on Foreign Relations.[52] There he proposed to define the shelf exclusively on the basis of the bathymetric criterion of 600 metres depth.[53]

A third type of suggestion would establish, between the area of exclusive national jurisdiction and the area outside national jurisdiction, an inter-

[47] The U.N. and the Seabed, Twenty First Report of the Commission to Study the Organization of Peace 12 (......).

[48] Treaty governing the exploration and use of the seabed, U.N. Committee of the World Peace through Law Center, Article 1, p. 5.

[49] E. Mann Borgese, *supra* note 46, at 10, 26.

[50] A Plan for Sequential Leasing of the Seabed – M.I.T. Group, December 1968.

[51] This draft has been distributed unpublished.

[52] Hearing before the Committee on Foreign Relations, U.S. Senate, 90th Congress, 1st session on S. J. Res. 111, S. Res. 172, S. Res. 186, 29 November 1967.

[53] 90th Congress, 1st session S.R. 186, p. 15.

mediate zone (buffer zone) with preferential rights for coastal states. This new idea for the revision of the Geneva Convention has one of its principal advocates in Professor Louis Henkin of Columbia University. Henkin's scheme is based upon the necessity of having narrow continental shelves, for he believes that broader ones in the long run ruin freedom of the high seas. He inclines towards the depth line of 200 metres, together with an X amount of miles from the shoreline, to satisfy those states that have practically no shelf. But, in order to avoid arguments based on national security, since foreign drilling towers could be erected near the shore, he proposes an intermediate zone of an X amount of miles. This zone would be regulated by the norms created for the exploitation of the sea floor beyond national jurisdiction, but, subject to this regime, only the coastal states could exploit the natural resources.[54]

This same theory of the intermediate zone is followed in the important "Stratton Report," which was prepared for the President of the United States and Congress, by a Commission on Marine Science, Engineering and Resources, set up under Public Law 89 - 154 of June 1966. This Commission, appointed by the President, was presided over by Julius A. Stratton, President of the Ford Foundation, and was composed of various well-known personalities.[55] The Commission recommends the revision of the Geneva Convention definition due to the uncertainties that, in its judgment, arise there. Among other things, it points out that the concept of exclusive access by coastal states to the natural riches of the seabed, up to the depth of 200 metres, is being doubted in those places where that depth is distant from the coast; such access would be inconsistent with the criterion of adjacency mentioned in the Convention.[56] The report rejects the interpretation based exclusively on exploitability, which tends to lead, in its view, to the division of the oceans by the median line. It also rejects the interpretation of the National Petroleum Council, based on the fact

[54] L. Henkin, *supra* note 38, at 42-48.

[55] Our Nation and the Sea. A Plan of Action. Report of the Commission on Marine Science, Engineering and Resources, at 148-151 (1969).

[56] Professor W. T. Burke seems to accept this same criterion. See Oda, *supra* note 45, at 27, where he says:

"First, it appears to have escaped notice that the definition in the Convention can be read so that the work 'adjacent' qualifies both the alternative formulations that follow it defining the shelf. In this view the area out to a depth of 200 metres is subject to certain sovereign rights of the coastal state only so long as that region is 'adjacent' to such a state. If such an interpretation were accepted, and unless the term 'adjacent' is to be deprived of any meaning, there are instances in which a part of the 200 metre region would be beyond coastal authority. Everyone accepts the idea that the exploitability criterion is subject to the limitations of adjacency."

that it did not adequately contemplate the interests of the United States; for, although the NPC interpretation would endow the United States with 479,000 square miles of sea floor with probably wealthy deposits, it would at the same time provide proportionately greater benefit to other states, According to the report, it appears to be safer and preferable for American private interests – and in accord with recent statements – that there be an international regime rather than a national one, for that will provide more guarantees. Furthermore, the National Petroleum Council's proposal presents an invitation, especially after the events following the Truman Proclamation, to certain states to feel justified in claiming the superjacent waters, their resources and the aerial space above them.

In brief, the Commission recommends defining the boundaries of the continental shelf at a 200 metre depth line or 50 nautical miles from the baseline, whichever is the greater area to the coastal state. The line should be established by geographical co-ordinates, in accordance with the best bathymetric research, and it would not be altered because of later changes stemming from new investigations or changes on the shore. This new definition is accompanied by a proposal to create an intermediate zone comprising the soil and subsoil of the sea floor up to the 2500 metre depth or up to 100 nautical miles from the baseline of the territorial sea, whichever gives the coastal state the greater surface, to exercise certain rights. The Commission chose the 2500 metre isobath because it understands it to be the average of the depth of the continental slope plus the continental margin. Under this proposal only the coastal state would have access to the natural resources of the intermediate zone. Nobody could explore or exploit the area except the coastal state, but its petitions would be registered in an International Register and the activity would be carried out according to an established regime. As it may well be appreciated, the plan is similar to that of Professor Henkin.

VI. THE LATIN AMERICAN 200-MILE SEA CLAIM

As was stated at the beginning of this study, the 200-mile territorial sea claimed by several Latin American States has some bearing on the claim over the seabed, particularly in those places where the 200-mile claim goes beyond the outer limits of the continental shelf. This is the case of the three South Pacific countries, parties to the Declaration of Santiago of 1952. Nine Latin American countries claim jurisdiction over 200 miles of sea adjacent to their coasts: Chile, Peru, Ecuador, Panama, El Salvador,

Argentina, Brazil, Nicaragua and Uruguay. But there is a substantial difference in the nature of their respective claims.

We should point out, in the first place, that none of these nine countries has become a party to the 1958 Geneva Convention on the Continental Shelf. Argentina, Chile, Panama, Peru and Uruguay signed the Convention, but did not ratify it. Only Colombia, Guatemala, Mexico and the Dominican Republic, which are not 200-mile states, are parties to the 1958 Convention.

Chile, Peru and Ecuador are parties to the Santiago Declaration of 18 August 1952, which states the following:

"II) As a consequence of these facts, the Governments of Chile, Ecuador and Peru proclaim as a norm of their international maritime policy, the exclusive sovereignty and jurisdiction pertaining to each one of them, over the sea adjacent to the shores of their respective countries, up to a minimum distance of 200 maritime miles from those shores.
III) The exclusive jurisdiction and sovereignty over the indicated maritime zone also includes exclusive sovereignty and jurisdiction over the soil and subsoil pertaining to it.
IV) In the case of insular territory the 200 maritime miles zone will be applied to the whole contour of the islands or group of islands. If an island or group of islands belonging to one of the declaring countries would be at a distance of less than 200 maritime miles from the general maritime zone pertaining to others of them, the maritime zone of this island or group of islands will be limited by the parallel of the point in which the land frontier of the respective states reaches the sea."

In national legislative instruments proclaiming the 200 miles' jurisdiction, claims differ. Brazil, Ecuador and Panama have extended their "territorial sea" over this distance. Brazil, by Decree-Law No. 1098, dated May, 1970, fixed the width of the territorial sea at 200 miles and added that:

"Brazilian sovereignty extends to the airspace located above the territorial sea as well as the soil and subsoil of that sea."

Article 4 of the Brazilian Constitution of 1969 declared the continental shelf to be property of the nation. Article 6 of the Ecuadorian Constitution declared the territorial sea and its subsoil to belong to the territory of the state. The 1951 and 1966 reforms to the Civil Code contain most of the rules regarding the territorial sea and the seabed, as follows:

Art. 625:
"The submarine shelf, continental and insular, adjacent to the Ecuadorian shore, and the resources to be found therein, belong to the State which will exploit them and exercise the necessary vigilance for the preservation of such resources and for the protection of the corresponding fishing areas.

Considered as submarine shelf will be the submerged land adjacent to the national territory covered up to a maximum of 200 metres of water.

Art. 628:

"The adjacent sea, up to a distance of 200 maritime miles measured from the most salient points of the Ecuadorian continental shelf and those of the most extreme islands of the Colon archipelago and from the points of the lowest tide, in accordance with the base line to be established by executive decree, will be considered territorial sea and under the dominion of the State...

The soil and the subsoil of the adjacent sea are also under the dominion of the State."

Article 209 of the 1946 Constitution of Panama establishes the continental shelf as the property of the State for public use and consequently not subject to private appropriation. In 1967, article 1 of Law No. 31 provided:

"The sovereignty of the Republic of Panama extends beyond her continental and insular territory and her internal waters to a territorial zone of a width of 200 maritime miles, the soil and subsoil thereof and the air space above it."

Even if these three nations have extended their territorial sea to 200 miles, their approaches to the seabed are different. It seems that Brazil and Panama have limited their national sovereignties on the seabed up to the same limits of the territorial sea. Ecuador, on the other hand, has used the 200 metres depth as the outer limit of national sovereignty.

The other six nations have not established the territorial sea, properly speaking, as their legislation has preserved freedom of navigation and overflight. Transit over the 200 mile zone of Brazil, Ecuador and Panama is subject to innocent passage, a traditional juridical feature of the territorial sea. Argentina and Uruguay have enacted similar legislation regarding their continental shelves, although Uruguay has extended her "territorial sea" over 200 miles and Argentina her "sovereignty," both preserving the freedom of navigation. Argentina has asserted, by Law 17.094 (1966):

Article 1:

"The sovereignty of the Argentine Nation extends to the sea adjacent to her territory up to a distance of 200 maritime miles, measured from the line of the lowest tides with the exception of the case of the Gulfs San Matias, Nuevo and San Jorge, where it will be measured from the line joining the Capes which form their mouth.

Article 2:

The sovereignty of the Argentine Nation extends likewise to the seabed and the subsoil of the submarine zones adjacent to her territory down to a depth of 200 metres or beyond that limit down to where the depth of the waters allow the exploitation of the national resources of such zones."

Uruguay enacted in 1969 Law No. 13.833, whose article 2 provides:

"The sovereignty of Uruguay extends beyond her continental and insular territory and her internal waters to a zone of 200 miles territorial sea measured from the base lines. The sovereignty of the Republic extends likewise to the air space located above the territorial sea as well as over the seabed and subsoil of that sea.

National sovereignty extends to the continental shelf for the purposes of the exploration and exploitation of the natural resources thereof. The continental shelf is formed by the seabed and the subsoil of the submarine zones adjacent to the shores of the country outside the territorial sea down to a depth of 200 metres or beyond that limit down to where the depth of the waters would allow the exploitation of the natural resources."

Both countries, Argentina and Uruguay, have thus taken their continental shelf definition from the 1958 Geneva Convention. This means that these countries claim the seabed and subsoil thereof when there is a continental shelf beyond the 200 mile limit, as is clearly the case of the Argentinian continental shelf, which ends several hundred miles from the coast.

Chile, on the other hand, has extended her national sovereignty over the continental shelf on the basis of a pure geological definition. The Presidential Declaration of June 23, 1947, provided:

"The Government of Chile confirms and proclaims national sovereignty over the continental shelf adjacent to the continental and insular shores of the national territory regardless of the depth at which it may be found and claims, consequently, all the natural resources that may exist above that shelf, within or underneath it, known or to be discovered."

Nicaragua has not fixed a definite outer limit to her continental shelf. A Declaration made by Congress in 1949 defined the continental shelf as:

"The area of land covered by sea water down to a depth of 200 metres from the level of the low tide."

Later, in 1950, the Constitution now in force laid down by article 5:

"National territory extends from the Atlantic to the Pacific Oceans and from the Republic of Honduras to Costa Rica. It also comprises the adjacent islands, the subsoil, the territorial sea, the continental shelf, the air space and the stratosphere."

In 1958 the Special Law on the Exploration and Exploitation of Petroleum included within the definition of the national territory the "zones of the continental shelf in both oceans," but without determining the limits of the continental shelf. (Article 4d).

In 1962 the Constitution of El Salvador incorporated within the territory of the country, the adjacent waters up to 200 miles, including the corresponding subsoil and continental shelf. The Constitution preserved freedom of navigation in this zone. Article 8 of the Constitution provided:

"The territory of the Republic within its present limits is irreducible; it comprises the adjacent sea up to the distance of 200 maritime miles to be counted from the line of the lowest tide and it includes the corresponding air space, the subsoil and the continental shelf. The above-mentioned applies without prejudice to freedom of navigation in accordance with the accepted principles of international law."

Peruvian legislation also presents special features. It should be remembered that Peru is a party to the 1952 Santiago Declaration. In 1947 Peru declared its sovereignty and jurisdiction over the continental shelf, taking into account a geological definition. With regard to the adjacent waters, sovereignty and jurisdiction were extended to 200 miles, retaining freedom of navigation. Decree no. 781 of 1st August 1947 stipulated:

1) It is declared that national sovereignty and jurisdiction extend to the continental and insular shelf adjacent to the continental and insular shores of the national territory, regardless of the depth and distance to be reached by that shelf.

2) National sovereignty and jurisdiction are also exercised over the sea adjacent to the shores of the national territory regardless of its depth and over the necessary distance.

3) As a consequence of the previous declarations, the State reserves the right to establish the demarcation of zones for the control and protection of the natural resources in continental or insular seas that remain under the control of the Government of Peru and also to modify that demarcation in accordance with developing circumstances resulting from research studies and national interests that may arise in the future; and, moreover, it is declared that such control and protection will be exercised over the sea adjacent to the shore of Peruvian territory in a zone extending between those shores and an imaginary line parallel to them and drawn over the sea up to a distance of 200 maritime miles, to be measured following the line of the geographical parallels. Respecting the national islands the demarcation will be drawn to cover an area of sea contiguous to the shores thereof up to a distance of 200 maritime miles measured from each point of their contour.

4) This declaration does not affect the right of free navigation by ships of all nations, in accordance with international law.

In 1952, article 14, paragraph 4, of the Petroleum Law 11780 defined the continental shelf as follows:

"the zone comprised by the western limit of the Coastal Zone and an imaginary line drawn towards the sea at a constant distance of 200 miles from the line of low tide of the continental shore."

The Supreme Resolution of 12th January 1955 mentioned the Santiago Declaration of 1952 and referred to the maritime zone as follows:

"The indicated zone is limited at sea by a line parallel to the Peruvian shore and at a constant distance from it of 200 nautical miles. In accordance with Paragraph IV of the Declaration of Santiago, that line could not go beyond the parallel corresponding to the point where the Peruvian border reaches the sea."

It seems, that the Peruvian claim to the continental shelf extends up to 200 miles.

As can be seen from this survey, as we have said before, the positions of the so-called 200 mile countries differ not only with regard to the territorial sea, sovereignty and freedom of navigation, but also regarding the outer limit of national jurisdiction over the seabed. However, the nine countries tried to unify their positions in Montevideo in 1970. The Declaration adopted at this meeting chose a flexible formula. The Declaration laid down:

"The States represented at the Montevideo meeting on the Law of the Sea

....

Recognising ... that rules relevant to delimination of national sovereignty and jurisdiction over the sea, the seabed and the subsoil thereof, and that measures concerning exploitation of resources, must always be mindful of the geographic realities of coastal States and of the special economic and social requirements of the less developed States;

....

Whereas the declarations, resolutions and treaties, principally inter-American as well as in multilateral declarations and agreements celebrated between Latin American States, legal principles have been incorporated which justify the right of the States to expand their claims to sovereignty and jurisdiction in the measure required to conserve, develop and exploit the natural resources of the maritime zones adjacent to their coast, of their seabeds and the subsoil thereof;

....

Do declare, as Basic Principles of the Law of the Sea;

1. The right of littoral states to exercise control of the natural resources of the sea adjacent to their coasts and of the seabed and subsoil thereof in order to achieve the maximum development of their economy and to raise the living standards of their peoples;

2. The right to delimit their maritime sovereignty and jurisdiction in conformity with their own geographic and geological characteristics and consonant with factors that condition the existence of marine resources and the need for national exploitation;

....

4. The right to explore, conserve and exploit the natural resources of their respective continental shelf out to where the depth of the superjacent waters admits of exploitation of said resources;

5. The right to explore, conserve and exploit the natural resources of the sea-bed and of the subsoil of the ocean floor out to where the littoral state claims jurisdiction over the sea;
6. The right to enact regulatory measures to achieve the aforecited goals applicable within the zones of their maritime sovereignty and jurisdiction without prejudice to freedom of navigation and to the passage of vessels and overflight by aircraft of any flag . . ." [57]

The rest of the Latin American countries, which have not adhered to the 200 miles rule, have adopted two different approaches to the problem of the outer limits of the continental shelf. Some have defined the continental shelf in the same terms as the 1958 Geneva Convention. Others have provided in their internal legislation for a renvoi to rules of international law. Among the first class are Honduras, Venezuela and the Dominican Republic. The 1965 Constitution of Honduras laid down, in article 5, paragraph 3:

"The subsoil, the air space, the territorial sea up to a distance of 12 nautical miles and the soil and subsoil of the continental and insular shelves as well as other submarine area adjacent to its territory beyond the zone of the territorial sea down to a depth of 200 metres or down to where the depths of the waters, beyond that limit, would allow the exploitation of the soil and subsoil, also belong to the State of Honduras and are subject to its jurisdiction and control."

Article 7 of the Venezuelan Constitution of 1961 provided:

"The sovereignty, authority and vigilance over the territorial sea, contiguous maritime zone, continental shelf and air space, as well as the dominion and exploitation of the resources contained therein, will be exercised to a distance and under conditions to be determined by law."

The 1956 Law on the Territorial Sea, Continental Shelf, Protection of Fisheries and Air Space had provided:

"Belonging to the Republic of Venezuela and subject to her sovereignty [are] the soil and subsoil of the submarine shelf adjacent to her territory, outside the territorial sea zone and down to a depth of 200 metres or down to the point where the depth of the waters beyond that limit allow the exploitation of the resources of the soil and subsoil, in accordance with advances in techniques of exploration and exploitation. The existence of tunnels, depressions or irregularities on the submarine soil does not interrupt the continuity of the said shelf, which also comprises the banks that by their position and natural conditions are related to them.
The continental shelf of the Republic of Venezuela comprises also that of the islands under the above mentioned conditions." (Article 4)

[57] Full text and translation, by Helen L. Clagett, in 9 Int'l Legal Materials 1081-83 (1970).

The Dominican Republic Constitution of 1966 provides:

"The territorial sea, the corresponding submarine soil and subsoil as well as the air space above them are also part of the national territory. The extension of the territorial sea, the air space, the contiguous zone and the defence thereof as well as that of the submarine soil and subsoil and their exploitation will be established and regulated by law." (Article 5)

Law 186, dated 13 September, 1967, laid down:

"The Dominican Republic will exercise rights of sovereignty over the continental shelf for the purposes of exploration or exploitation of its natural resources. No one will be entitled, therefore, to pursue the said activities without the express consent of the Dominican State."

The same defines the continental shelf as:

"a) the seabed and the subsoil of the submarine zones adjacent to the shore but outside the territorial sea zone, down to a depth of 200 metres or, beyond that limit, down to where the depth of the waters would permit exploitation of the natural resources of those zones.
b) the seabed and the subsoil of similar submarine zones adjacent to the shores of islands under Dominican sovereignty." (Article 7)

Colombia, Costa Rica, Guatemala and Mexico refered to international law in defining internally the continental shelf. The 1886 Colombian Constitution, modified in 1968, declared:

"Also constituting part of Colombia [are] the air space, the territorial sea and the continental shelf, in accordance with international treaties or agreements approved by Congress or in accordance with Colombian law in the absence thereof."

The 1949 Constitution of Costa Rica provided:

"The State exercises complete and exclusive sovereignty over the air space above its territory and over its continental waters and continental shelf, in accordance with the principles of international law and treaties in force." (Article 6)

Guatemala stipulated by article 3 of its 1965 Constitution:

"Guatemala exercises full sovereignty and dominion over her territory which is composed of the soil, subsoil, continental shelf, territorial waters and the space above them and it also extends to the natural resources that may exist in them, without prejudice to free maritime navigation in accordance with the law and provisions of treaties and international conventions."

Article 1 of the Guatemalan Petroleum Code of 1955 asserted:

"All oil deposits to be found within the land or sea limits of the Republic or up to the reach of its continental shelf, belong to the Nation. Dominion over them is inalienable and imprescriptible."

The Mexican Constitution of 1917 was amended in 1960. Its new article 27 included the continental shelf in the national territory and added, as belonging to the nation, direct dominion over certain resources such as "the natural resources of the continental shelf and the insular shelf" and the "oil and all solid, liquid and gaseous hydrocarbons as well as the space above the national territory to the limits and in the terms fixed by international law."

In August 1970 several Latin American countries met in Lima to discuss problems of the law of the sea. All Latin countries were invited, regardless of their position towards the 200 miles rule. Haiti did not attend the meeting and Costa Rica was represented by an observer. The meeting adopted the Declaration of Lima, the pertinent parts of which are:

"The Latin American Meeting on Aspects of the Law of the Sea ...
Whereas, ... the right of coastal states to establish the scope of their maritime sovereignty or jurisdiction in accordance with reasonable criteria has been recognised, taking into account their geographical, geological and biological realities and their socioeconomic responsibilities;

....

Declares as common principles of the Law of the Sea:
1. The inherent right of the coastal state to explore, preserve and exploit the natural resources of the sea adjacent to its shores and the soil and subsoil thereof, as well as the continental shelf and its subsoil, to promote the maximum development of their economies and raise the standard of living of their people;
2. The right of the coastal state to establish the limits of their maritime sovereignty and jurisdiction in accordance with reasonable criteria, taking into account its geographical, geological and biological characteristics and the need for a rational utilization of its resources."

This Declaration received the 14 affirmative votes of Argentina, Brazil, Colombia, Chile, Ecuador, El Salvador, Guatemala, Honduras, Mexico, Nicaragua, Panama, Peru, Dominican Republic and Uruguay. Three countries voted against: Bolivia, Paraguay and Venezuela. Trinidad and Tobago abstained. Barbados and Jamaica were absent. This is the most recent multilateral document agreed upon by Latin American countries.

VII. CONCLUSIONS

Advances in technology for the exploitation of the resources of the seabed, especially as far as petroleum deposits are concerned, have led to difficult legal questions, the principal one being the definition of the continental shelf. These problems are of an especial complexity and delicacy because of the very important economic interests at stake, the importance being attributable to the decisive role played by petroleum in contemporary economies. The involvement of these substantial interests has generated conflicts that must be resolved if an efficient system of exploitation is to be achieved. The problems are subject to pressures so intense that states hesitate to formulate a definite policy. The United States, the most advanced country with regard to the exploitation of mineral resources of the sea floor, has not yet defined its policy, and proof of the extent of the interests in question is the controversy that has started among powerful sectors of opinion in that country on the limits of the shelf. In a recent speech at the United Nations Seabed Committee, Ambassador Phillips, the United States Deputy Permanent Representative, recognised the indeterminacy of his country regarding this subject in this way:

> "Within the Government, we are giving the whole range of possibilities the most intense examination, because it is clear that the United States cannot best represent its own interests in the continuing discussion of the seabed until it has arrived at a position on the precise outer limit of national jurisdiction." [58]

This worry does not, of course, only affect the United States, but the great majority of members of the international community; and it has been reflected in the debates of the United Nations Seabed Committee. It should not be forgotten that it was the Delegation of Malta, a small nation, that introduced this provocative subject to he General Assembly.

What is the present situation? There is agreement that there is an area of the seabed which is situated beyond the national jurisdiction of states. In the absence of disagreement, consequently, the theory of division may be discarded. There also appears to be agreement that national jurisdiction ends beyond the 200-metre depth line. This norm is established in the 1958 Convention and in general international law, and is followed in state practice. The theory that the notion of adjacency can also be applied to the 200-metre depth does not prevent it from being a mere theoretical

[58] United States Mission to the United Nations, Press Release USUN 25 (70), p. 8, March 4, 1970.

exercise, not corresponding to the practice of states, the great majority of whom have systematically proclaimed their uncontested right to sovereignty over the continental shelf up to 200 metres. On the other hand, variation of the 200-metre formula would modify already existing, heavily financed developments and would endanger the security of investments made or planned. It is true that the 200-metre depth standard could lead to inequities between nations with an extensive shelf and nation without a shelf, but the argument has no validity; for these inequities and inequalities already exist among all states, some being more and some less economically and geographically endowed.

Meanwhile, national security reasons and efficiency in exploitation counsel that, up to the 200 metre depth, the ties between the coastal state and its shelf should not be broken.

Having established that the 200 metre limit is a norm in force, we ask ourselves in the first place if, with the present state of technology, there exists any urgency in redefining the shelf. To this we answer that we believe it to be premature to accelerate the process without previously having made detailed preparations that would assure the success of the process of redefinition. The 1960 Conference on the Law of the Sea that dealt with the limit of the territorial sea is an example to be remembered. However, it is most probable that in a reasonable period of time technology will make such progress that it will be necessary to fix precisely the limits between national and non-national jurisdiction of the seabed. When we have to fix a limit, we should, we believe, discard the horizontal criterion. That criterion might appear objective and equalizing, but it has the inconvenience of being able to leave outside national jurisdiction areas that are already in it when the 200 metres standard is applied.

The combination of depth and distance tends to balance things, but if a bathymetric criterion of 200 metres is adopted it will be prejudicial to the coastal states which have, according to laws in force, an anticipated right beyond 200 metres. The formula of depth and distance would only be acceptable with a greater bathymetric criterion. Which brings us to the conclusion that, in essence, the problem centres around the criterion of depth, the difficulty being that the criterion of depth has, since its origin, always been intimately identified with the notion of shelf, geologically as much as legally.

It is difficult to adopt a defined depth line, but not difficult to find a criterion. This should essentially be as objective as possible. That is, if the prolongation of the continent below the sea is divided into three recognizable sectors – continental shelf, slope and margin – we can accept one of them as the criterion, not forgetting that this whole legal doctrine of the shelf is, in essence, based on a geological fact. The continental shelf is already within national jurisdiction up to 200 metres. We must choose between slope and margin. Any line, let us say at 300, 400 or 500 metres, taken arbitrarily, would, I believe, bring more problems than solutions, not forgetting, of course, that the placers do not end in a determined depth, but tend to follow the geological phenomenon. We believe that the base of the continental slope gives us a adequate criterion, taking particularly into account its geological correspondence with the continent and the possible economic connection with the shore facilitating efficiency for exploitation.

Also defense reasons can be invoked, which, if legitimate, are received without protest, for the purpose of establishing a claim over the superjacent waters, as in the case of the Reciprocal Assistance Treaty of Rio and the Treaty of Tlatelolco. We must not forget that, following the Jennings Doctrine, this area would already be incorporated by general international law into the sovereign rights of the coastal state, with regard to its exploitation and exploration, as a result of recognition in the recent judgment of the International Court of Justice in the North Sea Continental Shelf cases.

If this objective criterion is valid, in reality and in law, and if a definite figure is searched for, the limit of the legal notion of the continental shelf could be at the 2500 metre depth isobath, which seems to be the median of the baseline of the continental slope. The continental margin is not yet sufficiently known, even geologically, to be able to be taken as an objective criterion.

THE U.N. DECLARATION OF PRINCIPLES GOVERNING THE DEEP SEA-BED

by

ATWOOD C. WOLF, JR.

Perhaps the most important aspect of the intensive consideration being given to the subject of the exploitation of the sea-bed beyond the limits of national jurisdiction stems from the fact that the difficulties faced by the international community in its efforts to resolve the problems associated with this subject constitute a model of all of the difficulties which it faces in dealing with almost every other subject on the international agenda. For example, one can begin with the fundamental question of whether or not the sovereign powers of states should be subjected to still further internationally imposed limitations. There follow questions concerning the nature and extent of proposed limitations, the motivations of those advocating and those opposing them, and the relevance of any one or all of them to the activities affected. Competing political and economic interests and prejudices must be reconciled and compromises of language and substance effected if agreement is to be reached, not merely on the nature of a legal regime to be created, but also on the nature and organization of the machinery, if any, to be established to administer the regime. It must also be noted that efforts to achieve a viable international agreement will be successful only if based upon a shared understanding of the realities of the area and of the subject matter under consideration.

Another interesting aspect is the fact that the question of the exploitation of the sea-bed beyond the limits of national jurisdiction transcends regional boundaries. Latin American states once concentrated their efforts on the development and codification of regional international law applicable to the Western Hemisphere. Here a supposed community of interests counseled the development of rules not necessarily recognized by *general* international law, since the latter was felt to reflect the interests of the great powers, including the United States. Although Latin American states have not given up their efforts to develop a body of regional rules, they have increased their efforts in the development of general international law through the United Nations. Here they have found an increasing number of allies among many of the new states, who share their suspicions of traditional international law, and because of the weight of their numbers in international conferences, feel themselves in a position to change that law.

Since the 1967 session of the United Nations General Assembly, when Ambassador Pardo of Malta requested that there be included on the agenda an item which ultimately became entitled, "The Examination of the Question of the Reservation Exclusively for Peaceful Purposes of the Sea-bed and Ocean Floor, and the Subsoil thereof, Underlying the High Seas Beyond the Limits of Present National Jurisdiction and the Use of Their Resources in the Interests of Mankind",[1] the significance of the subject has grown to the point where its importance in the development of international law and organization far transcends the material benefits to be realized in the near future from the exploitation of the mineral resources of the area.

In 1967, the XXII Session of the General Assembly, in response to the Maltese initiative, established an *Ad Hoc* Committee to Study The Peaceful Uses Of The Sea-bed And The Ocean Floor Beyond The Limits Of National Jurisdiction.[2] It was requested, *inter alia,* to prepare an account of the legal aspects of the item,[3] and an indication regarding practical means to promote international cooperation in the exploration, conservation and use of the area.[4]

The *Ad Hoc* Committee's Legal Working Group adopted a program of work which included an examination of legal principles relating to the deep sea-bed, including existing regulations, the consideration of legal principles which should govern international cooperation with a view to the preparation of an agreement on the use of the sea-bed exclusively for peaceful purposes, and the consideration of legal principles which should govern international cooperation in the use of sea-bed resources. A similar approach had been successfully employed in the early stages of U.N. consideration of outer space, and it appeared to be an appropriate elaboration of the *Ad Hoc* Committee's terms of reference.

On December 17, 1970, the XXV General Assembly adopted a "Declaration of Principles Governing the Sea-bed and the Ocean Floor and the

[1] Note verbale adressed by Permanent Mission of Malta to Secretary-General, dated August 17, 1969, U.N. Doc. No. A/6695.

[2] General Assembly res. 2340 (XXII).

[3] *Id.*, operative para. 2(b).

[4] *Id.*, operative para. 2(c).

Subsoil thereof Beyond the Limits of National Jurisdiction," [5] by a vote of 108 in favor, none against, with 14 abstentions.

The importance of this document stems from the fact that by its terms, it is to be the basis of an international regime applying to the deep sea-bed and its resources. It declares that "international machinery to give effect to its provisions shall be established by an international treaty of universal character, generally agreed upon." [6] While this forthright statement may be considered the expression of a hope rather than of a rule of law, it will be recognized that the creation of an acceptable regime and the operation of effective machinery will serve as remarkably novel precedents for the further development of international law and organization. The world community may have taken a major step forward in its continuing search for a system of world order.

The first of the fifteen principles, a declaration that "the sea-bed and ocean floor, and the subsoil thereof, beyond the limits of national jurisdiction. . ., as well as the resources of the area, are the common heritage of mankind," [7] constitutes what might well be considered, when its implications are accepted, a concept new to international law. The expression "common heritage of mankind" had its origin in a public statement concerning sea-bed affairs made by President Johnson some time before the subject was introduced to the General Assembly. Since then what probably struck Mr. Johnson and his staff as a nice turn of a phrase has taken on an importance and acquired the beginnings of a legal substance that were probably not anticipated by the President or his speech-writers when he uttered it.

It was introduced to the *Ad Hoc* Sea-bed Committee in a draft resolution of principles presented by India,[8] and was incorporated in a later formulation of proposed principles submitted as a working paper by most of the less developed countries serving on the Committee during the first year.[9]

Most of the developed countries, or at least those outside of the socialist bloc, first took a cautious and hesitant view of the formulation, principally on the grounds that the phraseology was unknown to international

[5] General Assembly res. 2749 (XXV).

[6] *Id.*, operative para. 9.

[7] The enumeration of the principles used in this paper corresponds to that of the operative paragraphs of General Assembly res. 2749 (XXV).

[8] U.N. Doc. No. A/AC. 135/21.

[9] Report of the *Ad Hoc* Committee to Study the Peaceful Uses of the Sea-Bed and the Ocean Floor beyond the Limits of National Jurisdiction, pp. 62-64 (U.N. Doc. No. A/7230).

law, and therefore ought not to be used until agreement on a definition could be reached. Furthermore, it was argued, a definition of the legal status of the sea-bed should logically be based on the nature of the international arrangements to be made with respect to its exploration and exploitation. Thus efforts to reach an agreement on a definition should await agreement on the arrangements. To the less developed countries, references to precedent, or rather to the lack of it, in the formulation of a new body of international law, were unacceptable. The political attitude toward traditional international law frequently displayed by many representatives of developing countries is well known: their countries played no part in its creation; many of its tenets serve no purpose except to legalize imperialism, and certainly do not meet the needs of contemporary international policy. This is not to suggest that developing countries reject traditional international law in its entirety. Nonetheless, it must be noted that its citation in the course of political discussion with respect to activities having potential economic significance will frequently arouse suspicions in the minds of representatives of developing countries.

While western international lawyers may regret this attitude, the validity of the underlying aim, to prevent a new outbreak of competitive imperialism, has been accepted in the context of international sea-bed policy. However, the fact that President Johnson had made the American attitude on that subject quite clear was overlooked when U.S. representatives in the early stages of the U.N. debates questioned the meaning and legal significance of the new phrase. When these questions were reiterated by other states, the phrase took on an added importance for those who had first advocated its inclusion in the lexicon of international law. It cannot be considered a coincidence that the principal advocates were those with the most sensitive feelings on the subject of imperialism, the developing countries.

As the discussions on the legal status of the sea-bed continued through three years of debates and consultations, the varying interests of the several groups of states participating came to be reflected quite clearly in numerous formulations of proposed principles on the legal status of the area, and in the comments each received. The fears of the Latin American and other less developed countries that their interests in the anticipated wealth to be derived from sea-bed activities might be prejudiced by a legal structure created by, and thus for the benefit of the rich and powerful states, underlay almost each and every one of the LDC's interventions in the debates. Fundamentally, they were seeking an acceptance of the concept that even though they might not directly participate in the development and exploitation of the resources of the area, they should share in the benefits. They are not so naive as not to recognize that if an international regime does not comprise a body of rules restricting the freedom of individual states to exploit sea-bed resources, a race would inevitably develop, and the less developed countries would not likely be among the winners. They do not, of course, accept the notion that "mankind" as a whole benefits when material advantages directly accrue solely to the powerful members of the class. This should not be a shocking thought in 1971 – the idea that what is good for private industrial or financial interests is necessarily good for the country has long been questioned on domestic scenes throughout the world. The LDC's were thus seeking new rules based on new concepts and expressed in new phraseology.

The discussions in the Sea-bed Committees [10] and the First Committee of the General Assembly are therefore helpful in clarifying the meaning and implications of the phrase intended by its advocates. It was argued that "common heritage of mankind" included the notions of trusts and trustees; the indivisibility of the heritage; the regulation of the use of that heritage by the international community; the most appropriate equitable application of the benefits to be derived from the area to the developing countries; as well as the principles of freedom of access and use by all states and the peaceful use of the area. It was also said that the concept implies an international machinery for the regulation and management of the seabed, and even that the area be deemed to be vested in the United Nations for the benefit of mankind as a whole.[11]

To suggest that any or all of these notions were or are generally accepted would be misleading. They are, however, of importance in identifying many of the problems to be faced in the course of the making of international arrangements with respect to the exploration and exploitation of the sea-bed.

As we have noted, the major western powers approached the work of the Sea-bed Committee with hesitancy born of caution, or, perhaps, with caution born of hesitancy. Viewed realistically, the recovery of wealth from the sea-bed beyond national limits of jurisdiction appeared, and still appears to be an expectation to be realized many years in the future. It was

[10] The XXIII General Assembly accepted the Report of the *Ad Hoc* Committee, and created (Res. 2467A [XXIII]) an enlarged Committee On The Peaceful Uses of the Sea-Bed and the Ocean Floor Beyond the Limits of National Jurisdiction.

[11] 1969 Report of the Legal Subcommittee, paras. 19-20 (U.N. Doc. No. A/7622, Part Two).

suggested that the creation of a legal regime designed to govern as yet undetermined types of activity in an as yet undetermined area was *ipso facto* premature. The sincerity of this position during the early stages of the discussions was, perhaps, more clearly established when it became quite clear that the major developed countries had not as yet determined policy on the major questions the subject presented. It was not until the end of May 1970, for example, that President Nixon, having resolved intra-government conflicts, enunciated a basic American position on the subject.[12] As of the adjournment of the XXV General Assembly in December 1970, the Soviet Union's position was unknown. Their principal contributions to the early discussions related, first to advocacy of a complete ban on the military use of the sea-bed,[13] second, to advocacy of freedom of scientific research, and third, to a statement that the creation of international machinery to govern sea-bed activities was not feasible so long as there existed in the world two conflicting social and economic systems. One is left with the impression that the development and exploitation of the non-living resources of the sea-bed do not hold a high priority in Soviet planning in view of the tremendous opportunities they have to develop mineral resources inside their own territory.

However, political pressures, principally based on the fear that in the absence of international arrangements, the powerful states would expand their jurisdiction to the entire sea-bed, and thus deprive the less powerful of their rightful share in the benefits to be derived therefrom, proved overwhelming. These pressures appeared to become increasingly sophisticated as there developed a remarkably successful effort, achieved principally in the Economic and Technical Subcommittee, to acquaint all members with the realities of oceanography. The Subcommittee, chaired until the close of the 1970 session by a particularly dynamic representative of Belgium, probably succeeded in influencing the work of the Legal Subcommittee, as well as the main Committee, to the point where progress could be made

[12] President Nixon's announcement of May 23, 1970 was transmitted to the Chairman of the Sea-Bed Committee by letter dated 25 May 1970 from the U.S. Representative (Amb. C. H. Phillips), U.N. Doc. No. A/AC. 138/22; 9 Int'l Legal Materials 806 (1970).

[13] In 1968 the U.S.S.R. introduced a draft resolution on this subject (U.N. Doc. No. A/AC. 135/20) in the *Ad Hoc* Committee. The U.S. countered with a draft resolution prohibiting the emplacement of weapons of mass destruction (U.N. Doc. No. A/AC. 135/24). The U.N. Disarmament Committee's subsequent discussions of this subject culminated in a Treaty on the Prohibition of the Emplacement of Nuclear Weapons and Other Weapons of Mass Destruction on the Sea-Bed and the Ocean Floor and in the subsoil Thereof, commended by the General Assembly in resolution 2660 (XXV); 10 Int'l Legal Materials 145 (1971).

in both the legal and political arenas, despite the difficult attitudes exhibited by the Legal Subcommittee's chairman.

Certainly, the implications of legal positions upon activities in the area became more clearly recognized and those positions became more clearly related to the realities of the subject. In due time, the objections of Latin American and newly-independent states to some long-established concepts of international law came to reflect somewhat more closely the real problems of developing countries. It was, for example, only after a period of gestation that the economic significance of deep-sea mining on national sources of minerals was recognized as a factor in the consideration of the legal status of the deep sea-bed.

From the outset, however, the applicability to the area of two traditional doctrines of international law was all but rejected. The concept of the sea-bed as *res nullius*, the notion that it belonged to no one, but that portions could be appropriated and subjected to sovereignty by any state effectively occuping them, was never considered acceptable by the states participating in the discussion. In fact, the second principle in the Declaration finally adopted by the General Assembly, that "the area shall not be subject to appropriation by any means by States or persons, natural or juridical, and no State shall claim or exercise sovereignty or sovereign rights over any part thereof," was considered generally acceptable from the beginning, and the differences that were expressed on the subject were largely semantic.

Similarly, it was urged at a very early stage by many states that the application to the sea-bed of the doctrine of *res communis* was of little "practical value." [14] This doctrine does, of course, reflect the notion that the rights of ownership are vested in all states, and, when applied to the sea-bed, that all states would be entitled to a share of their resources. It is the manner in which the latter aspect of the doctrine has been implemented in its application to the living resources of the high seas which, the writer believes, lies at the root of the objections to extending the doctrine to the sea-bed, for traditionally it included the notion that any state was entitled to capture, and thus to appropriate to itself a share of the resources.[15]

[14] 1969 Report of the Legal Subcommittee, para. 19 (U.N. Doc. No. A/7622, Part Two).

[15] It has been suggested that if the resources belong to everybody, no one may extract them without the permission of the international community (Bellman, *Address* before ABA Nat'l. Institute on Marine Resources, June 8, 1967, cited in 3 Panel Reports of the Commission on Marine Sciences, Engineering and Resources VIII-20). This view appears supportable only on the unrealistic assumption that

The doctrine was generally acceptable when the comparatively small amount of capital and skill required to harvest fish, then the area's sole resource of any importance, was available to all, and when, as Dr. Garcia-Amador had pointed out,[16] the idea that the supply of fish available for capture was not inexhaustible had occured to no one. Today, when as a practical matter only a fortunate few, the highly developed states, could exercise a right of capture of the mineral resources of the sea-bed, the implications of the traditional doctrine of *res communis* are, in the view of the less advantaged states, of "little practical value." It is an ownership interest in resources, before and after capture, that must be shared.

In the argument against the application of the traditional doctrines, consideration should also be given to the effect of the successful recovery of deep sea-bed resources upon states economically dependent on the export of internally-exploited minerals, an effect potentially so grave that even the concept of sharing the benefits to be derived from off-shore exploitation is not a fully satisfactory solution to the resulting problem. It should here be noted in passing that the XXV General Assembly, in another resolution (Res. 2750A), requested the Secretary-General to:

"(a) Identify the problems arising from the production of certain minerals from the area beyond the limits of national jurisdiction and examine the impact they will have on the economic well-being of the developing countries, in particular on prices of mineral exports on the world market;
(b) Study these problems in the light of the scale of possible exploitation of the sea-bed taking into account the world demand for raw materials and the evolution of costs and prices;
(c) Propose effective solutions for dealing with these problems;"

By 1969, a report of an Informal Drafting Group (which included representatives of LDC's and both western and socialist bloc members of the Sea-Bed Committee) could state that those states supporting acceptance of the "common heritage" doctrine were "insistent that it was the basis on which a formulation regarding (the legal status of the sea-bed), and for that matter the statement of principles, should be based." [17]

The Legal Subcommittee thereafter considered the work of the Informal Drafting Group, and in its 1969 Report stated:

states' fishery rights are subject to a "general license" granted by the international community. The Report of the Commission's International Panel, however, states that "most international lawyers seem to agree" with an analysis similar to that presented in this text, citing L. Henkin, Law of the Sea's Mineral Resources 30 (1968).

[16] F. V. Garcia-Amador, The Exploration and Conservation of the Resources of the Sea 22 (1959).

[17] U.N. Doc. No. A/AC. 138/SC. 1/3, para. 6.

"It was said that this expression lacked legal content, was imprecise, and, being novel, could not be interpreted on any generally accepted basis. It was argued on the other hand that once it had been enshrined in a declaration the concept would have universal validity as had been the case with the similar expression 'province of all mankind' used in the outer space treaty. . . . Furthermore, new technology and problems required the development of new concepts. . . . It was suggested that the concept that the area belongs to humanity as a whole is the basis for the prohibition of the exercise or claim of sovereignty and of all forms of appropriation. Some delegations doubted whether a general concept was required or desirable at that stage of the Sub-Committee's deliberations since the area would have first to be weighed and agreed upon; such process of analysis and agreement logically preceded the question whether there is any general concept by which all the aspects of the legal status of the area may be summarized." [18]

The Legal Subcommittee's 1969 Report thus reflected the continuing inability of its members to reach agreement on appropriate principles, but closed with a "synthesis of the related formulations," offered as an attempt "to determine insofar as possible common denominators." [19] It could only state at the close of the 1969 sessions: "The over-all concept that the sea-bed and ocean floor and the subsoil thereof beyond the limits of national jurisdiction are the common heritage of mankind (or part of the common heritage of mankind) was widely supported but not acceptable to all." [20]

Consideration of the concept was not, of course, conducted in a vacuum. Formulations of other principles concerning the legal status of the area were offered to supplement or clarify the legal meaning of the phrase. What became the second principle in the final Declaration, that dealing with appropriation of the area and sovereignty, achieved acceptance at an early stage of the deliberations. The third principle, "No State or person, natural or juridical, shall claim, exercise or acquire rights with respect to the area or its resources incompatible with the international regime to be established and the principles of this Declaration," does, however, constitute a resolution of what had been a major difficulty. The term "rights" considered in this context relates principally to the right to use the area; i.e., to explore and exploit, and the right to acquire exclusive property interests in its resources. There had been no problem with the thought that all states, whether coastal or land-locked, rich or poor, should have the right to use the area. What was at issue was the right to enjoy the benefits derived from that use. Not certain that a ban on the appropriation of the area, and on the claim and exercise of sovereignty would protect their interests in

[18] U.N. Doc. No. A/7622, Part Two, para. 29.
[19] *Id.*, para. 84.
[20] *Id.*, para. 88.

the resources, the LDC's urged adoption of a supplementary principle to the effect that no one might acquire any property rights in the area. As the Report of the Legal Subcommittee put it,

"It was however pointed out that acceptance of the non-appropriation principle would be of no practical value if it were linked with an unqualified concept of freedom of exploration and exploitation, since it would only benefit the very few countries which have the capability of exploiting the sea-bed resources, without due compensation to the international community as a whole and the developing countries in particular."[21]

On the other hand, the developed countries, or at least those among them whose nationals are the most likely to engage in deep-sea mining operations, proceeded from the assumption that investment capital would not be available in the absence of security of tenure and security of property rights. If an operator could not be assured of its right to remain in an area it was developing, and of its title to the minerals it recovered, it was not likely to undertake the operation. The developed countries were, of course, prepared to accept provisions barring national appropriation of the sea-bed or any part thereof, and the exercise or claim of sovereignty or sovereign rights. Similar principles governed both outer space and Antarctica. It is one thing to say that no one may ever own the area, but quite another to say that no one may ever own the resources. If the latter concept were to be accepted, serious questions concerning the feasibility of an international regime would be raised.

By the time the subject was reached by the First Political Committee of the XXIV General Assembly, the lines had been clearly drawn. Political suspicions colored the exchange to the point where agreement on legal principles appeared unattainable, for the LDC's had long felt that their adversaries were determined to delay agreement until development of sea-bed activities had progressed to the point where an international regime and machinery for its administration would either not be created, or would exclude them from effective participation both in its administration and in its benefits .

Resolution 2574D (XXIV) was the result. By vote of 62 in favor, 28 opposed, with 28 abstentions and 8 states absent, the General Assembly declared:

"Pending the establishment of the . . . international regime:

(*a*) States and persons, physical or juridical, are bound to refrain from all activities of exploitation of the resources of the area of the sea-bed and ocean

[21] *Id.*, para. 26.

floor, and the subsoil thereof, beyong the limits of national jurisdiction;
(*b*) No claim to any part of that area or its resources shall be recognized."

Other than Sweden, all states voting in favor were members of either the Afro-Asian or the Latin American and Caribbean groups. All western Hemisphere states except Canada and the United States, who opposed, and Cuba and El Salvador, who abstained, voted in favor of the resolution. The socialist bloc joined the western group of developed countries in opposition.

Following the vote, the United States announced that it rejected the resolution, and did not consider itself bound by its terms.

In addition, the 1969 General Assembly once again called upon the Sea-bed Committee to expedite its work of preparing a statement of legal principles, but in the event, the Legal Subcommittee was not able to report substantive progress. During 1970 the Subcommittee held only nine formal and ten informal meetings. Efforts to reach agreement were largely undertaken in a series of consultations carried on by groups of states with little apparent success. Indeed, the Subcommittee's 1970 Report even noted that a number of delegations had expressed doubt that the consultative procedure was "conducive to progress." [22] Nonetheless, experience had shown that formal meetings were not a satisfactory alternative.

The 1970 discussions and continuing efforts to draft an acceptable formulation did, however, prove valuable in at least one respect. It will be recalled that the early formulations of principles related to the legal status of the sea-bed did not distinguish between the area; i.e., the sea-bed, the ocean floor and the subsoil thereof, and the resources to be recovered from the area. The basic dispute can thus be seen to stem from the fact that while the concept of shared ownership of and control over the area was generally acceptable from the beginning, many states felt that the extension of that concept to the resources themselves would make the resulting regime impractical. An international regime governing states' access to and payment for the resources was one thing; internationally imposed clouds on title to the recovered resources and restrictions on their use had to be avoided.

The distinction between the area and the resources had, of course, long been recognized. It was, in fact, the basis of the conflict. The failure of the various draftsmen to find language that would both reflect the distinction and meet their various needs can now be seen to have played an important role in the failure of the Committee to reach agreement before the XXV

[22] Report of the Sea-Bed Committee (U.N. Doc. No. A/8021), Annex I, para. 11.

General Assembly. During 1970, however, two draft statements were formally presented, one by a group of developing countries,[23] the other by Norway.[24] While both proclaimed that the area and its resources are the common heritage of mankind and are not subject to national appropriation, both recognized that states and persons may acquire rights in the area and to the resources but included the requirement that such acquisitions not be incompatible with the regime to be established and the Declaration of Principles. The final Declaration accepted this approach.

Lest it be inferred that too great a responsibility for the Committee's slow progress has been placed on the draftsmen, it must be pointed out that agreement became possible only after general acceptance of the idea that the regime would include the establishment of international machinery to administer the regime. With that thought in mind, it can also be said that the final formulations served merely to postpone a solution to the underlying dispute until the terms of reference of the administering agency are agreed upon.

Following the close of the August 1970 session of the Committee, consultations continued. It was not until well after the opening of the XXV General Assembly that the Committee Chairman, Ambassador Amerasinghe of Ceylon, was able to present a generally acceptable statement of the fifteen principles and see it adopted in the closing days of the General Assembly.

It will be observed that a fundamental question of law, the legal status of the area and its resources, is not fully or unambiguously answered by the Declaration of Principles. Ultimately, of course, the answer will come from analyses of state practice. In the meanwhile, a definition in legal terms of "common heritage of mankind" will depend for its substance on the nature of the legal regime and the international machinery which the ninth principle declares shall be established by "an international treaty of a universal character, generally agreed upon." This principle itself offers a few criteria:

"The regime shall, *inter alia,* provide for the orderly and safe development and rational management of the area and its resources and for expanding opportunities in the use thereof and ensure the equitable sharing by States in the benefits derived therefrom, taking into particular consideration the interests and needs of the developing countries, whether landlocked or coastal."

Limitations of space do not here permit a detailed analysis of the myriad of alternatives, in both scope and structure, available to the draftsmen of

[23] U.N. Doc. No. A/AC. 138/SC. 1/L. 2.
[24] U.N. Doc. No. A/AC. 138/SC. 1/L. 4/Rev. 1.

the treaty, almost all of which, it could be argued, would meet these criteria. In a report [25] submitted at the request of the XXIV General Assembly by the Secretary-General, four types of machinery are envisaged: (1) machinery for the exchange of information and the preparation of studies; (2) machinery with intermediate powers, defined as a structure to which have been assigned tasks greater than those provided in the first type, but less than those in the third and fourth; (3) machinery for registration and licensing; and (4) machinery having comprehensive powers, which presumably would include extensive regulatory authority.[26]

Under the first type, states would be free to pursue their own interests in the area. Under the fourth, the "comprehensive powers" of the international organization could even include the conduct of exploitation (and presumably marketing) activities. Directly related to these substantive alternatives are the procedural or structural features of a regime which will directly affect the manner in which it will function and in which it will be controlled. The choices will be political, and the law will, as is so often and so properly the case, stem from politics.

The eleventh principle deals with the prevention of pollution. States are called upon to take appropriate measures and to cooperate in the adoption and implementation of "international rules, standards, and procedures for, *inter alia,*" the prevention of pollution and contamination and other hazards to the marine environment, including the coastline, of interference with the ecological balance of the marine environment, as well as for the protection and conservation of the natural resources of the area.

This principle probably enjoys, in theory at least, a wider measure of acceptability than any of the others, except, perhaps, those dealing with the applicability of international law and the United Nations Charter. The international community has agreed that marine pollution is a problem, but there is still little agreement on how to solve it. First steps toward the creation of a body of international dealing with pollution by oil and by radioactive materials have been taken, and these must be considered major steps, since oil is and radioactivity could be the major sources of difficulty. However, scientists have not yet been able even to identify all pollutants. Technologists have not yet established the means to be used to exploit the non-living resources of the sea-bed, other than oil, so the effect on the environment of these unknown technologies obviously cannot yet be measured. The means of measuring the effect of a given amount of a pollutant

[25] Originally issued as U.N. Doc. No. A/AC. 132/23, and included as Annex III to the Sea-Bed Committee's 1970 Report (A/8021).

[26] *Id.,* para. 42.

upon the ecological balance of a given portion of the marine environment, let alone the whole area, have not yet been satisfactorily developed. There is certainly no agreement upon the consequences to humanity, or for that matter, to the living resources of the sea, of a given amount of ecological imbalance. Above all, there is no agreement as to the relative importance of those consequences. In short, there is no agreed evaluation of the pollution problem or of proposed anti-pollution measures. Thus, a general understanding as to the priority to be assigned anti-pollution measures in the context of an international regime dealing with all of man's interests in the uses and resources of the high seas and the sea-bed will not be easily reached.

Any constructive discussion of the environment and of anti-pollution measures must include consideration of conflicting interests and their consequences upon the participant's policies. For an example, it may be said that it is not a coincidence that the interventions in the Sea-bed Committee's debates by the representatives of Iceland have been largely devoted to the subject of pollution. Iceland's economy and its people are fishery oriented. It is not a highly industrialized nation, and its famous natural sources of steam substantially reduce its dependence on imported fossil fuels. One can assume, therefore, that Iceland is prepared to accept international restrictions on the transport of oil and on deep sea mining operations rather more readily than are many other states. Other examples can easily be found. There are probably as many as there are sovereign states, for each has its own set of priorities based on its own evaluation of its own interests. In the context of the exploitation of the sea-bed itself, there are of course, countries whose geography or domestic sources of minerals are such that they are not as likely to accept the risk of pollution inherent in sea-bed operations as are states that would find such operations profitable, either as entrepreneurs or as consumers.

The evaluation of that risk, as of any other, is, of course, a highly subjective activity. The reward must be balanced against the danger. Each member of the international community is hesitant to allow the other members to make a determination which could vitally affect its own interests. That a realistic and universally applicable international standard of acceptable pollution of the marine environment can ever be achieved is questionable. Not only are there bound to be differing opinions as to the priority to be assigned to the problem in the light of inconsistent political and economic interests, but also there is validity to the argument that the nature and extent of the damage caused by pollution will vary from one portion of the seas to another. For this reason, much is heard of an international regime founded on regional arrangements for the prevention of pollution. Advocates of this approach take the position that the natural or biological factors in the limited portion of the environment directly affecting a regional grouping of states will be similar. It is also urged that the mutuality of interests presumed to exist among neighboring states, and their shared experience of cooperation would make it easier to reach agreement on specific standards and measures. One might, however, note in passing that existing regional arrangements were not always developed on a basis of common climatic or environmental factors. The ecological balance and physical characteristics of the southeastern Pacific have little in common with those of the southwestern Atlantic. If one state is fishery oriented and a neighbor has off-shore oil resources, agreements on anti-pollution measures will not be easily reached.[27]

There is a further difficulty inherent in the regional approach. Regulations promulgated by the coastal states will, if they are to be effective, have to be accepted by states outside of the region. In the absence of the consent of those states using the high seas, the imposition of regulations by coastal states could prove to be still another source of international friction. Participation by the users in the development of any legal regime, and the acceptance by the users of the jurisdiction of that regime are thus prerequisites to any successful regulatory system affecting the activities of states on or under the high seas.

A distinction between a unilateral proclamation of law governing portions of the high seas and one which is based on agreement among a number of states, appears relatively immaterial unless the participants in the multilateral arrangement include states whose interest in the subject matter of the regulations is not confined to the protection of coastal areas.

The traditional principle that acceptance of a doctrine by two or more states has more impact on international law than unilateral promulgations remains an important part of international law, and one which ought not to be discarded, nor has it been. Thus, implicit in Canadian policy statements with respect to its 1970 Arctic waters legislation, which unilaterally extended its jurisdiction beyond previously recognized limits, is its desire to regularize its initiative by agreement with the presumed principal future user of the Northwest Passage, the United States. In fact, Canada has long sought a conference of all states having an interest in Arctic waters, and

[27] An apparent loosening of regional and political ties could be noted in the March 1971 session of the Committee as states came to perceive that their respective national interests in and priorities assigned to sea-bed activities were not always consistent with those of other members of the established blocs to which they belong.

while presumably it is thinking of those states whose territories border on those waters, the interests of users would in fact be represented by that limited group of participants. Circumstances could thus make the distinction referred to above irrelevant in this instance. Elsewhere, however, unilateral or regional attempted efforts to enforce international law could create rather than lessen friction.

The twelfth principle calls upon states engaging in the exploration and exploitation of the resources of the sea-bed beyond the limits of national jurisdiction to pay due regard to "the rights and legitimate interests of coastal States in the region of such activities, as well as of all other States which may be affected by such activities." There is an additional provision that consultations shall be maintained with the coastal states concerned with respect to such activities with a view to avoiding infringement of such rights and interests.

This statement does not attempt to define the rights and interests with which it is here concerned, although it does seem to suggest a distinction between the rights and interests of coastal states in the region and those of others, both coastal and landlocked, when it refers to consultations with the former class and not the latter.

While the Declaration as a whole is based upon the concept of a universally shared right to conduct activities in the area, the recognition here given to the special interests and rights of coastal states is not necessarily inconsistent with the underlying concept, if they be deemed to relate solely to those activities which might have a physical effect upon coastal waters and territories. This principle may, however, be construed as granting all states an influence over off-shore activities merely because, for example, the resources recovered might have adverse effects upon their exports of domestically recovered or processed natural resources, and that this influence may be exercised outside of the regime to be established. On the other hand, it may be inferred from the fact that the statement calls for consultation only with "coastal States in the region," and not with "all other States which may be affected," that this principle relates to environmental interests alone and is simply an elaboration of the preceding principle's reference to cooperation in the prevention of pollution. If this inference should prove unjustified, the twelfth principle could serve as the basis for still greater unilateral limitations upon the sovereign rights of the users, who presumably would otherwise be exercising those rights in conformity with the international regime. It is one thing to recognize the "special interests" of coastal states in activities beyond their national jurisdiction if their environment may demonstrably be adversely affected, but quite another to suggest that national jurisdiction may be extended by unilaterally proclaimed redefinitions of "legitimate interests."

In conclusion, mention should be made of the omission from all fifteen of the principles of any reference in geographic terms to a definition of the area concerned. The second preambular paragraph of the Resolution affirms merely that "there is an area of the sea-bed and ocean floor, and the subsoil thereof, beyond the limits of national jurisdiction, the precise limits of which are yet to be determined." By way of contrast, the draft resolution submitted by the United States to the *Ad Hoc* Committee in 1968 included the statement that "there shall be established, as soon as practicable, a precise boundary . . . beyond that over which coastal States may exercise sovereign rights . . ." In the course of the search for agreement, the American proposal was dropped, although it originally appeared troublesome only to those delegations whose states had advanced claims of jurisdiction, sovereignty or patrimonial rights over an extent of the high seas not generally recognized by the majority.

The fervor with which these claims were protected included the advocacy of principles of international law which many lawyers could reasonably consider inconsistent with the establishment of any viable sea-bed regime. Thus a group of Latin American states meeting in Lima in August 1970 declared as a "common principle" of the Law of the Sea, "the right of the Coastal State to establish the limits of its maritime sovereignty or jurisdiction in accordance with reasonable criteria, having regard to its geographical, geological and biological characteristics, and the need to make rational use of its resources." [28]

Even overlooking the fact the reference to "its" resources can be deemed to be a self-serving assumption of title to a disputed asset, it is clear that these coastal states would effectively reserve for themselves the right to fix their own national limits of jurisdiction, for the degree of reasonableness to be used in choosing and applying the assumedly relevant criteria is to be self-determined. The results suggest an elasticity to the boundaries as great as that which has been read into the exploitability clause of the Continental Shelf Convention.

The sensitivity of certain of the Latin American states is reflected in the five resolutions adopted at the Lima conference, which included opposition to the establishment of an interim regime and to an agenda for an international conference on the law of the sea which would not include all aspects of the subject. Each aspect of the law of the sea would presumably be the

[28] Declaration of the Latin American States on the Law of the Sea, 10 Int'l Legal Materials 207, 8 (1971).

subject of extensive negotiations, and acceptance of an agreement on one could be dependent on acceptance or rejection of an agreement on another. The resolutions on treaty provisions barring nuclear weapons from the area [29] and on scientific oceanographic research each emphasized the preservation of "maritime sovereignty," the latter to the point of declaring that all samples obtained in the course of scientific research of the sea-bed "shall be the property of the State" in whose jurisdiction the research is carried out.[30]

The real difficulty, however, lies in the fact that protection of the claim to 200 miles of sovereignty has transcended the need to reach agreement on any other aspect of the proposed sea-bed regime. No proposal of substance made in the Sea-bed Committee proved acceptable until it was tested for its possible effect, no matter how remote, upon those claims. They have assumed an importance which outweighs in the minds of their advocates the advantages the world community may realize from these new steps toward the organization of the peace.

[29] *Supra* note 13.
[30] *Supra* note 28, at 208-14.

COMMENTARY

by

DOUGLAS M. JOHNSTON

I thought I might break down my comments into two segments – unusual segments.

The first segment would be a voyage of discovery – a voyage of imagination, and I invite you to join me on that voyage. Imagine with me what we would have seen, if we had sailed together from Toronto to New York. First, we would have encountered technology. I had some conception of the dominant role of technology in this whole theory of discussion because there is still ice in Lake Ontario and some solution would have had to be found to carve our way through that ice, since Spring has still not arrived in Canada.

Assuming we solve that problem, we find ourselves sailing down the St. Lawrence River. Ontario Province is on our left; New York State is on our right. This would have given us, at least, some passing familiarity with the harmonization or parallel legislation approach to the problem of managing international non-maritime water resources. Further down the river, we would have found Quebec replacing Ontario – reminding us that in the law of the sea, too, and not just in non-maritime water areas, we will have to deal with subnational entities as well as national governments. We might have time, sailing serenely down the river, to speculate on the further complications in organization, not merely governments, national and subnational and perhaps supranational, but perhaps many other kinds of organizations.

Further down the river still, the water becomes saltier. We're in the region where all kinds of fishery disputes are now becoming evident – disputes between inshore fishermen and off-shore fishermen, between national fishermen and foreign fishermen – disputes between little boats and big boats, between diferent kinds of fishing gear. We would have discovered in the Gulf of St. Lawrence peculiar fishery problems and disputes. We would have found that the existence of tiny little dots called St.

Pierre et Miquelon in the Gulf of St. Lawrence are French territory creating problems in the context of fishery rights, but beyond that creating problems in projecting the extent of the Continental Shelf from little dots that are scattered throughout the world. And the assumption of mere territorial presence justifies a linear projection of any concept of the Continental Shelf.

We are now in the waters where the Canadian Government will be treating with a variety of foreign governments in an attempt to persuade them to negotiate out of their present fishery rights, which exist allegedly on different kinds of bases – treaty bases, customary bases, and fanciful bases. Varying sectors of economic interests are involved: a negotiating problem. We would be reminded that most of these issues cannot be solved without some kind of negotiation. Quid pro quo. We might remember, in waiving to St. Pierre et Miquelon as we passed, that deals will have to be made – will soon be made – where fishing benefits will have to be traded off against mineral exploitation benefits; and the deals must be politically saleable to electorates back home. Then we move on, coming South, one of the most fished areas in the world; a slight diversion takes us to the Grand Banks. We might even have the good luck of witnessing a real fishery dispute in process. We would see seventeen countries fishing together, many of them using the most up-to-date equipment in the world. We could have fun on deck imagining when we have passed that line – that notional line that separates the Canadian Continental Shelf from the American Continental Shelf. Going down the New England coast, we could grieve at the decline of the New England fishing industry, remembering it has been declining and dying for the last forty years, but is not quite dead. We could consider the multiple factors that go into the state of health of a fishing industry at any one time. If we were Canadians, we would be glad to note, however, that the fishing boats out there – the Canadian fishing boats – catching fish which are now frozen and saleable to mid-western America as fish foods – a new found market because of developments in refrigeration technology. When we become bored with that, we can look overhead and see aircraft flying over the high seas being identified in aircraft identification zones over the high seas where freedom prevails and we wonder about the need for abstractions and absolutes in international law.

We might be boarded by United States officials concerned about public health requirements or fiscal regulations. We might wonder how twelve miles can stretch quite so far out from sea. We find ourselves in a contiguous zone and are bound to consider how contiguity relates to functional problems, how far it goes. Then, we are in the territorial sea, enjoying the right of innocent passage, convinced that we are innocent. But we would be bound to consider whether a non-military vessel is necessarily engaged in innocent passage – innocent if it is carrying radar equipment from a country that has a threatening ideology. Is it innocent passage if it is carrying oil – a pollutant – and might be a threat to the seas. Instead of entering internal waters, we might decide that this is too much fun – let's go further down the coast – after all, we have just seen a tiny bit of the Western Hemisphere.

So we turn South. I'll leave it to your imagination now – how many law of the sea problems we would encounter. We're still in the Atlantic Ocean, but then we're in the South Atlantic. We have entered warmer waters and we will pass into less warm waters. Scientists who come with us would tell us how important that was. It affects the concentration of fishery stocks. It may or may not affect the results of oil spillage in waters. It may have innumerable effects which should be the basis of law and not fanciful ideas and abstractions. And then we turn the corner at the bottom and come up. It's a different seabed. Does that matter? It's called the Pacific Ocean. The coastal states now have a very narrow continental shelf. That reminds us of the inequity of nature – how far need law go – can law go – to counter the inequity of nature. Then we pass up the Western Coast of North America. We recognize the difference between long-range interests, near fishing interests, the complexity of a fishing industry whose vessels are registered in a foreign country.

Passing up the border into off-Canadian waters, in the Pacific, we will recall the history of conservation agreements between Canada and the United States, the long record of cooperation between these countries, and recollect many other records of cooperation between other states working bilaterally, recalling the scientific effort and time invested in conservation regulation. We are reminded of the problem – the real problem – of the newcomer to an area, the difficulty of keeping out the newcomer – the moral questionability of keeping out a newcomer.

If we go much farther we are in the sub-Arctic and then the Artic and waters turn to ice. And yet we are still told we are in an ocean. The Arctic Ocean. It has no oceanic properties but it's been arbitrarily designated an ocean. And being an ocean matters. I mean, it being an ocean, you are on the offensive, if you wish to justify exclusive authority by a coastal state or the nearest adjacent state. By now my head is reeling, my imagination is boggling.

My modest and tentative conclusion at this point in this voyage of discovery is that lawyers are not enough – most of us would agree with that presumably – critical contributors but not enough. The problems we are talking about now are not legal problems – but policy problems and human problems. It is the future of the world we are concerned with. Not the future of concepts and words. And it is not very helpful either to say that. But it helps to put things in perspective. And, therefore, now in my second segment, I would like to talk about perspectives. A cowardly way out, perhaps. The papers that went before dealt in some detail with technical matters – all interesting and inviting and deserving of comment. But my feeling is that since this is a conference that deals with international law of the Western Hemisphere, we must first pause on the question of hemisphere. How relevant, if at all, is a hemispheric perspective in international law, specifically, the international law of the seas? Irrelevant would be my answer. Irrelevant also the semi-hemisphere if we are considering the international law of the seas as a whole; yet not necessarily wholly irrelevant if we are beginning now to break down the law of the sea into special kinds of problems. It would certainly be easy to argue, if we look first of all at the land, that there is a good deal of sense in encouraging the development of international law on a continental or semi-hemispheric basis, when you are dealing with problems that are exclusive to the land, where the societies on that continent – in that semi-hemisphere – are relatively homogeneous and where common customs can be established on the basis of common expectations. It does not disturb me in the slightest at this theoretical level that Latin American states should have developed on their own certain practices in the field, let's say, of diplomatic asylum. It seems to me unsurprising and desirable and a healthy kind of contribution to international law. I am not so clear, however, why that should necessarily be so, if, *a priori,* we are talking about the sea; unless, of course, one begs the question and says that the sea is an extension of the land. And that seems to be a denial of common sense. The sea is the sea.

If you look over the history of the international law of the sea, it is very clear that it has been dominated by the concept of the nation-state. And, therefore, until modern times, what one could do in the sea had to be answered by the logic of national authority. Either you had national authority or you had the denial of national authority in the sea.

We have seen a series of modifications in the twentieth century to the simple bifurcation of the oceans. Yet still, in all our legal thinking about the sea, we are dominated by the concept of the nation-state. I would not deny, not being a visionary, that the nation-state is the most important single actor in the treatment of international problems. But this fact certainly does not justify our placing the nation-state on a pedestal. And therefore it does not justify our putting a premium on the national perspective in the way that runs through most international legal literature. And yet reality tells us that one of the areas most seriously neglected in the international law of the sea is that there has not yet been a serious effort made by man to develop studies in national marine policies. It is an incredible situation. Ideally, every maritime country in the world should be intensively studied, first of all to discover what its stake really is in the ocean. This would require all the disciplines in the social and natural sciences to collaborate. It sounds somewhat visionary but, in practice, obviously, one would begin with a sample of maritime nations representing different situations and different perspectives. And that would throw much more light on the national perspective on the sea than anything that is contained in international legal literature. And it should precede the making of final – or allegedly final – settlements of a legal character on a treaty basis.

Then you ask, "What are the alternatives to the national perspective?" Four, I think. And they are not mutually exclusive. All can be regarded as legitimate perspectives, relevant to the full inquiry into the future of the sea.

The first alternative, rather obviously, is the region – as a unit, as a basis of organization, as a locale within which concepts, norms, can be developed independently of the national contribution.

Second, the environment: a new concept in thinking about the seas. And that is a very difficult one. Quite distinguishable both from the national perspective and the regional perspective is the environmental. In the Arctic, should we have a regional or environmental approach? That is a meaningless question. It might not be. The Canadian Marine legislation referred to by previous speakers – the antipollution legislation in the Arctic – has been both hailed and criticized (sometimes by the same people at the same time). Most people sympathise with the need for action and everyone, without exception, I think, would regret that the Canadian Government found it necessary to act unilaterally. People differ on whether they had any real political choice in the matter. But, of course, if we adopt, without thinking of it that way, a regional perspective on the Arctic then it seems more feasible to say that Canada should of course have entered into a regional arrangement with the United States – at least as far as passage through the North American sector of the Arctic waters concerned. If you think of the Arctic as environment then you come out with a different suggestion that the Canadian Government's position should have been a wholly Arctic policy where environmental protective legislation should have been part of a comprehensive Arctic policy – which in fact has not fully been worked out – involving choices between development on the one side, and conservation and environmental protection on the other. If the Arctic were regarded as an environment, including the waters of the Arctic, it should have involved the participation of all the Arctic countries, and arguably even the Sub-Arctic countries and perhaps even those countries possessing the technology to use the Arctic marine environment.

The third alternative to national perspective, if you like, is the oceanic perspective, which has accompanied the national perspective over the years in international law of the sea. I think, probably, the idea of an ocean should be discarded for policy making purposes and much of the discussion of the Continental Shelf problems, without intending to, is making the concept of the ocean obsolete. Presumably the more you break down a body of water called the ocean, into compartments and segments, the less it can be regarded as a whole – as an ocean, the less meaningful it becomes.

The fourth alternative is what I would call a systemic perspective. It is one that has been mentioned by Dean Hayton in his paper, talking of hydro systems and this is carrying functional logic further along the line than if you adopt any of these other perspectives on the sea: the national, the regional, the environmental and the oceanic, but it creates other problems. The systemic perspective is a partial perspective. It only deals admittedly, with one function, with one kind of need. Any hydro system presumably could only be argued as part of a larger life-supporting system and, therefore, it might be that scientists could argue that the logic that prevails in the systemic approach to the sea is the logic of the environment; and then, if we go back to the environmental perspective, which environment, how many environments are there? There is only one environment, of course, the whole ocean, the whole body of waters in the world. And yet this falls through our fingers. This is no benefit. We are told by the scientists that the real environment is the biosphere. There are still problems of organization and the global level is not necessarily the level at which most things can be done as economically and equitably as possible.

My view at this level of generalization is that we should first of all start to develop marine studies rationally, employing all four perspectives on the sea, using all the disciplines that man has developed. And the lawyers right now should be chiefly concerned with freezing existing arrangements which cannot be shown by the sciences to be harmful, unnecessarily harmful. Where existing arrangements can be shown scientifically to be unnecessarily harmful, they should be remedied on a temporary basis, until the national policy-making studies have been carried further. This would be a five-to-ten-year plan, I suppose, that I would advocate.

The lawyer brings to his tasks many advantages and some disadvantages. Two disadvantages bother me more than others. One is the lawyer's proclivity for uniformity. His obsession with the notion that justice and equity lie close to equality and that uniformity is likely to be clear. In the context of the law of the sea, this is not necessarily true *a priori*. One is not entitled to the assumption. I think that attempts to formalize the limits of the territorial sea have been stultified over the years by the concept that somehow the laws of the territorial sea must be uniform throughout the world and that until you have uniformity you do not really have any clear understanding of the applicable international law.

The second disadvantage he brings to the task is an excessive zeal for formalism, which I find most disturbing in certain contexts. Being from Canada, I might take the liberty of suggesting that much of the criticism that has been directed against the Canadian Government's pollution control legislation in the Arctic reveals formalistic fervor in the critic. Less important than the unilaterial form of the Canadian Government's action is the substance of the legislation. And I cannot understand why critics cannot take this point that the substance is *more* important than the form. They stand up and concede generously at the beginning that the substance of the legislation is irreproachable. And that it is very much of the kind that one would expect to see developing internationally under international auspices. And yet, to their mind, overweighing that is the heinous offence of resorting to unilateral form. And even though there can of course be differences of opinion about the need to resort to unilateral form, which is not *a priori* desirable, many critics end up by assuming that it is such a great evil that it virtually overrides the virtue of the substance of the legislation. This kind of formalism seems to me inherent in much legal thinking and is an obstruction in the way of rationalism in dealing with the future of the oceans.

COMMENTARY

by

F. V. GARCÍA-AMADOR

For those of us who only a few years ago pleaded for recognition of the special interests of coastal states, particularly those in the process of development, it is difficult to comprehend that technological progress today once again advises adoption of a different attitude, specifically with regard to the definition of the continental shelf or submarine areas contained in Article 1 of the Geneva Convention. Along this line, remember that this same argument, plus that of the legitimate needs and interests of coastal states, during the decade of the '50's advised recognizing for those states the interests and rights covered by the Geneva Convention.

Our reluctance to abandon our former posture is also justifiable on other grounds. From the technical point of view, if the criterion of exploitability is today not considered sufficiently precise, current uncertainty as to the nature and volume of activities contemplated in the exploitation and exploration of the resources of the seabed and ocean floor, and the subsoil thereof, also fails to provide us with a solid basis on which to establish a new international legal regime for these submarine areas. Mr. Wolf refers to this uncertainty in his paper. And, from a political point of view we must not underestimate the fact that the Convention on the Continental Shelf was approved by an overwhelming majority at a conference attended by 86 countries, only a little over ten years ago. Although it is true that new states have come into being, there is no ground for thinking that they and the older states are willing to renounce the vast rights the Geneva Convention recognizes for coastal states.

Without delving into any one specific problem I should only like to raise one question with regard to the limits of national jurisdiction. Within the context of resolutions of the United Nations General Assembly on this topic, what is dealt with is the limits on marine and ocean floors and their subsoil. How then shall we handle the question when we are dealing with maritime claims that extend to the submarine areas the same jurisdiction claimed over the waters? For example, the Declaration of Montevideo on the Law of the Sea recognizes as a basic principle of the law of the sea:

"5. The right to explore, conserve and exploit the natural resources of the seabed and of the subsoil of the ocean floor out to where the coastal state claims jurisdiction over the sea."

Furthermore, with all due respect I want to express my disagreement with Professor Johnston who has just refused to accept the idea that the sea can at times be considered as a continuation of the land. For many countries of the world this is a biological and economic fact in the sense that the development and sometimes the very subsistence of the country depends on the natural resources found in the waters, the seabed, or the subsoil of the seas adjacent to its coasts. Therefore it has always seemed reasonable to us that every claim of maritime jurisdiction should be examined in the light of the real and genuine interests of the coastal state in order to determine its justification and validity.

Finally, I should remind you that to date, when the Latin American countries have agreed to take or to launch new positions on the law of the sea, including times when these have been audacious positions, they have been successful. Bear in mind what happened at the Conference of Rome in 1955, in the International Law Commission when it drew up its final draft in 1955 and 1956, and at the two Geneva Conferences on the Law of the Sea, in 1958 and 1960. These are very encouraging experiences and one may hope they will be repeated in the future if the coastal states in the process of development agree on formulae and solutions that can be sustained on the strength of their merits.

PART II

SUPER POWER INTERVENTION: MILITARY AND ECONOMIC

REGIONAL INTERVENTIONISM BY THE SUPERPOWERS: A STUDY OF WORDS AND ACTS AS INCHOATE LAW MAKING

by

THOMAS M. FRANCK AND EDWARD WEISBAND

An old common law tradition holds that actions speak louder than words and that it is what is done, rather than what is said, that matters. To some extent this philosophy underlies also the viewpoint of the Office of Legal Adviser, at least in the United States. Insofar as the Office concerns itself with law derived from state conduct, it is the prior action of nations, rather than the characterization and conceptualization of that occasion, to which the legal advisers traditionally tend to lean.

It is our belief that this is essentially a disfunctional approach. Elsewhere,[1] we have shown the remarkable congruence between the concepts enunciated by the United States during four hemispheric crises and the concepts of the Brezhnev doctrine developed by the Soviet Union in 1968. We believe that that congruence is of substantial importance to lawyers and that these matters should have been taken into account in formulating the United States' conceptualizations. What the congruence has created is not a more viable coincidence but a new systemic relationship between each of the two superpowers and their regional aggregation of states: a system which we believe to be disadvantageous to the United States, and wholly ill-concieved. The task, now, is for the United States to use a mixture of concepts and acts to amend this systemic inaction and to replace it with one more congenial both to the US and to the nations who must perforce live in the proximity of the superpowers.

I. THE TWO-GHETTO SYSTEM: COSTS AND BENEFITS

The principles of conduct formulated and enunciated by the verbal strategy of the U.S. Government during the Guatemalan situation of 1954, in

[1] Frank & Weisband, 22 Stanford L. Rev. 979 (1970).

the Cuban Missile crisis of 1962, and in the Dominican intervention of 1965, have now been confirmed as an applied doctrine of world order by the Soviet invasion of Czechoslovakia. Through our behavior, military and conceptual, we helped develop principles of a world in which superpowers are licensed to operate ghettos of subservient states. By invading Czechoslovakia, Moscow agilely agreed to these principles. This acceptance does not necessarily make the Johnson-Brezhnev principles a permanent or irreversible contractual basis for world order. Rather, a foundation has been laid, but the cement has not hardened. This paper is addressed to the reversal of the two-ghetto principle and the possible emergence of a different norm.

There are, of course, things to be said for a two-ghetto system or rule: an arrangement making Latin America, or in any event the Central American and Caribbean portions of it, subservient in perpetuity to the overriding interests of the United States, and Eastern Europe to those of the Soviet Union. *First,* it may be argued that such an arrangement protects the national interest of the United States by excluding communism from the hemisphere and preserving established U.S. economic and military interests in the Americas. *Second,* the two-ghetto system, by drawing a line between "theirs" and "ours," might help stabilize the world political system and perhaps reduce cold war tensions.[2] *Third,* it may be argued that, since the Soviet Union will, in any event, keep Eastern Europe "ghettoized," the United States must do the same in Latin America lest the world balance of power be upset.[3] *Fourth,* it is conceivable that the propensity for trouble-making by small states which are dependents of the superpowers is such that, if the Great Powers are not to be dragged into dangerous squabbles, each must maintain strict discipline over its dependents.

Each of these is an arguable, though, in our opinion, unproved proposition. But it must at least be asked by Americans whether a people can long endure a double life of democracy at home and despotism abroad. History indicates that nations, like individuals, must seek an integrated lifestyle. This poses no present dilemma to Soviet authorities. The suppression of Czechoslovakia was readily paralleled by a revival of politico-cultural despotism at home. The tap of repression still turns readily in modern Russia. But for the United States, a policy of regional repression

[2] Cf. S. Brown, The Faces of Power 243 (1968).

[3] For a further discussion of these advantages and disadvantages cf., R. N. Rosecrance, *Bipolarity, Multi-polarity, and the Future,* 10 J. Conflict Resolution 313 (1966).

would almost certainly create social and political conflicts at home that could end only in the restoration of democratic ideals to our foreign policy or else in a domestic regime as authoritarian as any we might impose on the hemisphere.

From the point of view of U.S. self interest, therefore, the bargain struck, intentionally or unintentionally, by the confluence of the Johnson and Brezhnev Doctrines, seems to many Americans a bad one. But in order to begin to work our passage back from this bad bargain, it is necessary to understand how we got there: how the international system transforms the unilateral conduct of states into reciprocal norms which have, at least in relations between the superpowers, the force of near-law.

Assistant Secretary of State Richard N. Gardner has observed, "The law you make may be your own." President Johnson explained our invasion of the Dominican Republic in terms of a doctrine of limited sovereignty and regional self-defense against an alien ideology. It ought to have been recognized by American planners that he thereby, implicity, "offered" the Soviets the right to depose any regime in Eastern Europe which appeared to threaten socialist orthodoxy. In August, 1968, this implied "offer" was accepted. Strategically it means little to argue – however true – that we did not intend this systemic consequence. We knew, and the Russians knew that we knew, that the Brezhnev Doctrine was the reciprocal of the Johnson Doctrine. Estoppel, in such circumstances, is not merely a legal but also a systemic and strategic concept.

By failing to take into account the reciprocal system-transforming effect of the principles we enunciate and by which we purport to act, by not "listening to ourselves as if we were the enemy speaking," we are likely to misperceive our opponents' strategic position, which, in turn, conduces to serious strategic miscalculations. Several theoretical strategists, including George Kennan,[4] Marshall Schulman,[5] and Zbigniew Brzezinski,[6] for example, began to conclude, by 1965, that the Soviet Union's rigid domination of a united international communist movement was giving way, particularly in Eastern Europe, to a pluralistic, nationalistic pattern of socialist states relatively free to pursue their perceived self-interest. None of these experts seems to have realized that our reassertion between 1960 and 1964 of a doctrine of bloc discipline *vis-à-vis* Cuba and, particularly,

[4] C. F. Kennan, On Dealing with the Communist World (1966).

[5] M. D. Shulman, Beyond the Cold War (1966).

[6] Z. Brzezinski, Alternative to Partition: For a Broader Conception of America's Role in Europe (1965).

in the Dominican Republic might help pave the way for its reciprocal reassertion by the Soviet Union within its own bloc.

To the degree a superpower fails to think reciprocally about its own behavior, it fails to be realistic in its understanding of how that behavior, through the operation of mutually shared expectations and the systemic norm of reciprocity, affects and alters the system. The survival of some element of system or of predictable patterns in the interaction between the superpowers is to everyone's advantage, not least to the United States.[7] In the summer of 1968, the Soviets, under the rules of the system, were entitled to assume that we would not use force to deny them recourse to their equivalent of the Johnson Doctrine. A sudden shift in signals and a repudiation of an implied reciprocal obligation on our part would have created an extremely serious crisis, perhaps pushing the world to the brink of nuclear war.

The Soviet leaders undoubtedly knew this, and took it into account in calculating the probable risks and costs involved in their intended act.

Reciprocity is also essential to making credible a nation's commitment to a deterrence norm in any particular confrontation. The credibility of a deterrence strategy in any particular superpower confrontation depends upon military capability plus commitment. These two ingredients, although related, are also significantly independent of each other. Thus, for example, the Soviets perceived us to have military capability with which to meet their invasion of Czechoslovakia but little or no commitment to use it. In the event, they proved to be right. But it is never easy to manifest a commitment in a way persuasive to the other side. Stating an intention is not enough. Merely rattling sabres is not, either. As Schelling notes, "The hardest part is communicating our own intentions." [8] The most effective way to make manifest a commitment to deter, and thus to have an effective deterrence strategy, is for the state to conduct its foreign policy in consistent accord with certain enunciated, reciprocal principles even when, in a single encounter, it is not necessarily to its short-run advantage to do so. On the other hand, the credibility of a deterrence strategy is undermined

[7] What is an equivalent situation to which reciprocity applies? The question is discussed, and rules for determining equivalence are proposed, in an article by the authors which supplements this study: Franck and Weisband, *The Role of Reciprocity and Equivalence in Systemic Superpower Interaction,* 3 N.Y.U.J. Int'l L. & Pol. 263 (1970). For a relevant discussion from the perspective of legal philosophy see P. W. Taylor, *Universalizability and Justice,* in H. E. Kiefer and M. K. Munitz, eds., Ethics and Social Justice 142, 163 (1968). Also consult A. W. Gouldner, The Coming Crisis of Western Sociology (1970), especially pp. 231-245 for a discussion of some sociological implications.

[8] T. C. Schelling, Arms and Influence 35 (1966).

whenever the United States, in a single encounter, pursues a short-term strategy which violates its own proscriptive norms. Principled abstinence or self-denial by a superpower in an encounter with its opponent is perhaps the strongest evidence of that superpower's commitment to use force, if necessary, to enforce the same proscriptions against its rival.

Any commitment to a policy of deterrence becomes manifestly less credible if the deterring superpower fails to deter itself from doing the kinds of things it seeks to prevent its opponent from doing. In this strategic sense, to be credible, deterrence must also be reciprocal. This is quite aside from the systemic, social and moral implications of reciprocity.

The Cuban missile crisis offers an opportunity for speculative application of this theory. Although it has generally been treated as a completely successful instance of U.S. strategic planning, the very fact that the crisis arose at all must be seen as a failure of deterrence, and was so treated by President Kennedy. As Seyom Brown notes,

> "Kennedy had been insisting publicly that the United States could not allow Cuba to become a base for Soviet 'offensive' weapons. It was as much the fact of this drawing of the line in public as it was the actual military situation created by the Soviet deployments that underlay Kennedy's definition of the deployment as intolerable." [9]

Why did the Soviets nevertheless persist? Why did the President's warnings fail to carry credibilty? It is at least possible that the Soviets did not expect the United States to go to the brink of war to force the removal of Russian missiles from Cuba so long as American missiles continued to be stationed in Turkey.

Robert Kennedy and Roger Hilsman [10] have both indicated that the President, at the beginning of his administration, had ordered the evacuation of the Turkish missiles and had entered the Cuban missile crisis believing the order to have been carried out. It appears that he was furious to discover the missiles were still in place. It is interesting to speculate what might have happened had Kennedy known the facts somewhat earlier, before the crisis arose. Had the warning against the installation of Soviet missiles in Cuba been coupled with the enunciation of a reciprocal proscriptive norm, and had that norm been applied by the United States against itself, had our missiles been publicly withdrawn from Turkey, would the Soviets have been deterred and the crisis averted? Certainly the credibility of the President's warnings would have been enhanced. It would have been

[9] Brown, *supra* note 2, at 259.

[10] R. F. Kennedy, Thirteen Days: A Memoir of the Cuban Missible Crisis (1969); R. Hilsman, To Move a Nation (1968).

apparent to an inveterate politician like Krushchev that Kennedy meant business and was staking his career on the reciprocal proscriptive principle. Moreover, it would have been clear that the United States was offering Russia a reciprocal principle with reciprocal benefits, and not merely a unilateral threat with all the costs on one side and the benefits on the other. As Thomas Milburn has said:

> "One would ordinarily expect that he could change the direction of behavior of another more effectively, not alone by blocking the other's subjective probability of achieving success in one direction, but by increasing the subjective probability for success, and even its meaning, for taking some other path or direction." [11]

Although U.S. conduct and concepts helped pave the way for the two-ghetto system, it is still possible for an imaginative administration in Washington to make a beginning towards reciprocal U.S.-Soviet de-ghettoization, or, if you like, to make an offer of a new reciprocal norm in superpower relations. The process of transforming national unilateral initiatives, properly located within a conceptual framework, into reciprocal norms got us where we are today. It can also get us out of there.

For example, as the Revolutionary Junta of Peru or the elected Socialist Government of Chile embark on a leftist course of economic change, nationalizing U.S.-owned industry and, in general, moving towards a socialist society, the United States will have an opportunity to begin to move away from the Johnson Doctrine, one step at a time, while pausing between steps to see whether there is any comparable tendency on the part of Moscow to modify the Brezhnev Doctrine. We can begin by stating unequivocally, even while pressing our demands for compensation, that on no account would military force be used to interfere with Peruvian or Chilean sovereignty so long as no other superpower establishes its military presence on Peruvian or Chilean soil. It has already been quite clear to most Americans for some time, despite the overreach of the Johnson Doctrine, that we would be extremely unlikely to try to remove a socialist government of Peru or Chile by military force. It is probably far less clear, however, to the rest of the region: for example, to Peru or Chile. Nor is it clear to the Soviets. A ringing affirmation of Peru's or Chile's right to go it's own way, however well or ill-advised that may be, so long as it does not serve as a base for a foreign state nor for the subversion of other states in the hemisphere, would be a highly significant and credible initiating gesture in any strategy to alter the Johnson-Brezhnev norm.

[11] T. W. Milburn, *The Concept of Deterrence: Some Logical and Psychological Considerations,* 17 J. Soc. Issues, No. 3, p. 3 (1951).

A significant beginning in this direction has already been made by President Nixon. In his foreign affairs message to Congress of February 18, 1970,[12] he put the United States' position *vis-à-vis* the Americas rather differently from the Johnson Doctrine:

"Within the broad communality of our relationship, there is great diversity. In a period of such profound social and cultural change emerging domestic structures will differ by country, reflecting various historical roots, particular contexts and national priorities. We can anticipate different interpretations of reality, different conceptions of self-interest and different conclusions on how to resolve problems.

The United States must comprehend these phenomena. We must recognize national interests may indeed diverge from ours rather than merge."

In an obvious reference to the Johnson Doctrine, the Nixon statement declared that "Our power overshadowed the formal relationship of equality and even our restrained use of this power was not wholly reassuring. As a result, tension between us grew."

On January, 4. 1971, in the televised discussion with network correspondents, the President went further. Although noting, in reference to Chile, that "what happened is not something that we welcome," the President made it clear that "for the United States to have intervened in a free election and to have turned it around, I think would have had repercussions all over Latin America that would have been far worse than what has happened in Chile . . . (W)e recognized the right of any country to have internal policies and an internal government quite different from what we might approve of. What we (are) interested in (is) their policy towards us in the foreign policy field." [13]

This appears to indicate a well-calculated attempt to alter our conceptual strategy *vis-à-vis* Latin America. It seems also to be a beginning of a deliberate effort to alter America's image and the climate of international relations. This effort is characterized, above all, by the Nixon Doctrine [14] which sets a theme developed by Secretary Rogers in relation to Latin America as a determination on our part to "be less intrusive and less domineering. We can speak with a less strident voice," he noted, particularly "by conducting our international affairs with a bit more modesty . . . ." [15]

[12] *United States Foreign Policy for the 1970's: A New Strategy for Peace*, in *The New York Times*, Feb. 19, 1970, pp. 19C-30C at pp. 21C-22C, contains specific reference to the propositions of the Nixon Doctrine.

[13] *The New York Times*, Jan. 6, 1971, p. 42.

[14] Cf. President Nixon's address to the Nation on Nov. 3, 1969, 61 Dept. State Bull. 437 (1969).

[15] Secretary of State Rogers' address before the Department of State's national

The Soviets might reciprocate. Etzioni has shown, for example, that in every instance President Kennedy's gestures beginning with the Johns Hopkins speech were in fact reciprocated. The "Russians responded not just by reciprocating American initiatives but by offering some initiatives of their own," [16] and "(f)or each move that was made, the Soviets reciprocated." [17] There is some reason to hope that such reciprocation would also follow a small, concrete U.S. initiative to back away from the Johnson-Brezhnev Doctrines; the Soviets, too, could conceivably be beginning to feel embarrassed by the constant pointed reminders of their fraternal leaders, such as President Ceaucescu, that solidarity and mutual aid presupposes relations of equality, that no country has the right to interfere in the affairs of others and that when such interference occurs, it greatly prejudices socialism at large.[18] "By the world socialist system we understand not a bloc," they are saying, "in which the states are fused into a whole, giving up their national sovereignty, but the assertion of Socialism as an international force by its victory in several independent states, which develop independently . . ." [19] The assertions are not very different from those of leading Latin-American democracies in response to the Johnson Doctrine.

With such rebukes stinging their ears, the United States and the Soviet Union are, in fact, both at present stopping short of a rigid, consistent application of the Johnson-Brezhnev Doctrines to their respective regions. The United States has not invaded Cuba, Peru, or Chile; the Soviets have not attacked Romania, Yugoslavia or Albania. What is at first needed to initiate a change in climate leading to the eventual repeal of these norms is not a radical shift in actual conduct [20] but for each state to formulate and publicize concepts of behavior that emphasize the limitations it is in practice already imposing on its previously-asserted ghetto doctrine.[21]

But before the two-ghetto system can be decisively transformed into a reciprocal pattern of de-ghettoization and respect for sovereign self-deter-

foreign policy conference for editors and broadcasters on Jan. 15, 1970, 62 *id.* 118 (1970).

[16] A. Etzioni, *The Kennedy Experiment,* 20 The Western Pol. Science Q. 361 (1967).

[17] *Id.* at 368.

[18] President Ceaucescu of Romania, opening the Quadrennial Congress of the Romanian Communist Party, *The Times* of London, Aug. 7, 1969, p. 3.

[19] President Ceaucescu, Quadrennial Romanian Party Congress, *International Herald Tribune,* Aug. 7, 1969, p. 2.

[20] Cf., *U.S. Foreign Policy for the 1970's: A New Strategy for Peace; A Report to the Congress by President Richard M. Nixon,* Feb. 18, 1970, 62 Dept. State Bull. 290 (1970).

[21] Cf. *Id.* at 293.

mination, the two superpowers' images of each other will need to be changed: not necessarily the total spectrum of perceptive set by which the people and leaders of the one see the other, but at least those aspects of the image which directly block a genuine mutual change of policy.

It is thus necessary first to identify those aspects of each superpower's "way of seeing" which have been responsible for getting us into the two-ghetto system, and then to look for new "ways of seeing" that will help get us out.

The Soviet Union invaded Czechoslovakia believing that the radical reforms in that country constituted a conspiracy by "the forces of internal and external reaction" to wrest Czechoslovakia away from the Eastern European security system and draw it into the "imperialist camp." Thus the reforms in Czechoslovakia appeared to Moscow as a manifestation of the expansionistic "policy of ruling circles in the United States."

To Russians, the reform movement in Czechoslovakia was serving the imperial intentions of the United States. This implies an image of the Czechoslovak reformers as "agents" of the United States and West Germany and images of the United States and West Germany as imperialist nations anxious to employ the Czechoslovak reformers to Western advantage. It cannot, of course, be known whether these were the real reasons for the Soviet invasion, or whether this was really how the Kremlin perceived the Prague Spring and the intentions of the West. But these were the reasons advanced by Soviet apologists, and they were apparently accepted by all but a tiny radical minority of the Soviet population. This indicates a perceptive set which expects and thus sees reformist elements in the satellite states to be in league with U.S.-capitalist-imperialist interests and which expects the United States to take advantage of reformist movements in Eastern Europe in order to expand its sphere of military-imperialist hegemony to the common danger of the socialist commonwealth. Such an image of the West and of liberalizing movements has long been promoted by Soviet rhetoric. Justifying the crushing of the moderate socialist Nagy Government in Hungary in 1957, the Kremlin had even then railed against "intervention" by "international forces of reaction and counter-revolution." [22]

The United States appears to perceive radical movements within its

[22] Ralph K. White cites a study showing that Soviet Citizens "indicated a complete acceptance of official propaganda with regard to foreign affairs," R. K. White, *Images in the Context of International Conflict: Soviet Perceptions of the U.S. and the U.S.S.R.*, in Kelman, ed., International Behaviour: A Social-Psychological Analysis (1965).

region in almost exactly the same way. The Arbenz Government of Guatemala was early branded by the State Department as an "intervention of international communism in this hemisphere." The use of force against it was thus justified in terms of hemispheric self-defense. Although no Soviet military units were ever introduced into Guatemala, it was a "given" of U.S. policy that communism is *ipso facto* an alien ideology, subservient always to Moscow's imperialist interests, and that any "activities" of an "international communist movement" in the Western Hemisphere *per se* constitutes "intervention in American affairs." These activities were seen as being pursued "in the interests of an alien despotism" i.e., the Soviet Union. Our verbal strategy made it appear inconceivable that a radical leftist government in our hemisphere could be anything but an agent of Russia, or that Soviet leaders would fail to use any such government to establish their own military-imperial hegemony. This image was widely shared by U.S. policy-makers and the public.

Only in the instance of the Cuban missile crisis was there factual justification for the assertion that a radical revolutionary regime in the Western Hemisphere really was leading its nation towards becoming a base for the Soviets. Nevertheless, before Soviet missiles where introduced, the United States had already branded Castro's regime as one "dominated by international communism" and had both openly called on the hemisphere to use sanctions to "prevent the establishment" of this regime and covertly tried to overthrow it by force at the Bay of Pigs. It may be contended, although definitive proof is lacking for both sides of the argument, that Washington's refusal to distinguish between Castro's and the Kremlin's interests, our insistence that Cuba had become a captive of Soviet imperialism, constituted a self-fulfilling prophecy. Whether this is so or not, the experience of Cuba did undoubtedly strengthen the U.S. image of Russia as the sponsor and exploiter of all radical revolutionary movements in the Western Hemisphere.

This image played an important part in shaping our perception of, and reaction to, the events of 1965 in the Dominican Republic. We readily justified our intervention as hemispheric self-defence against Dominican revolutionaries whom we saw to be agents of an "international conspiracy" and "inspired by an outside power." There was scarcely more evidence of this in the Dominican crisis than in the Czechoslovak or Hungarian cases. Rather, as in these other instances, it was a presumption derived from passing mixed facts through the selective filter of a perceptive set. We derived our understanding of the "enemy's" actions from our image of the invariable motives and nature of "international communism."

Before any significant change in the Johnson-Brezhnev pattern of interaction can be achieved, it will be necessary for the leaders and opinion-shaping mass media of the Soviet Union and the United States, in a deliberately achieved, mutually shared climate of relaxed tension, to promote two crucial image changes:

1) each superpower must change its fixed *a priori* impressions of the nature of revolutionary or radical reform movements within its own region, and,
2) each superpower must change its fixed *a priori* impressions of the use made of radical movements in its region by the rival superpower.

It is well documented that many national communist movements, both in and out of power, no longer slavishly subordinate their own to Moscow's interests. Nor does Moscow invariably establish military bases or try to take over control of countries in which radical revolutionary movements gain power. There are instances and bits of evidence which reinforce the stereotype and more evidence which does not. So too, with the Soviet stereotype of radical reform movements in their region and our intentions to exploit them.

What shape might a restructured mututal image realistically be expected to take? Any backing away from the image underlying the Johnson-Brezhnev Doctrines would require Soviet-U.S. leaders to re-educate their own and the other superpower's publics to be able to make a clear distinction between, on the one hand, regimes which do not conform to the orthodox political norm in their sphere and, on the other, regimes which ally themselves militarily with the rival superpower. Such a distinction would permit the superpower to continue to employ force if necessary to prevent the establishment of regimes in its region which are strategically allied with a rival superpower, while excluding the use of force to prevent the establishment of genuinely national but politically-deviationist regimes.

Russia, for example, seems to have been willing to make this distinction in the case of Finland and Austria, both of which are in the outskirts of Russia's security region, both of which have non-communist regimes and essentially western political, social and economic institutions, but both of which cooperate with the Soviet Union to the extent of remaining strictly aloof from western military alliances and avoiding all contact with the West that could give rise to legitimate Soviet strategic apprehensions. To some extent the United States and Cuba have, in fact but not yet in rhetoric, tentatively begun to move towards a similar "mutual accommodation." President Nixon, in particular, has been careful to link his tentative concession to radical social experimentation within Chile to an insistence that Chilean foreign policy not link that member of the hemispheric sub-system to the Soviet "family of nations." Concurrent with Nixon's assumption of a "low profile" towards Chile has gone his firm public affirmation of an "understanding" with Russia "that they would not put a military naval base into Cuba." [23] In effect, Cuba, Chile or Peru can regard themselves as free as, but no freer than Austria or Finland. Austria and Finland, it should however be noted, are states which have never been members of either superpower ghetto. Chile, Cuba and Peru are all traditionally members of the U.S. sphere. It is now up to the Soviets to reciprocate by permitting nations within their traditional family also to opt for the Austrian or Finish model. The effect of current U.S. strategy appears to be to encourage such a reciprocation by the Soviets and to begin, with or without specific Russian participation, to lay a very tentative base for a system and strategy of partial de-ghettoization.

Sensing the new rules of the game in Latin America, President Allende has been insisting on his country's right to follow a Marxian economic policy and a neutralist foreign policy. But at the same time he has been at pains to reassure Washington: "we will never provide a military base that might be used against the United States. Chile will never permit her territory to be used for a military base by any foreign power – by anybody." [24] In this, the Chilean Marxist regime appears to be "accepting" the new form of partial de-ghettoization for Latin America proposed by the Nixon administration. It remains to be seen whether any parallel rethinking of its relations with Eastern Europe is on the agenda of the Kremlin. In any event, for the present, the Chileans appear determined to prove that there are still "different roads to socialism" [25] and that the Chilean model would help to dissolve, rather than reinforce, the cold war image of a monolithic Moscow-dominated international communist hegemony. If they succeed, the task of de-ghettoization will be considerably eased.

If, then, we have decided to move the U.S.-Soviet sub-system away from its present commitment to rigid dual ghettos, our strategy will have to concern itself with a general change in the climate of sub-systemic interaction, that is, in the mood of U.S.-Soviet relations; it will next have to make a start in the slow and complex process of reshaping our long-held

[23] Transcript of the Nixon Interview with Television Correspondents, *The New York Times*, Jan. 6, 1971, p. 42.

[24] *The New York Times*, March 26, 1971, p. 1.

[25] *Id.* at 24.

and much-reinforced image of *all* socialist movements as part of a monolithic aggressive international-communist conspiracy controlled and invariably subservient to the strategic interests of Moscow. Such a change of image can only come as part of a similar Soviet effort to amend the images that prompt them to perceive all liberalizing movements striving to make socialism more humane, national or democratic, as part of a world-wide capitalist-imperialist conspiracy to encircle the Soviet Union and overthrow its regime.

We are at the crossroads. If they, and we, so choose, the United States and the Soviet Union can now move from the dual-ghetto pattern of subsystemic interaction to a new norm which safeguards the superpowers' justified, essential strategic interests, while yet permitting much greater expression of the national individuality of smaller states within each superpower's region.

THE NATIONALIZATION BY PERU OF THE HOLDINGS OF THE INTERNATIONAL PETROLEUM COMPANY

by

NIGEL S. RODLEY

"In the damp forests beyond the Bío-Bío river, the Spaniards met the fierce resistance of the Araucanian Indians, whose leader Lautaro had learned to manage horses and devised tactics for engaging the Spanish cavalry in successive combats until they were exhaused. In 1554 Valdivia was captured by the Araucanians and executed." [1]

If it was hurtful to the Spaniards that horses should be so used against them, it was doubtless as galling for the United States to find the Peruvian army, so painstakingly trained and supplied by the Pentagon – an organization often perceived as the moral successor to the *conquistadores* – coming to direct power 414 years later on a platform that challenged the basic interests of its mentor. Within a few months after the army seized power, under the presidency of General Juan Velasco Alvarado, the military junta had seized all the properties of the International Petroleum Company, Ltd. (IPC).

The IPC is a 99.9% owned subsidiary of Standard Oil of New Jersey, incorporated and with its principal headquarters in Toronto, Ontario. Richard N. Goodwin, from whose "Letter From Peru" [2] much of the historical background for this paper is taken, has observed:

"By the time of the seizure, the company's interests in Peru extended far beyond the La Brea y Pariñas field near Talara [the extent of the IPC's property rights over this field constitutes the basis of much of the legal and political discord in question]. It also owned a half interest in the more productive Lobitos field. It had a refinery in operation at Talara and controlled fifty-five per cent of the marketing and sale of gasoline in Peru. In addition IPC had reasonable expectations of obtaining concessions to explore for oil in the potentially rich jungle lands east of the Andes."

[1] G. Pendle, A History of Latin America 47 (1963).

[2] R. Goodwin, *Letter From Peru,* The New Yorker, May 17, 1969 [hereinafter cited as "Goodwin"].

When I first thought of examining the nationalization of IPC, I had hoped for a vehicle to demonstrate the increasing unreality of the western position regarding the responsibility of states in their treatment of foreign economic interests. What I thought I needed for my thesis was a simple act of uncompensated expropriation of a major foreign enterprise as part of a third world country's attempt radically to restructure its economy for domestic public purposes. This approach was strengthened by the plan annouced in the summer of 1969 to nationalize the largest sugar plantations in the country, including two owned by United States' interests.[3] What I found was a situation that is extremely complicated and in many respects *sui generis*. Indeed, the title of a booklet published by the Peruvian General Bureau of Information is "Petroleum in Peru – for the World to Judge: The History of a Unique Case." [4] It is not difficult to understand why the Peruvians should have attacked the problem in terms of its particular complexities. As I shall return to show, these complexities were very much a part of the political texture of the country. Nevertheless, regardless of much of the rhetoric surrounding the bloodless Peruvian "revolution," the new government was not interested in a direct confrontation with the United States. Its leaders were genuinely anxious to avoid the application of the Hickenlooper amendment that would cut off a potentially substantial amount of aid and of the amendment to the Sugar Act that would eliminate Peru's sugar quota, since its exports of that product to the United States constitutes a major source of foreign, hard currency exchange. Furthermore, within the limits of what Ambassador Perez de Cuellar [5] has characterized as economic "dirigisme," [6] the new government has shown itself to be more than anxious to encourage the inflow of United States' capital for the promotion of productive industrial investment [7] and has passed comprehensive legislation, complete with incentives, to stabilize the terms of operation of such investment.[8] In brief, then,

[3] See Texto Unico de la Ley de Reforma Agraria, Decreto Supremo No. 265-70-AG of 18 August 1970) [Consolidated Text of the Agrarian Reform Law], incorporating Decree Laws No. 17716 and No. 18296.

[4] (1969).

[5] Permanent Representative of Peru to the United Nations.

[6] Interview, March 12, 1971.

[7] Several prominent advertisements in recent issues of the *New York Times* attest to this anxiety.

[8] Ley General de Industrias, Decreto-Ley No. 18350 of 27 July 1970. [General Law of Industries, Decree Law No. 18350, which is also issued in translation by the Oficina Nacional de Información] Unofficial translations of this and other decree laws governing the financial and mining industries may be found in 8 Int'l Legal Materials 1178-1196 (1969). See also Decreto Ley Normativo de la Industria Minera,

Peru wanted neither to antagonize the United States government nor to chill any further its own "investment climate."

If results are any criterion the strategy may be said to have worked, at least as far as inter-governmental relations with the United States are concerned.[9] Certainly the Nixon Administration was reluctant to use Hickenlooper because of the "domino effect" it would have in Latin America. When the President used that term at his March 4, 1969, News Conference, he invited the Peruvian Government, in a tone suggesting more of a plea than a threat, to take "some steps . . . to deal with the expropriation matter" so that the United States would "not have to go down [the Hickenlooper] road." [10] A little over a month later, after Peru had agreed to hold discussions over "current issues" with President Nixon's Personal Representative, John N. Irwin,[11] particularly the issue of "effective compensation" for the IPC holdings,[12] and had agreed to permit IPC to make representations through an administrative process within the Ministry of Energy and Mines, the United States announced that these measures constituted "appropriate steps within the meaning of the Hickenlooper amendment [13] to the Foreign Assistance Act and of the amended Sugar Act."

Decreto-Ley No. 18225, of 14 April 1970 [Decree law establishing fundamental principles governing the mining industry].

[9] I have not examined the statistics on U.S. investment in Peru.

[10] 60, Dept. State Bull. 245 (1969).

[11] *Id.* at 282.

[12] Secretary Rogers' statement before the Senate Committee on Foreign Relations, *id.* at 310.

[13] The relevant part of the Hickenlooper amendment to the Foreign Assistance Act of 1962, 22 U.S.C.A. sec. 2370 (e) (1), reads:

> The President shall suspend assistance to the government of any country to which assistance is provided under this chapter or any other Act when the government of such country or any government agency or subdivision within such country on or after January 1, 1962
>
> (A) has nationalized or expropriated or seized ownership or control of property owned by any United States citizen or by any corporation, partnership, or association not less than 50 per centum beneficially owned by United States citizens, or
>
> (B) has taken steps to repudiate or nullify existing contracts or agreements with any United States citizen or any corporation, partnership, or association not less than 50 per centum beneficially owned by United States citizens, or
>
> (C) has imposed or enforced discriminatory taxes or other exactions, or restrictive maintenance or operational conditions, or has taken other actions, which have the effect of nationalizing, expropriating, or otherwise seizing ownership or control of property so owned, and such country, government agency, or government subdivision fails within a reasonable time (not more than six months after such action, or in the event of a referral to the Foreign Claims Settlement Commission of the United States within such period as provided herein, not more

Accordingly the sanctions contemplated by Hickenlooper would be "deferred pending the outcome of this process." [14] Less than six weeks later the talks between Ambassador Irwin and the Peruvians "recessed" with "no substantive agreements hav[ing] been reached." [15] Some four years after the deferral of Hickenlooper had been announced, the IPC has received no compensation, while Hickenlooper seems to have been confined. to a dusty grave in some State Department archive. The recommendation of Governor Rockefeller, in the report that developed from his turbulent trips to Latin America [16] in the late spring and early summer of 1969, to the effect that the Executive Branch should seek the suspension or modification of, *inter alia*, the Hickenlooper amendment, doubtless helped hasten the demise of that particular piece of legislation – at least, as far as Latin America is concerned.

Accordingly, one is inclined to feel that possible "domino effects" and the urgings of the New York Governor (one wonders whether he might, not even have made one or two suggestions to Jersey Standard) might have had more to do with U.S. self-restraint than the peculiar nature of the IPC's history.[17] Still, in turning to that history, it should be borne in mind that states wishing to expropriate foreign property may well seek to emulate the Peruvian example. In a way, it will be seen to be a variation on the "creeping expropriation" [18] theme. A "unique case" approach, like confiscatory taxation or the prohibition of vital imports, presents a far more elusive target for the heavy and predictable armoury of the State Department's legal office.

than twenty days after the report of the Commission is received) to take appropriate steps, which may include arbitration, to discharge its obligations under international law toward such citizen or entity, including speedy compensation for such property in convertible foreign exchange, equivalent to the full value thereof, as required by international law, or fails to take steps designed to provide relief from such taxes, exactions, or conditions, as the case may be; and such suspension shall continue until the President is satisfied that appropriate steps are being taken, and no other provision of this chapter shall be construed to authorize the President to waive the provisions of this subsection.

[14] Secretary Rogers' News Conference, 7 April 1969, 60 Dept. State Bull. 357 (1969).

[15] *Id.* at 472, 3 (1969). The "administrative procedure" culminated in the denial of IPC's claim by the Ministry of Energy and Mines, Oficio No. 073-69-EM/SD, 9 July 1969.

[16] Rockefeller's scheduled trip to Peru which was considered "inconvenient" by the junta did not materialize; 61 *id.* at 523 (1969). His personal connections with the "parent" of IPC and other major enterprises operating in Latin America were lost on few in that sub-continent.

[17] I know of no official U.S. statement acknowledging any validity to Peru's special claims.

[18] See H. Steiner & D. Vagts, Transnational Legal Problems 363-8 (1968).

THE NATURE OF THE TAKING

The reason I have dwelt on the historical special nature of the Peruvian government's action is that the seizure of IPC's properties was ostensibly aimed at the settlement of past grievances rather than at the implementation of a new social order. The dispute revolves around the oilfield at La Brea y Pariñas in northern Peru. IPC claims its title to the property, the suboil and the fruits thereof through a chain of transactions going back to 1826.[19] In that year the Peruvian government, grateful to one Don José de Quintana, who had helped finance Bolívar's struggles against a recalcitrant Spain, granted a deed to the gentleman in question whereby the agents of the government

"abdicate, strip and separate from the state which they represent all right, title and dominion held by or appertaining to it over the said mine of "pitch," and they cede, renounce and transfer the same to the purchaser." [20]

The pitch (*brea*) referred to was the product made of the oil which seeped to the surface of the property and into trenches dug by the Spanish who wanted more of it than their Indian predecessors. Whether the title deed ought to be interpreted to include a grant of *subsoil* rights should be seen in the context of this technological fact,[21] as well as of the more formal legal status of mining rights. As the Peruvian publication, "Petroleum in Peru," points out, "In Peru, mines have not been subject to private ownership, during the Incaic period, the Viceregency or the Republic." [22] Indeed, the Peruvian revolutionaries after declaring independence from Spain in 1821, but prior to ousting the last of the Spanish troops in 1824, reconfirmed the colonial ordinances so that ownership of the subsoil rights to all minerals, and other substances in the earth, belonged to the state." [23]

When the matter first became a bone of contention in 1888, it would appear that the then owner acquiesced in the Government's characterization of him as a concession holder for the purpose of the registration un-

[19] A more complete history may be found in Goodwin. Most of the relevant documents are reproduced in translation in 7 Int'l Legal Materials 1201-64 (1968) and 8 *id.* at 264-330 (1969). A thorough analysis of the domestic Peruvian Law implications of the taking is to be found in D. Furnish, *Peruvian Domestic Law Aspects of the La Brea y Pariñas Controversey,* 59 Ky. L. J. 351 (1970).

[20] Quoted from Goodwin.

[21] Goodwin notes that the first oil well was not to be drilled for another 28 years.

[22] *Supra* note 4, at 17.

der the mining laws. He then sold his property to British interests who, on deciding to sell to IPC, needed clarification of the tax status of the holding. The British government eventually pressured the Peruvian government into agreeing to an arbitration, whose award was a deal worked out by two Peruvian and British representatives, adopted by the English and Peruvian arbitrators and the Swiss umpire. The "award," which provided for exceptionally low tax treatment, has, in Goodwin's words, provided a vehicle by which "[l]awyers and politicians have built reputations and careers analyzing, attacking and defending the award . . ." Once the Peruvian dictator whose regime had promoted the "settlement" was overthrown, the award became a matter of continuing controversy until, in 1963, the Peruvian Congress passed legislation declaring the award void. They no doubt had in mind that the award did not address itself to the crucial question posed in the *compromis,* namely, whether or not the "Mineral Property of 'La Brea y Pariñas' " had a "legal status distinct from that of mineral property acquired and held in the usual manner under the Mining Ordinance or the Mining Code of Peru." [24]

In 1951, IPC submitted to regular income taxation, but still did not fall within the normal regime of royalty payments for mining concessions. Then just before the Army took over (indeed it was the major public reason for the takeover), the constitutional government of President Fernando Belaúnde Terry, after about two years of suspended U.S. aid on account of IPC and then another suspension because of Peruvian acquisition of French Mirage aircraft, arrived at an agreement, the Act of Talara, with IPC. It settled in Peru's favour (the "award" had avoided this fundamental question) the question of Peruvian ownership of the subsoil at La Brea v Pariñas. It also granted sizeable long-term further concessions to IPC,[25] and it provided that Peru would forego the taxes it had claimed on the basis of operating under the "illegal" regime of the award. According to the Peruvians, an eleventh page which stipulated the price to be paid for the oil, a guaranteed minimum price for the Empresa Petrolera Fiscal (State Petroleum Enterprise) which would sell crude oil to the IPC, had disappeared.

Thus, the military government took over the country and within a few days occupied the oil complex at Talara. They promised compensation,[25A]

[23] Goodwin.

[24] Award of the Tribunal, Article I, 7 Int'l Legal Materials 1203 (1968).

[25] *Id.* at 53.

[25A] Diplomatic Note No. 112 from the Foreign Office of Peru to the United States government, 28 November 1968, 7 *id.* at 1262, 1264 (1968).

which they deposited into a blocked account. The compensation would be payable when the IPC paid the back taxes they alleged would have been payable since IPC's purchase in 1924, had the enterprise operated under a normal regime. The amount of such taxes ($690, 524, 283) not only exceeded the amount of compensation offered (about $70 million), it exceeded the value of the assets of the enterprise (about $100 million).[26] Assuming the accounting accuracy of the sum claimed by Peru, the legitimacy of its claim depends on the effect of the 1826 deed, the 1922 "award" and the Act of Talara. The deed is subject to reasonable interpretation by either side, and since the Peruvian view is at least as persuasive as the Company's, I should think the public claim ought to be preferred over the private.[27] The award failed to decide the very question of the legal status of La Brea y Pariñas it was set up to decide. Perhaps the award, or, at any rate, the arrangement arrived at by the representatives of Peru and the U.K., could be seen as a valid agreement between Peru and the United Kingdom. Whether IPC, or the United States, could have founded an anomalous legal claim on such an agreement seems a dubious proposition. The Act of Talara may be incomplete and accordingly becomes as legally controversial as it has been politically.

I am not trying here merely to adopt the view of the present Peruvian government. For example, the Peruvian government adduces several arguments in support of its case that are factually or legally specious. Thus, it claims inaccurately that there is no certified copy of the award in existence.[28] The evidence regarding the existence of an eleventh page of the agreement between IPC and Peru, promulgated by the Act of Talara, is not conclusive. Its complaints regarding IPC's role in "abus[ing] and scoffing [at] . . . and violating Peruvian laws [29] are of doubtful juridical value, though reminiscent of similar claims made by Mexico when trying to overcome U.S. resistance to its nationalizations of U.S. oil interests.[30] Peru's computation of the taxes owing to it, even accepting the validity of the rest of its legal brief, is subject to challenge.[31] Nor do I wish to infer that these matters are not amenable to impartial judicial scrutiny, a

[26] Furnish, *supra* note 19, at 353.

[27] See, e.g., Article 25 of the International Covenant on Economic, Social and Cultural Rights, quoted *infra*, p. 121.

[28] See Va. J. Int'l L., *Foreign Investment in Latin America: Past Policies and Future Trends,* Regional Meeting of the American Society of International Law, March 13 & 14, 1970, p. 54.

[29] Message of the President of the Republic of Peru, 6 February 1969, 8 Int'l Legal Materials 309, 312-13 (1969).

[30] Person, Mexican Oil (1944).

[31] See Furnish, *supra* note 19, at 370, note 65 & accompanying text.

process which has been denied to IPC (though not through any wrongdoing by the Peruvian judiciary, which seems to have been precluded by various decrees and legislation from examining the facts). Rather it is my intention to describe the strategy followed by the Peruvian government in presenting its case to the U.S. and the world. The claim that this is a "unique case" might in an impartial forum have turned out to be fallacious. It may be that what has occurred is a simple uncompensated expropriation. I offer some observation on the legal implications of that kind of act in the following sections. My purpose here has been to suggest that the very rigidity of U.S. practice in the field of state responsibility for economic injury to aliens has been to promote reliance on techniques of self-justification that, like recourse to methods of "creeping expropriation," merely confuse the international legal issues, thus making rational negotiation that much more difficult.

THE RIGHT OF DIPLOMATIC PROTECTION

If one were to assume the validity of IPC's claim to title over La Brea y Pariñas, thereby negating the validity of the tax debt claim by Peru, it would still be permissible to wonder about the ensuing position at international law. For the United States to make a formal international claim, on behalf of the IPC, it would have to show that the Company had exhausted local remedies. Although Goodwin has shown that the U.S. government has largely acted as unquestioning agent for the Company, at this stage it could be asserted with some confidence that Peruvian judicial and administrative mechanisms afford the IPC no further recourse for relief.[32]

Most difficult for the United States would be the necessity of demonstrating its right to exercise diplomatic protection of nationals abroad. Indeed, since the *Barcelona Traction* decision[33] was handed down by the International Court of Justice in February of 1970, this particular procedural hurdle would seem insuperable. In that case, the World Court had to decide whether or not Belgium had a right to exercise diplomatic protection in respect of her nationals who allegedly owned the majority of the shares in the Barcelona Traction, Light and Power Company, Ltd. This

[32] See the documents found in 8 Int'l Legal Materials 264 et seq. (1969), as well as the administrative procedure mentioned earlier. Given the particular non-concessionary nature of the regime under which IPC operated, there is, of course, no "Calvo clause" problem.

[33] *Barcelona Traction, Light and Power Co.* [1970] I.C.J. 3. The opinion of the Court is reprinted in 9 Int'l Legal Materials 227 (1970).

company, in awesome imitation of the present case, was registered in Ontario and operated in Spain both through branches and Spanish subsidiaries.[34] In determining the preliminary question of whether Belgium had *jus standi* to bring the claim before it, the Court made its answer depend on Belgium's right to espouse the claim of national shareholders. It decided that Belgium had no such right, although Canada's "right of protection in respect of the Barcelona Traction Company remains unaffected by the present proceedings." (Paragraph 83)

I do not propose to analyze the Court's reasoning in the case,[35] since whatever one's view of it, the IPC situation, I submit, falls directly within its ambit. The only possible escape [36] might be the Court's failure to decide what would have been Belgium's position had Barcelona Traction no longer been in existence (*in esse*). In holding Belgium's contention that Barcelona Traction was "practically defunct" to lack "all legal precision" and finding the Company to be indeed in legal existence, the Court observed that "[o]nly in the event of the legal demise of the company," which would deprive the shareholders of "the possibility of a remedy available through the company," could "an independent right of action for them and their government . . . arise." (Paragraph 66) Such wording might indicate that if IPC were interested in having the State Department pursue its claim unhindered by the obstacle of this decision, it might be valuable for Jersey Standard to commit corporate infanticide. I suspect that in such a case the plea of *volenti non fit injuria* might render such action unproductive.

EXPROPRIATION AND COMPENSATION

If we were to suspend disbelief and imagine Canada to espouse IPC's claim or, being a little less credulous, to imagine that the United States contrived to persuade Peru into an arbitration that would avoid the nationality problem, we might ask ourselves what view international law would take of an effectively uncompensated nationalization. This is a topic which has largely been crushed under the weight of the literature it has provoked. Since the camel's back has already been broken, I feel my

[34] The Court drew no distinction as between branch and subsidiary, being concerned only with the rights and interests of shareholders in the Canadian company.

[35] I have already done so in 47 Ind. L.J. 70 (1971).

[36] Conceivably Peru's negotiating with the U.S. might be perceived to estop her from denying the right of the U.S. to proceed, but estoppel is not a popular concept by which to determine the actions of sovereign states, especially where the negotiations, as in this case, can be easily characterized as political rather than legal.

straw – consisting of some recent thoughts engendered primarily by some interesting *dicta,* again, in the *Barcelona Traction case* – can do little damage.

The first thought is that the only way out of the conceptual tangle in which this area has become enmeshed is to draw a distinction between economic and human rights. By conceptual tangle I refer, *inter alia,* to the following hitherto intractable questions. Is there an international standard of behavior towards aliens? Is that international standard higher than mere equality of treatment between aliens and nationals. If so, how much? If not, how do you deal with foreigners who occupy an exceptional status in the society, such as a monopoly *à la* IPC? To what extent is the international standard co-extensive with the concept of denial of justice? What organs of the state, judicial, administrative, legislative, can commit a denial of justice? Does the concept refer only to defective or corrupt or negligent procedure? Or can it also comprehend the actual denial of a right? [37] Under which of these concepts, if at all, does the notion that an expropriation ought not to be discriminatory or arbitrary fall? What is its validity? Is a foreigner with shares in a domestic corporation to be protected in the same way as a resident-individual alien? If not, does this merely discriminate in favour of branch operations that do not owe their juridical existence to domestic law?

By distinguishing between economic rights and human rights, I do not mean any disrespect to economic rights, whatever they are. Indeed certain economic rights are human rights that actually provide the infrastructure upon which civil and political rights may be meaningfully enjoyed. But in a case such as the IPC's complaint with Peru, I doubt that any tribunal would have much trouble in reconciling in favour of Peru the apparent tension between Article 17 of the Universal Declaration of Human Rights

1. Everyone has the right to own property alone as well as in association with others.
2. No one shall be arbitrarily deprived of his property.

and Article 25 of the International Covenant on Economic, Social and Cultural Rights

"Nothing in the present Covenant shall be interpreted as impairing the inherent right of all peoples to enjoy and utilize fully and freely their natural wealth and resources."

I realize that it is one thing to sneer when Jersey Standard, whose annual

[37] Belgium's claim against Spain alleged a denial of justice *lato sensu* and *stricto sensu;* it also alleged abuse of rights and usurpation of jurisdiction!

revenues are three and a half times greater than Peru's national product, loses an investment and another to contemplate the fate of a foreign resident individual who may have his whole livelihood tied up in a foreign country that mistreats him.[38] I realize further that it is unrealistic to draw distinctions between an individual's economic rights and those of a juridical entity or between greater or lesser sums of investment. But since the individual's case is insignificant in terms of world capital flows, it is invidious to use him as a pretext for securing a wholly unrealistic international legal regime for foreign capital.

Clearly, once the distinction has been made, the individual may have his person and his civil rights protected under the concept of international protection of human rights, subject to normal limitations for aliens such as immigration laws. Here diplomatic protection can be seen in terms of international implementation of human rights. The view [39] that the exhaustion of local remedies rule puts the local courts in the position of the initial and primary defenders of human rights gives theoretical balance to the rule. Discrimination, arbitrary treatment, procedural denial of justice, all constitute an international standard of behaviour that, though not often enforceable internationally for nationals of a country, may be enforceable, or at least assertable, for foreigners.

That the World Court seems to be edging towards making a similar distinction between economic and human rights, preferring the latter to the former, appears, I submit, in certain passages of the decision in the *Barcelona Traction Case*. Thus the Court observes:

"When a State admits into its territory foreign investments or foreign nationals . . . it is bound to extend to them the protection of the law. However, it does not thereby become an insurer of that part of another State's wealth which these investments represent. Every investment of this kind carries certain risks. The real question is whether a right has been violated . . .." (Paragraph 87)

The Court returns to the question of risk when, in alluding to the various tax or other advantages considered by the promoters of a company on establishing the company abroad, it states:

[38] If he is also resident in that country, there may be some question as to whether he has a "genuine" enough "connection" with the country of his nationality for the latter country to be able to exercise diplomatic protection in respect of him: see *Nottebohm, Second Phase* [1955] I.C.J. 4.

[39] See, generally, R. Falk, The Role of Domestic Courts in the International Legal Order (1964).

"It does not seem to be in any way inequitable that the advantages thus obtained should be balanced by the risks arising from the fact that the protection of the company and hence its shareholders is thus entrusted to a State other than the national State of the shareholders."

It is a short step from here [40] to balance the higher profits of companies operating in developing countries – often explicitly justified on the basis of the non-business risks the above quotations refer to – against such risks. The Court also felt that the area of nationalizations associated with "structural changes in a State's economy" and the compensation agreements resulting therefrom constituted a *lex specialis* (paragraphs 59 and 61), the implication being that in such cases bilateral or multilateral arrangements are required [41] to give precision to a law that, it noted elsewhere, "has been formed in a period characterized by an intense conflict of systems and interests .... Here as elsewhere, a body of rules could only have developed with the consent of those concerned." (Paragraph 89)

While the Court seems then to be fundamentally questioning the role of diplomatic protection of foreign economic interests, the underlying basis on which it does so is by stressing the primarily bilateral nature of the relationships involved. Thus, the Court observes that it "is essentially bilateral relations which have been concerned, relations in which the rights of both the State exercising diplomatic protection and the State in respect of which protection is sought have had to be safeguarded." (Paragraph 89) But the Court draws an "essential distinction" between such bilateral relations and "obligations toward the international community as a whole" where "all States can be held to have a legal interest in their protection; they are obligations *erga omnes*." (Paragraph 33) As examples of such obligations the Court cites those stemming from "the outlawing of acts of aggression, and of genocide, as also from the principles and rules concerning the *basic rights of the human person* .... " (Paragraph 34 – emphasis supplied)

If this approach is correct then it is possible that even seeing the IPC events as an expropriation would not help the position of the United States. While I am sure that the Court is not saying that in certain circumstances international law does not demand compensation for takings of foreign property, it is, I think, implicit that international law at best will

[40] I recognize that the nature of the risk that a country of incorporation may fail to exercise diplomatic protection is only secondarily a non-business risk in the usual sense of that term. It only comes into play if the primary non-business risks in the country of operation become realities.

[41] Paragraph 90 re-inforces this position.

only require compensation – it will not make certain types of taking illegal *per se* – and that the level of such compensation can only be worked out by *ad hoc* or *a priori* institutional agreement. It is a step forward when, even in a case such as this, where there are elements of discrimination, the position of the United States has been limited to a demand for compensation. There has been no challenge to the right to expropriate.[42] Whether the United States, or other capital-exporting States for that matter, demands "prompt, adequate and effective" compensation, as she has in the past, or "effective compensation," as Secretary Rogers did,[43] or simply a "fair amount," the term used by President Nixon,[44] there will be many claims, counterclaims and arrangements before international law develops any meaningful standards of compensation.

CONCLUSION

The conclusions to be drawn from this case study seem to be as follows:

a. The Hickenlooper amendment was not only useless to the United States government, in that its application would have entailed unacceptably hostile continental repercussions, it actually hampered the Administration, insofar as the latter could not negotiate in an atmosphere free of this particular "big stick."
b. The traditional posture of the United States probably tended to encourage the Peruvians to cloud the issues separating the two countries, with respect to this case, by resorting to the "unique case" stratagem that raises questions almost impossible of solution in the absence of judicial or quasi-judicial *fora.*
c. The *Barcelona Traction Case* must have made continued U.S. espousal of IPC's claim extremely difficult to justify.
d. The same case seems to suggest that international law, though perhaps demanding compensation in some cases of expropriation, is incapable at this stage of its development of providing any meaningful standards of determining what those cases are or how the level of compensation is to be measured.
e. An international claim regarding state responsibility for the protection

[42] In a taking clearly for public purposes, the U.S. had, as far back as her dispute with Mexico over agrarian and oil expropriations, recognized a right expropriate subject to compensation; see Bishop, International Law 851-63 (3d ed. 1971).

[43] Dept. State Bull. 310 (1969).

[44] *Id.* at 245.

of the human rights of aliens may nevertheless have the support of international law.

I am not unmindful of the fact that many developing countries, including Peru, as Professor Vagts points out subsequently, remain anxious to secure private foreign investment, by way of both capital and technological input, for productive purposes. In many ways, the problem of natural resources extraction by foreign interests, a sector which has long dominated the purposes to which capital-exporting states, or their nationals, have put their surplus capital in the capital-importing states, has distorted the political climate in which foreign investment has had to operate. The result, unfortunate as it may be, is that general international law is of little use in resolving conflict in this area. This becomes particularly difficult even with the use of procedures, such as those provided for by the Center for the Settlement of Investment Disputes set up under the recent World Bank Convention.[45] To the extent that an arbitral panel established under its auspices is to apply international law,[46] it may well encounter difficulty in finding meaningful guidance from that system of law. Perhaps the very nature of an arbitral procedure may admit of more flexibility than would be available to a strictly judicial organ. Certainly a conciliation panel of the Center might be less inhibited. This and other mechanisms suggested by Professor Vagts in this volume may ultimately contribute to the establishment of satisfactory bilateral arrangements. Norms may develop therefrom that would in time crystallize into meaningful norms or standards of general international law. I submit that there are none such now and that any durable arrangements will emerge at the initiative of states wishing to improve their investment climates, not under pressure of those wishing to defend the economic interests of their nationals abroad.

[45] Convention on the Settlement of Investment Disputes Between States and Nationals of Other States, T.I.A.S. No. 6090; 60 Am. J. Int'l L. 892 (1966).

[46] Sec Article 42.

COMMENTARY

by

ARTHUR W. ROVINE

The paper presented by Thomas Franck and Edward Weisband is excellent, both for its point of view and the subtlety of its analysis. I certainly find myself in sympathy with attempts to create a legal order in which intervention by the superpowers, whether within their own immediate spheres of influence or elsewhere, is substantially reduced. And as an international lawyer, I am persuaded of the importance of verbal formulations in the establishment of juridical norms. I think the authors have made a contribution by their emphasis upon the potential significance of the interaction between action and conceptualization in the field of limitations upon the use of force. Further, they have quite properly focused attention upon a particularly vexing problem of legal regulation of force, since superpower actions within their respective "regions" have at times, as we know, weakened the fabric of the rule of non-intervention.

However, I do have certain conceptual difficulties with the proposal as formulated by Franck and Weisband, all of which tend to diminish its prospects of restricting interventionism. If we are to make progress, it would be advisable, in my view, to give some thought to the problems posed by their approach.

As a general proposition, I have some trouble in appreciating the purported analogous nature of the Latin American and Eastern European blocs. It seems to me that when viewing American and Soviet interests, the two areas serve somewhat different purposes. The Latin American region is far more important economically and less significant militarily to the United States than the communist bloc in Eastern Europe is to the Soviet Union. Eastern Europe stands as a large buffer between a suspicious Russia and NATO; Latin America serves no such function for the U.S. This has had, and will continue to have, an impact upon Soviet perceptions of tolerable change in Eastern Europe that may well preclude the kind of arrangement suggested by Franck and Weisband. Images filtered through security considerations are more likely to include perceptions of foreign influence and attachments than those colored primarily by economic variables.

Even assuming, however, the appropriateness of the Latin American – East European analogy, there are significant problems. Rules of law in this area are desirable to the extent that they draw comparatively distinct lines between permissible and impermissible. Yet the formula proposed by the authors is extremely vague. I take it that the key distinction is that the formula "would permit the superpower to continue to employ force if necessary to prevent the establishment of regimes in its region which are strategically allied with a rival superpower, while excluding the use of force to prevent the establishment of genuinely national but politically-deviationist regimes."

There are a number of difficulties here. What does "strategically allied with" mean in this context? Suppose the freely-elected regime in Chile were to receive small arms from the Soviet Union. Would this be sufficient to justify force to overthrow the government there? The formula refers to "the establishment of" regimes. Once a regime is established, and *subsequently* becomes "strategically allied with" a rival superpower, is there still a right to use force against it? According to the wording of the formula, apparently not. Bases are clearly precluded, but what is the "military presence" alluded to in the text following footnote 11. Would technicians from Eastern Europe helping in a local armaments industry meet the definition? Is Cuba today "strategically allied with" the Soviet Union, and if so, do we possess the legal right to invade with our armed forces and eliminate the Castro regime?

These are not merely normal semantic obstacles found in most rules of law that require interpretation and application before their meaning is fully understood. These are questions necessitating substantial scope for subjective evaluation. Given the extraordinary political sensitivity of the issues involved, the normal tendency would be to err, as national security managers are often obliged to do, on the side of caution and national self-assertion. The rule as formulated actually legitimizes the right to utilize force for the overthrow of governments we or the Soviets don't like under far broader circumstances than are permitted by traditional international law and by the United Nations Charter.

In the name of non-intervention, the authors have constructed a rule that might well justify more frequent intervention than we have already experienced. Missile bases in Cuba present a clear case of strategic alliance and military presence, but world politics rarely present such clear cases, and the many degrees of lesser alliance and presence must also be considered. My objection is that the suggested rule, at least on its face, would justify forcible intervention in the lesser cases as well. I don't think the authors intended that result, but if not, their approach must be clarified.

There are also conceptual problems connected with the likelihood of reciprocal interaction in the proposed structure. It is perfectly true that intervention by one superpower provides justification for similar intervention by the other under like circumstances. To that extent, reciprocity works well. But is the converse equally true? Does non-intervention by one side act as a restraining force upon the other? Does restraint occur in the hope that restraint will become the rule? I think the likelihood of reciprocity on this side of the proposed structure is significantly small. Can one realistically imagine the Soviet Union not intervening in, for example, Czechoslovakia in the hope that perhaps some day the United States might not intervene in, say, Cuba?

The problem here is the non-reciprocal nature of the reward based upon the differing perspectives of what is important in the Latin American and Eastern European areas. Put most simply, the Soviet Union will not tolerate the establishment of non-socialist regimes in East Europe simply for the "gain" of new socialist regimes in Latin America. The one area is far more important to Moscow than the other. There is no reciprocal reward and, thus, little chance of establishing a pattern of reciprocal restraint. I do not believe that even the most restrictive pattern of behavior by the United States would succeed in inhibiting a Soviet intervention in a socialist bloc state that wished to eliminate its socialist structure.

The question is not simply a matter of a "politically-deviationist regime," but the deeper problem of the nature of the regime. To date the United States has not used force against Chile, notwithstanding a developing socialism, but did use force to some extent against Cuba and the Dominican Republic. The Soviets will permit a limited independence (Yugoslavia, Romania, Albania) but not a non-socialist system (Hungary, Czechoslovakia). In brief, the real test is whether each superpower will permit the establishment not just of political and economic independence, but the development of alien governmental and economic structures. To date, the Soviet Union has clearly indicated it will permit no such change; in the case of the United States the evidence has gone both ways. The differing values attached to Latin America and East Europe by the superpowers do not augur well for the system proposed by the authors.

Even if it were possible to respond satisfactorily to each of these objections, I am not persuaded that the world community would be better served by a less restrictive norm than that now found in the United Nations Charter. Article 51 of the Charter has its own set of problems, of course, but a limitation upon the use of force to self-defense in case of armed attack, or force in accordance with United Nations-sponsored sanctions, is the rule which is currently accepted law and, in my view, the preferable norm. That there have been violations of the rule is obvious, but a more permissive legal structure, notwithstanding beneficent intentions, is hardly likely to reduce the frequency and intensity of unjustified uses of armed force. Particularly in an era when the distinction between international and civil conflict is blurred, it is important to restrict the right of intervention within nations so far as possible to offset outside (international) intervention. The Franck-Weisband formula, I fear, would go very far toward the legitimization of intervention in purely civil conflicts.

It is not sufficient to argue that the proposed rule would be applicable only to the superpowers, and only within their own areas of greatest influence and concern. The precedent value of the recommended rule would be great, and would no doubt be tempting for the rest of the world community. If superpower concepts and actions may influence the other side, they may also influence middle and lesser powers. "The law you make may be your own." There is little hope of confining the proposed legal structure, even assuming its desirability, to the framework of United States and Soviet relations with Latin America and East Europe.

I do hope that the authors, in presenting their analysis for future consideration, will consider these issues and perhaps reformulate their recommendations accordingly.

COMMENTARY

by

DETLEV F. VAGTS

In subject matter, my remarks relate to Professor Rodley's presentation but in method I find myself closer to Professor Franck's. I am concerned with the role of law in creating a system through which foreign investment can play a useful role in economic development in Latin America and elsewhere. The controversy between Peru and IPC is thus of concern to me largely because of its potential impact on the relationships needed to make such a system work.

A preliminary question has to be grappled with – is there any merit to having foreign investment in the less developed countries? Quite a number of critics would give a negative answer to this. They would point to various past episodes in which foreign investors had obtained extravagant concessions from weak or unskilled officials, in which natural resources had vanished without discernible benefit to the local population. They would view with alarm the heavy drain on hard currency resources involved in servicing foreign investment. At a more subtle level, they would decry the depressing effect on local enterprise of trying to compete with the overweening power of great foreign enterprises.[1] They would stress the secondary effects of such inflows in discouraging the development of domestic entrepreneurship and the distorting effect on government policies of having a large foreign investment component in the country.

The positive case for foreign investment is familiar, too, from having been sounded in many voices from the unctuous to the doubtful. At certain times the stress has been on the capital inflow component and more recently it has been shifted to the technological and managerial skills side. As governmental flows come less generously than formerly private operations are to take up the slack, with or without governmental guarantees or other backing.

[1] A. O. Hirschman, How to Divest in Latin America – And Why (1970).

To resolve such a disputation would be impossible. Suffice it to note for present purposes that most governments, even the revolutionary regime in Peru,[2] profess to wish further private foreign investment. Some managements, though fewer than formerly, are still interested in plunging ahead. Thus there will still be bargaining about investments, which in general will be much more knowledgeable and sophisticated on the part of the government than it used to be and will force private investors to be on the alert. But such negotiations, formal or informal, tacit or explicit, need some sort of legal framework to support and sustain them through the years in which the results of such negotiations are executed, modified and developed.

The need for such a framework can best be seen from the side of the investor who, once he has committed his resources, is the most in need of legal protection. This fact is very apparent, especially after recent events, to the corporate planner evaluating an investment in a less developed country. If he is conversant with the latest formal planning techniques as taught on the other side of the Charles River he is apt to work out a diagram, that looks like that on the following page.[3]

Assigning odds to each of the forks in this tree, the planner can work out the political risk involved of the operation. This risk factor he subtracts from his estimates of the economic return he will probably derive from his investment. If he is not as disciplined and calculating, he is very apt simply to discard the opportunity once it appears that there is a significant risk of an expropriation. The manager in a large corporation is aware that his fellows will take a dim view of his recommendation if it ends in well publicized total loss. Thus the result of an inability to assure oneself of recourse against a taking is very apt to be a decision not to act. If the decision is affirmative it is likely to be either because a full government guaranty of the political risk can be obtained or because the promised return is exceedingly high. This latter is not a very healthy situation. If the expectation is realized, the high profits that are repatriated will cause not only foreign exchange problems for the host country but a vigorous feeling of being exploited and oppressed. This is just the sort of atmosphere in which cancellation and expropriations are most apt to result. It is similar to those situations common in the nineteenth century in which bondholders who had contracted for a large discount in advance plus high

[2] Abramovitz, Koven & Valdez, *The Peruvian General Law of Industries,* 12 Harv. Int'l L. J. 312 (1971).

[3] This analysis and the diagram are based upon Stobaugh, *How to Analyze Foreign Investment Climates,* 47 Harv. Bus. Rev., Sept.-Oct. 1969, p. 100.

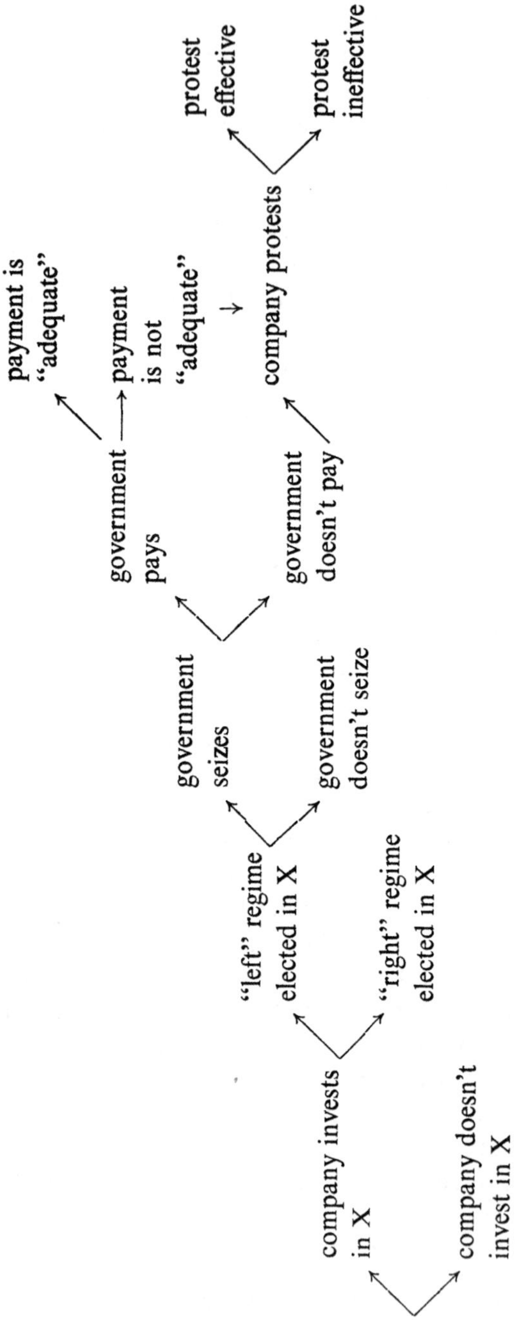
company invests in X
company doesn't invest in X
"left" regime elected in X
"right" regime elected in X
government seizes
government doesn't seize
government pays
government doesn't pay
payment is "adequate"
payment is not "adequate"
company protests
protest effective
protest ineffective

rates of interest found default almost inevitable.[4] In short, a high uncertainty system of law makes legitimate planning almost impossible and tends to narrow investment to unhealthy, exploitative schemes.

What is the impact of the Peruvian episode in the investor's outlook? It seems clearly to have changed matters for the worse and contributed to the reluctance of business to move into the troubled waters of Latin America. In a sense it ought not to deter new enterprise because it might be taken to represent one of the last episodes of expropriation of old property (held for years by IPC) and in the natural resources area at that. Nearly all takings in Latin America have involved investments made well before World War II and either in the natural resources, public utilities or land sectors. One might think that a firm contemplating a manufacturing investment now would tend to put matters like this to one side as only slightly errelevant. But the IPC case goes deeper than this. It is not just that it assails the validity of the "prompt, adequate and effective compensation" principle in which sophisticated business executives have not had much faith for some time. It goes further and strikes at two concepts that are critical to any investment decision. First, it undermines the principle of international adjudication by riding roughshod over an arbitral award. True, there were substantial objections to the validity of the award, as Professor Rodley's paper sets forth in detail. On the other hand, lawyers being what they are, some objections of a plausible character can be made against almost any award in a difficult and controverted matter. The fact that no appeal in a lawyer's usual sense lies from the award of an arbitral tribunal makes the problem a difficult one to unravel but investors' counsel would advise him that this means that it would be very hard to make a decision stick even after pursuing it to victory before a tribunal.

Second, and more basically, the Peruvian situation casts doubt on the fundamental concept that agreements between national governments and foreign investors ought to be carried out. It is not a satisfactory answer to say that there were doubts about the validity or interpretation of the agreements involved – both the original concession and the recent settlement under the preceding regime. To solve all such doubts in favor of the government is to offer cold comfort to the prospective signer of a development agreement. Whatever the present day weakness of the international law principle that a government must pay compensation for its takings, there is a much more general agreement on the concept that agreements freely entered into by governments should be respected. This emerges from

[4] M. Winkler, Foreign Bonds: An Autopsy Chs. IV, V (1933).

the United Nations Resolutions on Permanent Sovereignty over Natural Resources and seems to have survived almost unscathed all the rhetoric of the new international law.[5]

What is missing then, the IPC case tells us, is an effective and workable means of adjudicating such disputes. The traditional ad hoc and ex post arbitral commissions created under strong pressure from the investor's home government are, unlamented, a thing of the past. The International Court of Justice has proved disappointing in terms of its capacity to resolve controversies in the area of investor-government relations. Twice before it has avoided handling such disputes on procedural grounds: in the Nottebohm case and in the Interhandel litigation.[6] Finally, it found jurisdictional reasons not to take up the allegations of the Barcelona Traction Company that it had been ruthlessly mulcted of its property. The reasoning of the I.C.J. is defensible but again the net effect of the decision is to slam shut the doors of that court without suggesting any feasible alternate route towards obtaining a decision. The World Bank's proposed system, while it has amassed a very respectable number of signatory countries, has had no success whatever in Latin America.[7] The sense of the oppressive past of arbitration and of the inequality of acceding to a request not made of the governments of powerful capital-exporting countries is too great. Thus, while there is much that is valuable about the IBRD Convention – better than its predecessors – there is still no answer. And yet one cannot but feel that the sort of questions posed in the IPC controversy are eminently suitable to adjudication – clean cut issues such as whether there was a missing page to an agreement or what was the meaning of certain words relating to the grant of mineral rights. If the international legal system cannot work out a way of resolving problems such as this – if not to the satisfaction of both parties at least to their respect and acquiescence – it seems unlikely that it is capable of handling any of the truly complex and explosive inter-government tensions that threaten world peace and order.

[5] For the text of these resolutions and some of the background see H. Steiner & D. Vagts, Transnational Legal Problems 344-349 (1968).

[6] *Nottebohm, Second Phase,* [1955] I. C. J. 4; *Interhandel,* [1959] I.C.J. 6.

[7] See Rodley, *Some Aspects of the World Bank Convention on the Settlement of Investment Disputes,* 1966 Can. Y.B. Int'l L. 43; P. Szasz, *The Investment Disputes Convention and Latin America,* 11 Va. J. Int'l L. 256 (1971).

Part III

HUMAN RIGHTS

HUMAN RIGHTS AND THE ORGANIZATION OF AMERICAN STATES

by

ANN VAN WYNEN THOMAS AND A. J. THOMAS, JR.

HISTORICAL BACKGROUND

The historical idealistic basis of an American community of nations is posited upon the belief that the New World was to be dedicated to liberty, democracy, and peace, in contrast to the monarchy, tyranny, and belligerency which prevailed in the old.[1] Since the earliest days of American independence, her leaders have called for respect for and protection of those complementary aspects of democracy – popular constitutional government and human rights. Henry Clay in 1820 and again in 1821 appealed for a hemispheric system to serve as "a rallying point of human wisdom against all the despotism of the Old World," and as "a sort of counterpoise to the holy alliance . . . in favor of national independence and liberty." [2] Bolivar, in the 1826 Treaty of Union, League and Perpetual Confederation, would sanction any state which deserted the republican form of government by expulsion from the proposed inter-American organization. A continental citizenship was also to be established, and slavery in the Americas was to be abolished.[3] Pedro Felix Vicuña of Chile wrote in 1837 that a hemispheric union should be established to support popular revolutions against tyrannical governments.[4] Later, Juan Baptista Alberdi, then a refugee in

[1] A. Whitaker, The Western Hemisphere Idea chs. I, II (1954).

[2] *Id.* at 32.

[3] *See* Treaty of Perpetual Union, League, and Confederation between the Republics of Colombia, Central America, Peru, and the United Mexican States, July 15, 1826, in International Conferences of American States 1889-1928, at xix-xx (J. Scott ed. 1931). Article 29 of this treaty provides for exclusion if any of the parties should change its present form of government. Since the nations were all obstensibly possessed of a republican form of government it follows that substantial departure from the republican form would mean exclusion.

[4] *Id.* arts. 23, 24, 27.

Chile from Argentine dictatorship, maintained that intervention should be utilized to promote democratic governments in the Americas.[5]

Despite these and other declarations for a continent of liberty, declarations which were to be made over and over again in the forthcoming years, demands for specific and clear-cut protection of human rights through the medium of Pan America were not to be heard until the end of World War II. Throughout most of the continent, dictatorship had become the rule, democracy the exception, and with dictatorship came a consequent drastic deprivation of fundamental rights and freedoms. This pattern had repeated itself over and over again in every age from Rosas, Lopez, and Santa Ana to the even bloodier regimes of Gomez, Ubico, and Trujillo down to the present era. Today, we are presented with a spectacle of increasing numbers of military governments in leading South American states that should be well on the way to democracy.

Perhaps as a result of this dominance of military dictatorships, it was not until 1945 that human rights became of inter-American concern. At the Mexico City Conference on War and Peace, the Chapultepec Conference,[6] Guatemala demanded that collective non-recognition be used as a weapon against anti-democratic governments on the ground that such regimes endangered the peace and solidarity of the hemisphere and were the primary cause for the denial of the rights of man.[7] This proposal was sidetracked and ultimately forgotten.[8] Collective action against the internal regime of a fellow American state would conflict with the most sacrosanct principle of the Americas – the doctrine of non-intervention. Instead of the Guatemalan proposal, the conference adopted a weak resolution on International Protection for the Rights of Man.[9] It declared adherence to those international law principles for the safeguarding of essential human rights and vaguely supported a system of international protection for these rights. Strangely, the resolution was not really made for the enlightened purpose

[5] R. Burr & R. Hussey, Documents on Inter-American Cooperation, 1810-1881, at Nos. 19, 23 (1955). Tobar of Ecuador and President Wilson were also advocates of multilateral protection of democracy in the hemisphere. *See* A. J. Thomas, Jr. & A. V. W. Thomas, The Organization of American States 216-17 (1963) [hereinafter cited as Thomas and Thomas].

[6] P.A.U. Inter-American Conference on Problems of War and Peace, Mexico City, Report Submitted to the Governing Board of the Pan American Union by the Director General (Feb. 21-Mar. 8, 1945, Cong. and Conf. Series No. 47 1945).

[7] *See* P.A.U. Handbook for Delegates to the Ninth International Conference of American States 88-89 (1947).

[8] Resolution XXXVIII, Defence and Preservation of Democracy in America, P.A.U. *supra* note 6. On the conflict between intervention and human rights *see* M. Ball, *Issue for the Americas,* 15 Int'l Org. 21 (1961).

[9] Resolution XL, P.A.U., *supra* note 6.

of protecting human rights as such. Rather, it rested upon the assumption that protection of human rights was needed to eliminate diplomatic protection of citizens abroad and the intervention which had resulted therefrom. Thus, human rights and their protection were again placed in an inferior position to principles of sovereignty and non-intervention.

After the Mexico City conference, a doctrine was formulated by Eduardo Rodriguez Laretta, Foreign Minister of Uruguay.[10] He followed Emanuel Kant's theory by equating international peace with a republican form of government for all states.[11] Rodriguez Laretta called for collective intervention to assure democracy in the Americas. "Peace," he said, "is safe only where democratic principles of government prevail." He added that action to assure democracy "is really nothing more than the fulfillment of obligations freely assumed by the American republics, all of whom have proclaimed at inter-American conferences their devotion to democracy and the rights of man." [12] The Laretta Doctrine was rejected by the majority of American governments, although over one-third did express approval of its contents.[13] Objections covered several points. It was argued that it was often difficult to categorize a particular government as democratic or non-democratic; and that no nation could ever live up to the utopian ideals of democracy; and that democracy could not always be equated with peace, for democratic governments had on occasion constituted major threats to peace.[14]

[10] P.A.U. Consultation of the Government of Uruguay and Replies of the Governments on the Parallelism between Democracy and Peace, the International Rights of Man and Collective Action in Defense of those Principles (May, 1946). [hereinafter cited as P.A.U.].

[11] Although Kant laid down a doctrine of non-intervention he qualified it by his statement that the civil constitution in every state shall be republican. Thus, he believed that world peace could only be maintained if and when the republican form of government had become universal. For a statement of this thesis of Kant, *see* K. Lowenstein, Political Reconstruction 17-20 (1946). In A. Hershey, Essentials of International Public Law and Organization 243 n.18 (1935) the author claims that Kant in *Essay on Perpetual Peace* published in 1795 was first to state the principle of non-intervention. Hershey fails to mention the fact that Kant's prohibition of interventions might be considered as modified by his statement that the civil constitution in every state should be republican.

[12] P.A.U., *supra* note 10.

[13] *Id.*

[14] *Id.* Selte-Camaro Filho, *A Doutrina Larreta,* 3 Boletim da Sociedade de Direito Internacional 18 (1946).

THE CHARTER OF THE OAS

When the American republics met in 1948 in conference at Bogotá to reconstitute the inter-American system, they had before them the previously accepted Inter-American Treaty of Reciprocal Assistance (The Rio Treaty). In its preamble, this treaty affirmed "as a manifest truth ... that peace is founded on justice and moral order and consequently on the protection of human rights and freedom." [15] This language can hardly be understood as creating a legal obligation on the part of the American republics to maintain essential human rights within their respective borders. Moreover, the treaty provided no sanctions or measures of enforcement to be taken against a state violating human rights.

There was strong sentiment at Bogotá to remedy this failure through the creation of an inter-American norm for the respect of human rights. Power would be granted to the inter-American system, now to be called the Organization of American States (OAS), to enforce the norm.[16] An opposing view prevailed,[17] however. Thus, the Charter, the basic constitutional instrument of the OAS, set forth rather general and idealistic statements as human rights. American solidarity was declared to be founded upon liberty and social justice.[18] In a statement of principles, "the fundamental rights of the individual without distinction as to race, nationality, creed or sex" were proclaimed.[19] Language of a legally binding character was used, however, in Article 13 of the Charter which reads as follows:

> "Each state has the right to develop its cultural, political and economic life freely and naturally. In this free development, the state *shall* respect the rights of the individual and the principles of universal morality." [20]

[15] On the Inter-American Treaty of Reciprocal Assistance *see* P.A.U., Inter-American Conference for the Maintenance of Continental Peace and Security, Rio de Janeiro, Report on Results of Conference submitted to the Governing Board of the Pan American Union by the Director General (1947).

[16] P.A.U. Inter-American Juridical Committee Report on the Inter-American Council of Jurists concerning Resolution XXXI of the Conference of Bogotá 2 (1949).

[17] The opposing group argued that the Charter was in the nature of a constitutional instrument and should be confined to the establishment of the OAS and the functions of its organs. All other inter-American policies should be set up in separate agreements. Ninth International Conference of American States, Report of the Delegation of the United States with Related Documents, Dept. of State Pub. 3263, at 13 (1948).

[18] O.A.S. Charter preamble.

[19] O.A.S. Charter art. 5(j).

[20] O.A.S. Charter art. 13. (Italics supplied)

Use of the word "shall" in Article 13 appears to impose a legal obligation upon the members, but the rights of the individual to be respected and maintained are not delineated, and the additional duty imposed to respect the principles of universal morality is vague indeed, smacking of natural law. Moreover, the organization was not empowered to see that each nation lived up to the obligation of Article 13.

States demanding inter-American protection of human rights were not content with these generalized proclamations. At their insistence, a resolution was adopted entitled the "American Declaration of the Rights and Duties of Man" which constituted the first comprehensive statement of continental human rights.[21] Unfortunately, the declaration can be considered only as a statement of aims and hopes. It was not the intent of its authors to create a legally binding hemispheric bill of rights.

The rights listed in the declaration are extensive. Some are of a political nature while others are economic and social. Still others can hardly be classified as rights. They are ethical aspirations. As the title of the resolution indicates, the declaration also concerns itself with the "duties" of man, stating: "the fulfillment of duty by each individual is a prerequisite to the rights of all." [22] "Rights and duties are interrelated in every social and political activity of man." The duties of man are roughly classified into social duties, political duties, and economic duties. Underlying the inclusion of duties is the thought that each individual should recognize that he owes certain responsibilities to the society in which he lives, and that stress should not be placed solely upon the responsibility of the state to secure human rights. Nevertheless, one may question the utility of including such a concept in an international declaration, for the whole basic theory of the protection of human rights on the international level is that individuals can be easily overwhelmed before the aggregate collection of power lodged in a state. A sovereign state, on the other hand, still retains its power to exact from all individuals the duties which are owed to it.[23]

HUMAN RIGHTS AND COLLECTIVE SECURITY

No powers are given to the OAS to enforce respect for fundamental rights and freedoms in a state departing from the norm. Still, proposals have been

[21] Final Act, Resolution XXX, as contained in Ninth International Conference of American States, *supra* note 17, at 260.

[22] Preamble, American Declaration of the Rights and Duties of Man. For discussion of the rights and duties delineated *see* Thomas and Thomas, *supra* note 5, at 224-27.

[23] Thomas and Thomas, *supra* note 5, at 226.

made, and, in certain cases, collective action has been taken, which would, or did, permit the cat to be skinned. Inter-American protection of human rights through collective action rests upon the foundation that outrageous violations of human values by an American state will result in a threat to the peace of the hemisphere. By the terms of the Rio Treaty, collective measures may be taken against an American state which threatens or breaches the peace of the hemisphere or which commits an aggression so as to endanger the territory or the political independence of another American state.[24] Therefore, a state which violates human rights so as to threaten the peace of the Americas may be subjected to the collective enforcement measures of the Rio Treaty. Here is a return to the thought of Kant and Laretta – a parallelism is found between democracy and respect for human rights on the one hand and peace on the other.

This idea found expression again in 1959 at the Fifth Meeting of Consultation of Ministers of Foreign Affairs which was called to consider problems of political unrest in the Caribbean and the effective exercise of representative democracy in the hemisphere.[25] Attributes of a democratic regime were set forth by the meeting's Declaration of Santiago.[26] These included freedom of the press, radio, television, and, in general, freedom of information and expression. The American governments were called upon to ensure a system of freedom for the individual and social justice based on respect for fundamental human rights. They were also asked to protect by effective judicial procedures those human rights contained in domestic legislation.[27]

The declaration thus recognized the relationship between respect for human rights, fundamental freedom, and representative democracy on the one hand and inter-American peace and harmony on the other. It was noted that failure to adhere to the principles of democracy is "a source of widespread disturbance and gives rise to emigration that causes frequent grave political tensions between the state the emigrés leave and the state that receives them." [28]

Political tensions and emigration are by no means new to Latin America. The common denominator of political life in the Latin American republics has long been the presence of internal revolutionary disturbances as rivals

[24] Inter-American Treaty of Reciprocal Assistance at arts. 3, 6. *See also* Thomas and Thomas, *supra* note 5, at ch. XV.

[25] *See* 41 Dept. State Bull. 342-44 (1955). On the background of the Santiago Meeting, *see id.* at 279 *et seq.*

[26] *Declaration of Santiago,* 41 Dept. State Bull. 343 (1959).

[27] *Id.*

[28] *Id.*

have competed for political power. Losing parties are the "outs" and the "outs" are not only out of power, but they are often also out of the country. This is frequently the healthier course of action inasmuch as the "ins" have, in many instances, found it convenient to put the remaining "outs" out of the way in such a manner as to constitute a gross denial of human rights. Once out of the country, the "outs" conspire to return so as to overthrow those in power, the "ins." Such conspiracies and movements aimed at the overthrow of the "ins" have on countless occasions boiled over to embroil the government of the state to which the "outs" have emigrated either because the government of such state is in sympathy with the "outs" and aids them overtly or covertly in their endeavors to stir up civil strife, or because such government fails to use due diligence to prevent such rebellious activities. Thus, a threat or even a breach of the peace comes to pass in the form of an indirect or vicarious aggression – as called by Dr. Schwarzenberger, an aggression by proxy.[29]

In 1960, the Inter-American Peace Committee followed the Declaration of Santiago by finding hemispheric tensions and threats to peace in the flagrant denial of human rights and lack of representative democracy by the despotic Trujillo regime in the Dominican Republic. After investigation of the situation in the Dominican Republic, the committee found in that country denial of freedom of speech and assembly, arbitrary arrest, cruel and inhuman treatment of prisoners, and the use of intimidation and terror as political weapons.[30] International tensions in the Caribbean were said by the committee to be aggravated by these violations of human rights and it was believed that such tensions would continue to increase so long as these violations persisted.[31]

A short time later, U.S. Secretary of State Herter, taking this cue from the committee, sought application of the principle. The Sixth Meeting of Ministers of Foreign Affairs, acting under the Rio Treaty, was convened in August, 1960, to consider charges of aggression by the Dominican Republic against Venezuela.[32] Finding complicity of the Trujillo regime in an attempt on the life of Venezuela's president, the meeting agreed that the

[29] G. Schwarzenberger, Frontiers of International Law 155 (1962).

[30] Case presented by Venezuela relating to violations of human rights in the Dominican Republic (February 1960), P.A.U. Inter-American Peace Committee, Report of the Inter-American Peace Committee to the Second Special Inter-American Conference on the Activities of the Committee since the Tenth Inter-American Conference 1954-1965, at 24-26 (OEA/Ser.1.iii.ii 10, English, 1965).

[31] *Id.* at 26.

[32] P.A.U. Applicaciones del Tratado Interamericano de Asistencia Reciproca 1948-1960, at 393 *et. seq.* (1960).

enforcement measures of the Rio Treaty should be applied against the Dominican Republic. The measures authorized by the consultative meeting were an immediate and collective break of diplomatic relations and a collective partial interruption of economic relations.

Although agreeing that the Dominican Republic had committed serious acts against Venezuelan sovereignty warranting condemnation, Secretary of State Herter expressed doubt that sanctions were the best means to bring the Dominican Republic back into the inter-American fold. Harking back to the Inter-American Peace Committee's previous report which would link aggression and threats to the peace with denials of democracy and human rights, he sought OAS supervision of free elections in the Dominican Republic after a period of free expression and free assembly. If the OAS were refused the right to supervise by the Dominican Republic, then strong measures under the Rio Treaty could and should have been taken.[33] Here then was an effort to enforce democracy and human rights against a member state in violation of community principles. This OAS political trusteeship for an American nation received very little enthusiasm. Other American republics believed the OAS not to be so empowered and therefore viewed it as collective intervention of an illegal nature in the internal affairs of the Dominican Republic.[34] Immediate measures under the Rio Treaty were favored and voted.

There is difficulty in upholding the legality of an imposed OAS political trusteeship upon an American republic under existing OAS instruments. A state's free acceptance of such a trusteeship and supervision of elections would create no problem. Moreover, in an instance similar to the Dominican Republic case, when the delinquent nation has been found to have committed an aggression against which measures can be legally taken, those measures might be delayed or withheld on condition that the state would accept the offer of a political trusteeship. Through such trusteeship, democracy and human rights could be instituted and maintained in order more nearly to effectuate inter-American peace. Something of a sophistry is present in such reasoning, however, in that threat of measures which can legally be taken are held over the head of the delinquent to compel acceptance of a measure which could not otherwise be legally taken.

Real difficulty is encountered with legality if the derelict state has neither consented to the trusteeship nor committed a threat to the peace, breach of the peace, or act of aggression against another state. Assume a despotic state flagrantly violates the human rights of its inhabitants to

[33] 43 Dept. State Bull. 355-58 (1960).

[34] *See* Thomas and Thomas, *supra* note 5, at 236.

such an extent that a large exodus of these inhabitants has occurred. The despotic state has engaged in no illegal acts or acts threatening or breaching the peace in relation to other states. Other states, however, are aiding and abetting the emigrés within their borders to overturn the tyrannical regime. Although this regime has contributed to the whole tense situation by creating conditions within its frontiers that cause the emigration, the immediate threats to peace or acts of aggression emanate from those states which are supporting the emigrés and rebels to overthrow the dictator. Action under the Rio Treaty should be taken against those states, not against the dictator. It must be remembered that the Rio Treaty does not permit collective action in the case of acts endangering the peace alone. Article 6 calls for measures in the case of aggression, not of armed attack nature, or extra or intra-continental conflicts, or other situations endangering the peace which at the same time affect the "inviolability of the integrity of the territory or the sovereignty or the political independence of an American State." It is difficult to conceive how an authoritarian regime, albeit denying all human rights to its inhabitants, is affecting the territorial integrity, sovereignty, or political independence of another state, even though its violation of human rights creates international tensions through the emigration of those inhabitants.

In addition to suspending diplomatic relations or attempting to impose trusteeships, collective protection of democracy and human rights also might be pursued by the exclusion of an offender state from the inter-American system. Bolivar would have excluded from his American league any state which changed its form of government, i.e., from republicanism to some other form.[35] Brazil at the 1948 Bogotá Conference would have made membership under the Charter of the OAS conditional upon a state having a democratic form of government. The prerequisites of democracy were listed as plurality of political parties, freedom of the ballot, the opportunity of private enterprise, and the guarantee of the fundamental rights of man. Brazil's recommendation failed to be adopted, but the idea of isolating non-democratic states from the OAS did not die. At the Seventh Meeting of Foreign Ministers of 1960, President Betancourt of Venezuela called for a treaty which would exclude from the organization those states with governments not freely elected by the people. Additionally, a duty to respect the fundamental rights of man, guarantee freedom of the press and information, and recognize the rights of minorities to organize political parties were also requirements, according to President Betancourt.[36]

[35] *See* note 3, *supra.*

[36] See Ninth International Conference of American States, *supra* note 17, at 15.

1. Cuban Exclusion

To some extent, President Betancourt's recommendations were to be followed at the 1962 Eighth Meeting of Ministers of Foreign Affairs. Despite the fact that the Charter of the OAS contains no mechanism to depose a non-conforming member, the eighth meeting – called to consider problems created by the intervention of international communism in the hemisphere through Cuba [37] – ended up with a resolution which had the effect of expelling Cuba from the organization.[38] The ministers first approved, with only Cuba dissenting, a resolution which recognized that continental unity, democracy, human rights, and self-determination were jeopardized by the subversive offensive of communist governments, the purpose of which was to destroy democratic institutions and to establish totalitarian dictatorship in the Americas at the service of extra-continental powers. The principles of communism were declared to be incompatible with the principles of the inter-American system.[39] The principles were respect and preservation of the rights and freedoms of man, representative democracy, non-intervention, and a rejection of alliances and agreements that may lead to American intervention by extra-continental nations.[40] A second resolution declared that by associating itself with the principles of Marxist-Leninism, by establishing a political, economic and social system based on such a doctrine and by accepting military assistance from extra-continental communist powers, including the threat of military intervention in America by the Soviet Union, the Government of Cuba had acted contrary to inter-American principles and had thus violated its OAS membership obligations so as to be incompatible with the OAS. It was further noted that no member of the OAS can claim the rights pertaining to its membership if it fails to recognize the corresponding obligations. It was therefore resolved that adherence by any member state to Marxist-Leninism is incompatible with the inter-American system. Since the government of Cuba had identified itself officially as a Marxist-Leninist government, it was incompatible with

[37] N.Y. Times, Aug. 24, 1960, at 10, col. 3.

[38] On the Punta del Este Meeting, see P.A.U. Final Act Eighth Meeting of Consultation of Ministers of Foreign Affairs Serving as Organ of Consultation in Application of the Inter-American Treaty of Reciprocal Assistance, Punta del Este, Uruguay, January 23-31, 1962 (OEA/Ser.C/II.8, 1962); Thomas and Thomas, *supra* note 5, at 59-60, 238-39, 326-27.

Treaty of Reciprocal Assistance Applications 69 (1964).

[40] *Id.* at 75.

the principles and objectives of the OAS. This incompatibility therefore excluded the Castro regime from participation in the system.[41]

Following this resolution, it might be thought that an inter-American norm requiring adherence to democracy and respect for human rights is in being, enforceable by the OAS through the sanction of exclusion. This would be a doubtful conclusion. Stress was laid upon the actions of Cuba violative of inter-American principles which led to Cuba's incompatibility with those principles which in turn led to Cuba's automatic exclusion. In other words, Cuba by her own actions creating incompatibility had excluded herself. If Cuba's actions had led to self-exclusion, exclusion can hardly be considered as a collective measure by the organization to enforce respect for human rights or anything else. The exclusion order was simply a recognition of *fait accompli*. Actually, though, we have before us a speciousness. It is rather clear that the hope was that the resolution of exclusion of the government of Cuba would so isolate Cuba as to work hardship and disadvantage upon her so that she would be compelled to return to the fold, to return to legality, and to avoid new offenses.

Also opposed to any notion that democracy and human rights have suddenly become enforceable norms of the OAS through the exclusion of Cuba is the fact that the resolution of exclusion passed by only the bare two-thirds majority necessary for adoption. Cuba of course voted in the negative. Argentina, Bolivia, Brazil, Chile, Ecuador, and Mexico abstained.[42] The abstainers were motivated in part by the fact that they believed the exclusion to be illegal under the Charter of the OAS, since no provision was made for this procedure in that document.[43] Since the order was illegal, it would result in an illegal intervention in Cuba's internal affairs. These countries did recognize the incompatibility of a Marxist-Leninist government with basic American principles, but by failure to agree to any enforcement measures against a state departing from these basic principles, which include respect for human rights, respect for human rights seems to be relegated by the abstainers to an "ought" rather than regarded as an "is."

Finally, the exclusion action was taken against a communist government committed to the spread of its ideology through subversive intervention – a gross disregard of the American principle of non-intervention, particularly as it relates to a prohibition of extra-continental intervention – a mainstay

[41] Resolution VI, Exclusion of the Present Government of Cuba from Participation in the Inter-American System, 2 P.A.U., Inter-American Treaty of Reciprocal Assistance Applications 75 (1964).

[42] *See* Thomas and Thomas, *supra* note 5, at 60.

[43] *See* 2 P.A.U., *supra* note 39, at 79-80 for statements of these states as to their votes.

of hemispheric thought since the proclamation of the Monroe Doctrine. Thus, it would seem that the exclusion is directed toward a Marxist-Leninist government in violation of respect for human rights, democracy, and other inter-American principles such as that of non-intervention. Can this be considered as precedent for an enforceable norm which would be directed against a state in derogation of human rights and fundamental freedoms only? If exclusion is used to enforce representative democracy and respect for human rights in the Americas, there are other nations, in addition to Cuba, where neither is observed, and against which measures could and should be taken. Membership in the OAS would be considerably reduced – possibly to the breaking point – if all such trangressors were to be excluded.

2. Intervention in the Dominican Republic and the Inter-American Peace Force

Discussion has centered to this point upon the authority of the OAS to safeguard human rights in the American states, and thus international peace, through the collective security machinery of the Rio Treaty. OAS action during the 1965 crisis in the Dominican Republic illustrates that there may be other ways and means to maintain respect for human rights as a basic principle of the American community.[44] At that time, the Tenth Meeting of Consultation of Ministers of Foreign Affairs established an Inter-American Peace Force composed of member-state armed forces for service in the Dominican Republic.[45] This force was not organized for use against an aggressor or to prevent threats and breaches of inter-American peace. The Tenth Meeting was not convoked under the Rio Treaty at all, but under Article 39 of the Charter of the OAS,[46] which authorizes Meetings of Consultation of Ministers of Foreign Affairs not only to serve as the Organ of Consultation under the Rio Treaty, but also "to consider problems of an urgent nature and of common interests to the American States." The Tenth Meeting was to consider the "[s]erious situation created by armed strife in the Dominican Republic." [47] This nebulous statement made no

[44] For discussion of the crisis *see* A. J. Thomas, Jr., and A. V. W. Thomas, The Dominican Republic Crisis 1965 Background Paper and Proceedings of the Ninth Hammarskjold Forum (J. Carey ed. 1967). For account of the Tenth Meeting of the Consultation of Ministers of Foreign Affairs *see* 1 O.A.S. Chronicle, Aug. 1965, at 1-10, 19-41.

[45] Resolution, Inter-American Force, 1 O.A.S. Chronicle, Aug., 1965, at 23-24.

[46] Convocation of the Tenth Meeting of Consultation of Ministers of Foreign Affairs, *id.* at 19.

[47] *Id.*

mention of armed attack against an American state, aggression which is not an armed attack, or threats to or breaches of extra-continental or intra-continental peace, one of which would be requisite for an application of the Rio Treaty. To the contrary, the Tenth Meeting was concerned with armed civil strife in the Dominican Republic.[48]

Several Meetings of Consultation have been called under the urgent-nature-common-interest enabling clause, and from these meetings have come general resolutions and recommendations urging, requesting, or recommending certain courses of action on the part of the member states.[49] But unlike decisions for measures of collective enforcement under the Rio Treaty which, except for decisions made by the consultative organ to use armed force, are binding upon all member states, the resolutions and recommendations taken by the Meeting of Foreign Ministers to consider urgent and common interest problems are not usually thought of as creating obligations.[50] Moreover, the power of direct action under the Rio Treaty to prescribe a certain course of behavior by providing collective measures for the maintenance of hemisphere peace is exempt by the OAS Charter from the non-intervention principle of the Americas as well as the prohibitions against the use of force or military occupation.[51] A Meeting of Consultation grounded upon the urgent-problem-common-interest faculty has broad powers to discuss, deliberate, resolve, and recommend, but its competency here is not exempted from the basic OAS interdiction on intervention and use of force. If the OAS as a jural personality is obligated to respect these principles, it would be reasonable to assume, that in the absence of specific exception, any attempt by a Meeting called under the urgent-nature-common-interest power to impose the collective will of the OAS and its members against a state without that state's consent would be illegal intervention.[52]

Yet, in the *Dominican Republic* case, the Tenth Meeting, acting under the urgent-nature-common-interest power, authorized a use of armed force through the Inter-American Peace Force to restore democracy in the Dominican Republic and, to a lesser extent, protect human rights. This controversial Inter-American Peace Force resolution [53] requested the govern-

[48] *Id.*

[49] See discussion of the various Meetings of the Ministers of Foreign Affairs and the powers of the meetings in Thomas and Thomas, *supra* note 5, at 79-85 and ch. XVII.

[50] *Id.* at 86.

[51] O.A.S. Charter arts. 15, 16, 17, 19.

[52] For discussion *see* Thomas and Thomas, *supra* note 5, at 165.

[53] *See* note 45, *supra.*

ments of member states to make available to the OAS contingents of their armed forces to operate under the authority of the Tenth Meeting. Following this resolution, some United States military forces which had previously landed in the Dominican Republic upon the outbreak of civil strife were withdrawn, and the remainder were incorporated into the Peace Force under a unified command. Six Latin American nations supplied forces. With the exception of Brazil, their numbers were small.[54]

The Peace Force resolution gave no hint that it was an instrument of inter-American collective security for hemispheric peace or a measure of enforcement of such inter-American peace. It was declared that since the OAS was charged with the responsibility of interpreting the *democratic will* of its members, and with safeguarding the principles of its charter, it was also empowered to adopt appropriate measures in the instance presented by the Dominican Republic to assure the reestablishment of peace and normal democratic conditions. Since the OAS was competent to assist member states in the preservation of peace and the reestablishment of normal democratic conditions, it was also "competent to provide the means that reality and circumstances require and that prudence compels as adequate for the accomplishment of such purposes." It was therefore legitimate to form the Peace Force for service in the Dominican Republic which would have:

> "as its sole purpose, in a spirit of democratic impartiality, that of cooperating in the restoration of normal conditions in the Dominican Republic, in maintaining the security of its inhabitants and the *inviolability of human rights,* and in the establishment of an atmosphere of peace and conciliation that will permit the functioning of democratic institutions." [55]

The venture aimed specifically to permit the functioning of democratic institutions and to maintain the inviolability of human rights of the Dominican people.

As discussed previously, inter-American instruments do not specifically empower the OAS to use coercive measures to enforce democracy or respect for human rights or the maintenance of such rights in a state where they have disappeared. Since no such prerogative is granted by existing treaties, an exception to the non-intervention principle can hardly be spelled out if the action of the Tenth Meeting is considered as intervention. A use of force which controlled and affected the outcome of a civil strife in

[54] The peace force was composed of 1,115 men from Brazil, 21 from Costa Rica, 3 from El Salvador, 10,900 from the United States, 250 from Honduras, 164 from Nicaragua, and 183 from Paraguay. O.A.S. Chronicle, *supra* note 44, at 5.

[55] *See* note 45, *supra* at 24.

an American state would appear to be coercive in nature, altering the condition of things in the Dominican Republic, and thus violative of Article 15 of the OAS Charter which prohibits intervention.[56]

However, argument has been advanced that this forceful measure for democracy and human rights in the Dominican Republic falls outside the meaning of intervention. Some authorities distinguish collective intervention from collective action.[57] Any action taken by an international organization which is in the general interest of its members is technically not intervention. Providing the organization is acting within its constitutional competency, the action may be acceptable. The Secretary General of the OAS took this point of view. He stated:

> "The purpose of the Inter-American Force is clearly not one of intervention but rather one of rendering assistance to the people of a sister state." [58]

A similar contention was advanced before the Security Council of the United Nations where the Peace Force was designated by the Malaysian representative as neither intervention nor enforcement action but a conciliatory function, a type of action permitted to all international organizations to foster peace and tranquility and to permit a "people to establish a democratic civil government of their own choosing, to heal the wounds and the bitterness of civil strife, and to begin the path of relief and reconstruction." [59]

The debates before the Security Council were similar to those concerning the legality under the UN Charter of regional agency use of armed force against a member state within the region. Article 51 of the UN Charter permits member states to take measures including the use of armed force in the exercise of the right of individual or collective self-defense until such times as the Security Council takes the necessary steps to maintain peace. But in the *Dominican Republic* case, the OAS did not base its action on a collective right of self-defense. When states within a regional agency are not exercising a legitimate right of collective self-defense, the validity of regional measures taken without Security Council approval is doubtful. Article 53 of the UN Charter demands that enforcement action not be taken under regional arrangements without authorization by the

[56] *See* Thomas and Thomas, *supra* note 5, at 164-68, for discussion of the O.A.S. and the principle of intervention.

[57] *E.g.*, Lleras, *Report on the Ninth International Conference of American States*, 1 Annals of O.A.S. 25-27 (1949).

[58] As quoted by Mr. Yost of the United States before the Security Council, U.N. SCOR, S/PV. 1220 June 3, 1965, at 57 (1965).

[59] U.N. SCOR, S/PV. 1222 June 9, 1965, at 67-68 (1965).

Security Council. Thus, the validity of measures taken without such previous authorization appears to depend upon whether they fall within the meaning of "enforcement action."

The OAS has always maintained that non-forceful coercive measures permitted by the Rio Treaty do not fall within the meaning of "enforcement action" as the phrase is used in the UN Charter. The director general of the OAS has stated:

"Enforcement action, with the use of physical force, is obviously the prerogative of the Security Council with a single exception: individual or collective self-defense. But the other measures . . . are not; it may even be said that it is within the power of any state – without necessarily violating the purposes, principles, or provisions to the Charter – to break diplomatic, consular, and economic relations or to interrupt its communications with another state." [60]

Although issue has been taken with this viewpoint, in cases of hemispheric aggressions where the OAS has decided to take diplomatic or economic measures against an aggressor, Security Council authorization has not been sought nor thought to be required.[61]

Measures involving physical force, according to the thought of the director general, would be enforcement action. Thus, use of the Inter-American Peace Force in the Dominican Republic would appear to be beyond the powers of the OAS, for such force was not authorized by the Security Council. OAS precedent does exist, however, for a use of OAS force without authorization. The armed naval quarantine in the *Cuban Missile Crisis* case was based on an OAS recommendation under the Rio Treaty that members states take measures, including the use of armed force, to prevent Cuba from continuing to receive military material which threatened continental peace and security.[62] A spokesman of the United States at the time denied this use of physical force was enforcement action. It was called an action for the maintenance of hemispheric peace taken under the co-jurisdiction of the OAS with the Security Council.[63]

The International Court of Justice also seems to have restricted the meaning of enforcement action. In speaking of the United Nations armed

[60] Inter-American Conference for the Maintenance of Continental Peace and Security, *supra* note 15, at 41-42.

[61] For discussion of the various OAS cases in relation to the U.N. *see* MacDonald, *The Developing Relationship between Superior and Subordinate Political Bodies at the International Level. A Note on the Experience of the United Nations and the Organization of American States,* 2 Canadian Y.B. Int'l L. 21 (1964).

[62] 2 P.A.U., *supra* note 39, at 112.

[63] Chayes, *Law and the Quarantine of Cuba,* 41 Foreign Affairs 550, at 554-56 (1963).

operations in the Congo, the court construed the word "action" by saying such operations:

"did not include a use of armed force against a state which the Security Council, under Article 39, determined to have committed an act of aggression or to have breached the peace. The armed forces which were utilized in the Congo were not authorized to take military action against any State. The operation did not involve "preventive or enforcement measures" against any State under Chapter VII and therefore did not constitute "action" as that term was used in Article 11." [64]

This reason would support the legality of the Inter-American Peace Force. Its purpose was not to take action against an aggressor state or against a government which by its policies was threatening peace. The operations of the Peace Force were not preventive action or enforcement action against any aggressor state or peace-breaking or peace-threatening state. It was action taken against a "[a] civil disorder, political chaos, bloodshed and internecine war." [65] The action was called a conciliatory function, "a pacific settlement operation which may require a minimum use of force." [66] The OAS was preparing "the necessary conditions for the will of the people to find free expression so that it may ultimately prevail." [67]

If this line of thought is followed, the OAS can act legally to assure basic principles of democracy and respect for human rights in an American state undergoing civil strife by proceeding under its urgent nature-common-interest power – even to the use of armed force to reestablish democracy and the inviolability of human rights in the strife torn land.[68] Can we take this a step further and say that such action can be taken to protect and assure respect for human rights in an American state where rights have disappeared, or do not exist, or have been extensively violated, when a state is *not* engaged in civil strife? If so, the OAS has its work cut out for it.

THE INTER-AMERICAN COMMISSION ON HUMAN RIGHTS

At the Fifth Meeting of Foreign Ministers in 1959, the highly debated issue of safeguarding human rights to protect the stability of the continent

[64] *Advisory Opinion of 20 July 1962,* [1962] I.C.J. Reports, at 170-71.

[65] 20 U.N. GAOR Supp. 2 at 117, U.N. Doc. A/6002 (1965).

[66] U.N. SCOR, S/PV. June 9, 1965 at 66-68 (1965).

[67] *Id.*

[68] *See* Thomas and Thomas, *supra* note 44, at 59 for further discussion of legality of the Peace Force.

finally resulted in the creation of an Inter-American Commission on Human Rights, composed of seven members elected by the Council of the Organization.[69] The commission, an autonomous entity within the OAS, was to promote respect for human rights by preparing studies and recommendations on progressive measures in favor of human rights and also to serve the OAS as an advisory body.[70] The commission was established by mere OAS resolution. It has now become treaty-based. In 1967, the Protocol of Buenos Aires amended the Charter of the OAS and established the Inter-American Human Rights Commission as the consultative organ of the OAS on human rights.[71] The prime function of the organ was declared to be the promotion, observation, and protection of human rights. Moreover, the 1970 American Convention on Human Rights[72] recognizes the commission as one of the organs – the other being the Inter-American Court of Justice – with competence relating to the fulfillment of the obligations made under the convention. This convention continues the commission membership of seven. However, the members are to be elected by the General Assembly of the OAS from lists of candidates proposed by member states. The commission is also directed to prepare its own statute and regulations. The statute must be submitted to the General Assembly for approval. Since this convention is not yet operative due to

[69] Resolution VIII as contained in P.A.U., Fifth Meeting of Consultation of Ministers of Foreign Affairs, Actas y Documentos (OAE/Ser.F/II.5, 1961). *See also,* P.A.U. La Organizacion de los Estados Americanos 1954-1962, at 12 (OEA/Ser.D/ II.2, 1959).

[70] See functions and powers of the commission as contained in the Statute which was adopted in 1960 by the Council of the O.A.S. and as amended by the Second Special Inter-American Conference. Comision Inter-Americana de Derechos Humanos, Manual de Normas Vigentes en Materia de Derechos Humanos, p. 30 *et. seq.*, OEA/ Ser. L/V/II.23, doc. 21, 1970; the statute of the commission is also contained in 1 Revue des Droits de L'Homme – Human Rights Journal 144 *et. seq.* (1968). For discussions of the work of the Inter-American Commission on Civil Rights *see* A. Schreiber, The Inter-American Commission on Human Rights (1970); Thomas and Thomas, *supra* note 44, at 59-74; Cabranes, *The Protection of Human Rights by the Organization of American States,* 62 Am. J. Int'l L. 889, at 893-908 (1968); Sandifer, *Human Rights in the Inter-American System,* 11 Howard Law J. 508, 516-524 (1965); A.V.W. Thomas and A. J. Thomas, Jr., *The Inter-American Commission on Human Rights,* 20 S.W.L.J. 282 (1966). *See also* Van Boven, *The United Nations Commission on Human Rights and Violation of Human Rights and Fundamental Freedoms,* 15 Nederlands Tijdschrift voor Internationaal Recht 374 (1968).

[71] P.A.U. Charter of the Organization of American States as Amended by the Protocol of Buenos Aires in 1967 ch. XVIII, Treaty Series 1-c (OEA/Ser.A/2 Rev. 1968).

[72] *American Convention on Human Rights,* 5 Rev. of Int'l Comm'n of Jurists 44-62 (Mar. 1970).

a deficiency in ratifications, the old statute of the commission continues extant.[73]

The first Statute of the Inter-American Commission on Human Rights was adopted by the Council of the OAS in 1960.[74] Article 9 described its functions and powers as follows:

"a) To develop an awareness of human rights among the peoples of America;
b) To make recommendations to the Governments of the member states in general, if it considers such action advisable, for the adoption of progressive measures in favor of human rights within the framework of their domestic legislation and, in accordance with their constitutional precepts, appropriate measures to further the faithful observance of those rights;
c) To prepare such studies or reports as it considers advisable in the performance of its duties;
d) To urge the Governments of the member states to supply it with information on the measures adopted by them in matters of human rights;
e) To serve the Organization of American States as an advisory body in respect to human rights."

Almost at once, controversy arose as to the scope of the commission's functions and the interpretation of the statute. Many of the members believed a function confined to the making of reports for the promotion of respect for human rights generally throughout the Americas was too narrow. In debating the extent of their authority, a majority of the members of the commission decided that Article 9(b), which declared that the commission was empowered to "make recommendations to the governments of the members states *in general*," should be interpreted as meaning to make *general* recommendations to member states.[75] Despite the fact that the OAS Council had refused to grant individuals and groups the right to submit petitions to the commission, the commission resolved that it could accept written communications from individuals claiming violations of human rights because the commission was authorized to prepare studies and reports which it deemed advisable.[76] Thus, the commission determined it could recommend the adoption of general measures for the promotion of human rights within the framework of the domestic law of each state as well as recommend to individual states that they take appropriate measures to assure faithful observance of human rights within their borders. Complaints from individuals could also be received and accused governments could be requested to give information to the commission regarding

[73] Authorities cited note 70, *supra.*

[74] *Id.*

[75] P.A.U., Inter-American Commission on Human Rights, Report on the Work Accomplished During its First Session, Oct. 2-28, 1960, at 10 (OEA/Ser.L/V/II.I, doc. 32, 1961).

[76] *Id.* at 13.

the steps taken to remedy violations the commission had called to the attention of the violator.[77]

1. Commission's Experiences

a. Cuba

The commission's conclusions regarding its power in this respect have failed to be accepted as correct by certain states, and collisions between such states and the commission have resulted. The commission's experiences with Castro's Cuba have been most unhappy and disheartening. In 1961, the commission, observing that it had received communications requesting commission action in Cuba to a void irreparable violations of human rights, suggested to the government of that country that it respect the American Declaration of the Rights and Duties of Man, and requested that the commission be supplied a report on the measures Cuba was taking to maintain and advance human rights.[78] Cuba denied the commission's power to make such specific recommendations and requests and intimated that such was an illegal intervention in its affairs.[79] The commission replied that is was interpreting the legal precepts of its statute in their natural sense, implementing the statute's mandate to promote respect for human rights.[80]

The commission subsequently prepared and published two reports, the first in 1962 entitled, "Report on the Situation Regarding Human Rights in the Republic of Cuba" [81] and the second, in 1963, "Report on the Situation of Political Prisoners and their Relatives in Cuba." [82] These reports were based on information, communications, and complaints received by the commission. The second report contained testimony from men who had participated in the Bay of Pigs invasion and who had been released and returned to the United States. The men told ugly tales of human rights violations in Cuba. Those accused of crimes against the Cuban revolution were denied a right to hearing and appeal. Death penalties were meted out to those designated enemies of the regime and counter-revolutionaries. Ar-

[77] *Id.* at 12.

[78] P.A.U. Inter-American Commission on Human Rights, Reports on the Situation of Political Prisoners and their Relatives in Cuba ch. 1 (OEA/Ser.L/V/II.7, doc. 4, 1963).

[79] *Id.* at 4.

[80] *Id.* at 6.

[81] P.A.U. Inter-American Commission on Human Rights, Report on the Situation Regarding Human Rights in the Republic of Cuba (OEA/Ser.L/V/II.4, doc. 30, 1962).

[82] *See* note 78, *supra.*

bitrary arrests were reported as well as the tortures and cruelties occurring in Cuban prisons.

Despite Cuba's attitude, the commission persisted in its efforts. In 1964, the Cuban Government sent its last message to the commission, refusing to provide any information. It denied OAS jurisdiction because of Cuba's exclusion from the organization, which was, in turn, characterized as illegal. The commission replied declaring its continued competence, inasmuch as the present Cuban government had been excluded, not Cuba itself. Under the Commission's reasoning, Cuba as a state was still obligated to inter-America and its principles concerning human rights.[83]

In 1965, the Cuban government refused to respond to a request of the commission to visit Cuba,[84] and in 1966, when the chairman of the commission sought once again to obtain human rights information from Cuba, he was rebuffed.[85] Nevertheless, the commission did continue to issue damning reports on continued human rights deprivations in that unfortunate land, particularly as relating to death penalties for political prisoners, lack of fair criminal procedures and impartial trials, and the cruel treatment of persons in prisons.[86]

b. Haiti

The commission has fared little better in the treatment it has received from other countries. After receiving complaints in Haiti and Nicaragua, the commission decided to request permission to hold part of its 1962 session in those nations. Haiti refused, stating the request was a form of interference in Haiti's internal affairs.[87] Nicaragua assented but left the date open pending further conversations. When dates were suggested in December,

[83] *See* P.A.U., Inter-American Commission on Human Rights, Report on the Work Accomplished During its Ninth Session: Oct. 5-16, 1964, at 13 (OEA/Ser.L/V/II.10, doc. 21, 1965); P.A.U. Inter-American Commission on Human Rights, Report on the Work Accomplished During its Tenth Session 9-10 (OEA/Ser.L/V/II.11, doc. 19, 1965).

[84] P.A.U., Inter-American Commission on Human Rights, Report on the Work Accomplished During its Twelfth Session: Oct. 4-15, 1965, at 17-18 (OEA/Ser.L/V/II.13, doc. 26, 1966).

[85] P.A.U., Inter-American Commission on Human Rights, Report on the Work Accomplished During the Thirteenth Session: April 18-28, 1966, at 17 (OEA/Ser.L/V/II.14, doc. 35, 1966).

[86] P.A.U., Inter-American Commission on Human Rights, Report Regarding the Situation of Human Rights in Cuba (OEA/Ser.L/V/II.17, doc. 4, rev., 1967); O.A.S. Inter-American Commission of American States, Inter-American Commission on Human Rights, Second Report on the Situation of Political Prisoners and Their Relatives in Cuba (OEA/Ser.L/V/II.23, doc. 6, rec. 1, 1970).

[87] P.A.U., Inter-American Commission on Human Rights, Report on the Situation Regarding Human Rights in Haiti 2-3 (OEA/Ser.L/V/II.8, doc. 5, 1963).

1962, or January, 1963, the Nicaraguan Foreign Minister reported that a date during those two months would not be convenient because of circumstances of a national and international nature. The chairman of the commission in November, 1962, again sought permission to hold a part of its January special session in Nicaragua. A cable was received two months later stating it would be impossible to designate the current month of January for a commission session in Nicaragua. The commission concluded that Nicaragua had refused its assent for a Nicaraguan meeting for the purpose of ascertaining the observance of human rights there.[88] In both the Haitian and Nicaraguan instances, the commission through press release widely publicized that these nations were accused of violating human rights.

In 1963, the commission requested and was again refused permission to study the situation regarding human rights in Haiti on Haitian territory.[89] Haiti stated that the commision's visit might be interpreted as a form of interference in its internal affairs. The commission made it clear that it respected Haiti's sovereignty, but that it was empowered by Article 11(c) of its statute to visit the territory of an American state with prior consent of the government. Unable to investigate further, and, in accordance with Article 9(c) of its statute, the commission then prepared and issued a report on the situation regarding human rights in Haiti. The report contained complaints indicating serious transgressions by the Haitian government in its abridgement of a whole spectrum of rights.[90] Violations of the right to life, liberty, and personal property, particularly in the arrest and disappearance of persons and the mass execution of political prisoners, were reported. Suppression of freedom of investigation, opinion, expression and dissemination through the closing of newspapers and the jailing, torture, and expulsion of newsmen, was reported. The complaints went on and on alleging: denial of a right to a fair trial, arbitrary arrest and lack of due process of law, the denial of the right to asylum, restrictions on the right to vote and to participate in government through the elimination of opposition parties, the suppression of the right of assembly and association, denial of the right to residence and movement, and the violation of a right to education and culture. Information refuting certain of the complaints

[88] On the Nicaraguan case *see* P.A.U., Inter-American Commission on Human Rights, Report on the Work Accomplished During its Fifth Session, Sept. 24-Oct. 26, 1962, at 11-16 (OEA/Ser.L/V/II.5, doc. 40, 1963); P.A.U., Inter-American Commission on Human Rights, Report on the Work Accomplished During its First Sessions, Jan. 3-23, 1963, at 11 (OEA/Ser.L/V/II.6, doc. 18, 1963).

[89] P.A.U. *supra* note 87, at 4-6.

[90] *Id.* at 9 *et. seq.*

was received by the commission from the Haitian government, although such information, according to the commission, did not relate to all of the complaints.

A second report on Haiti's violations of human rights was released in 1967.[91] This document concerned accusations that Haitian citizens who were returned to Haiti from the Dominican Republic had been executed or imprisoned arbitrarily. One instance reported was the case of the Beauvoir-Florez family. According to a complaint received, a secret military court sentenced two members of the family to death after arbitrary arrest. The Haitian government rejected requests for information regarding returned Haitian citizens, but related that the persons concerned in the Beauvoir-Florez episode had been sentenced to death for attempted murder and treason, that the president had pardoned them, and they were free to depart from Haiti.

Still another report on Haiti was communicated to the American governments by the commission in 1969.[92] This document again listed the rights allegedly violated, the denunciations which had been received, requests for information, and the replies of the Haitian government.

c. Nicaragua

In the Nicaraguan situation, the refusal of the government to receive the commission in 1963 made it impossible for the commission to monitor Nicaraguan presidential elections in 1963. The commission believed the delays and maneuverings of Nicaragua were carried on to prevent it from making a determination as to whether the elections were conducted freely, with observance of the rights of suffrage.[93]

A report was prepared mentioning the denunciations against Nicaraguan authorities as to human rights, listing the rights which were held to have been violated, the commission's requests for information from Nicaragua, and the information that had been sent. This report was not made public.[94]

[91] P.A.U., Inter-American Commission on Human Rights, Requests for Information Transmitted to the Government of Haiti on the Case of Haitian Citizens Returning to their Country from the Dominican Republic and the Case of the Beauvoir-Florez Family (OEA/Ser.L/V/II.16, doc. 2, 1967).

[92] P.A.U., Inter-American Commission on Human Rights, Report on the Situation Regarding Human Rights in Haiti (OEA/Ser.L/V/II.21, doc. 6 rev., 1969).

[93] P.A.U., Inter-American Commission on Human Rights, Report on the Work Accomplished During its First Special Session: Jan. 3-23, 1963, at 4-8 (OEA/Ser.L/V/II.6, doc. 18, 1963).

[94] P.A.U., Inter-American Commission on Human Rights, Report on the Work Accomplished During its Sixth Session, April 16-May 8, 1963, at 8-12 (OEA/Ser.L/V/II.7, doc. 28, 1963).

Complaints in following years against Nicaragua were found not to constitute sufficient reason to continue commission study of deprivations of human rights in that country.[95] But in 1966, numerous complaints of flagrant human rights abuse by Nicaraguan authorities began to pour in. Violations of rights of free suffrage were also denounced. Several of the cases had been placed before Nicaraguan judicial authority where no verdict had been forthcoming. The government offered to transmit the verdicts when handed down.[96] The commission decided to continue to study the Nicaraguan situation. Later, in view of a conflict between Nicaraguan military personnel and government supporters on the one hand and the supporters of the opposing presidential candidate on the other, the chairman of the commission offered to visit Nicaragua to ascertain what was transpiring. No invitation was extended although the government did report on the incident.[97]

d. Guatemala

Complaints of denial of human rights by the government of Guatemala were received during the 1963-1966 tenure of the Peralta regime.[98] The complaints charged arbitrary arrests and executions, banning of political parties, suppression of free expression, forcing opponents of the regime into exile, and the terrorizing of the rural population. Requests for information by the commission were either ignored or answered in an unsatisfactory manner. The commission sought permission to make an on-the-spot examination of the situation. Permission was denied. The commission thereafter published a report based on the complaints received.[99]

Some greater degree of cooperation came from Latin American governments in certain other instances. After preparation of a report kept confidential by the commission regarding human rights in Paraguay, the chairman of the commission and the Executive Secretary were permitted to visit that nation.[100] Paraguay, however, did not prove so cooperative in its sup-

[95] P.A.U., Inter-American Commission on Human Rights, Report on the Work Accomplished During its Fourteenth Session, Oct. 3-21, 1966, at 12 (OEA/Ser.L/V/II.15, doc. 29, 1967).

[96] P.A.U., Inter-American Commission on Human Rights, Report on the Work Accomplished During its Fifteenth Session (Special) Jan. 9-20, 1967, at 9-10 (OEA/Ser.L/V/II.16, doc. 20, 1967).

[97] For report of this incident *see* Schreiber, *supra* note 70, at 74.

[98] P.A.U. Inter-American Commission on Human Rights, Solicitudes de informacion transmitidas al gobierno Guatemala (OEA/Ser.L/V/II.15, doc. 5, 1966).

[99] *Id.*

[100] P.A.U., Inter-American Commission on Human Rights, Report on the Work Accomplished During its Twelfth Session, Oct. 4-15, at 1965, 15-16 (OEA/Ser.L/V/II.14, doc. 35, 1966).

ply of information on certain complaints received by the commission: it replied in a manner unsatisfactory to the commission. Conditions which brought allegations of civil rights violation after the acquisition of power by military authorities in Ecuador[101] and Honduras[102] also resulted in complaints to the commission. In these two instances, the commission was invited to visit each of these countries, although the invitation was not accepted in either case.[103]

e. Dominican Republic

The commission was most successful in its relations with the Dominican Republic. In 1961, the commission was granted permission by the Dominican government to visit and to investigate complaints alleging violations of human rights. The Dominican government granted permission on the understanding that the comission would restrict its investigations to violations occurring since the departure of the Trujillo family from the island. The members gathered information on the arrests and disappearances of persons, the restriction on freedom of expression, and on the problems of conflict between governmental authorities and students, and government and labor unions. The commission then submitted a report to the Dominican government urging it to take immediate steps to advance human rights.[104]

Other visits were made by the commission to the Dominican Republic,[105] but the most important action of the body in that country came in 1965,

[101] P.A.U., Inter-American Commission on Human Rights, Report on the Work Accomplished During Its Seventh Session, Oct. 7-25, 1963, at 16 (OEA/Ser.L/V/II.8, doc. 35, 1964); P.A.U., Inter-American Commission on Human Rights, Report on the Work Accomplished During Its Eighth Session, April 6-20, 1964, at 12-14 (OEA/Ser.L/V/II.9, doc. 24, 1964); P.A.U., Inter-American Commission on Human Rights, Report on the Work Accomplished During Its Ninth Session, Oct. 5-16, 1964, at 20 (OEA/Ser.L/V/II.10, doc. 21, 1965); P.A.U., Inter-American Commission on Human Rights, Report on the Work Accomplished During Its Tenth Session 8-9 (OEA/Ser.L/V/II.11, doc. 19, 1965); P.A.U., Inter-American Commission on Human Rights, Report on the Work Accomplished During Its Eleventh Session (Special), July 21-23, 1965, at 14 (OEA/Ser.L/V/II.12, doc. 10, 1965).

[102] Report of the Eighth Session, *supra* note 101, at 16.

[103] *Id.* at 12-14; Report of the Ninth Session, *supra* note 101, at 19.

[104] See P.A.U., Inter-American Commission on Human Rights, Report on the Work Accomplished During its Third Session, Oct. 2-Nov. 4, 1961, at 4-5 (OEA/Ser.L/V/II.3, doc. No. 32, 1961). P.A.U., Inter-American Commission on Human Rights, Report on the Situation Regarding Human Rights in the Dominican Republic (OEA/Ser.L/V/II.4, doc. No. 32, 1962).

[105] *See* Pan American Union Symposium on Representative Democracy; Santo Domingo, Dominican Republic, December 17-22, 1962, at 19 (1963); P.A.U., Inter-American Commission on Human Rights, Report on the Work Accomplished During Its Sixth Session, April 16-May 8, 1963, at 14-18 (OEA/Ser.L/V/II.7, doc. 28, 1963).

when the commission was invited by the opposing factions engaged in civil strife to enter and to investigate violations of human rights.[106] The Secretary General of the OAS also believed that the commission should conduct the investigation.[107] Thus, the commission acted under Article 9(e) of its statute which permitted it to serve as an OAS advisory body on human rights. The commission demanded and received from both factions assurances that they would consider themselves obligated to respect and enforce human rights as contained in the American Declaration of the Rights and Duties of Man, and to extend to the commission those facilities needed for the fulfillment of its mission.[108] In carrying out its duties in the Dominican Republic, the commission requested the authorities of the two factions to halt alleged violations of human rights, visited prisons, and was instrumental in bettering the lot of and in freeing some political prisoners. Installation of boards of investigation and review was urged and reports of executions and inhumane treatment of prisoners were conveyed to the authorities. The commission also arranged for some persons to depart the country in safety and conducted others to political asylum in Latin American embassies.[109]

A special committee of criminologists was called in to aid the commission in the investigation of a mass execution. The deed was confirmed, the criminologist placing the blame on the Government of National Reconstruction and stating that this revolutionary faction had sought to eliminate its adversaries through a policy of mass executions without trial.[110] The

[106] P.A.U., *The Dominican Situation,* 1 O.A.S. Chronicle, Aug., 1965, at 6, 7.

[107] *Id.*

[108] *Id.* at 8.

[109] P.A.U., Tenth Meeting of Consultation of Ministers of Foreign Affairs, Situation Regarding Human Rights in the Dominican Republic (Preliminary Report), (19 OEA/Ser.L/V/II.12, doc. rev., 1965). For summary of work done D. Dunshee de Abranches, A Special Protection of Human Rights in the Dominican Republic 3 (Washington World Conference on World Peace Through Law, T 7/6, Sept. 15, 1965). *See also* P.A.U., Inter-American Commission on Human Rights, Report on the Activities of the Inter-American Commission on Human Rights in the Dominican Republic, June 1-Aug. 31, 1965 (OEA/Ser.L/V/II.13, doc. 14 rev., 1965); P.A.U., Inter-American Commission on Human Rights, Report of the Inter-American Commission on Human Rights on its Activities in the Dominican Republic, Sept. 1-July 6, 1966 (OEA/Ser.L/V/II.15, doc. 6 rev., 1966); *See also* Sandifer, *The Inter-American Commission on Human Rights in the Dominican Republic: June 1965 to June 1966* in The Dominican Republic Crises, 1965, at 132 *et seq.*; Thomas and Thomas, *supra* note 44, at 59 *et seq.*

[110] P.A.U., Tenth Meeting of Consultation of Ministers of Foreign Affairs, doc. No. 231, at 5-18 (OEA/Ser.F. 11.10, 1965); Situation Regarding Human Rights in the Dominican Republic (Preliminary Report), *supra* note 109, at 18.

commission was also authorized to remain in the Dominican Republic until the elected government took office, in order to assure compliance with the rights of suffrage and the holding of free and democratic elections.[111]

f. El Salvador – Honduras

A final case of commission activity worthy of note is that which arose from the 1969 conflict between El Salvador and Honduras. Previously the commission had concerned itself with situations primarily involving a violation of human rights of citizens of a state within the territory of that state by its government. No dispute between states was involved. But, in 1969, El Salvador accused Honduras of committing "genocide such as murders, persecution, outrages, personal injuries, damages to property and massive expulsions of Salvadorian citizens residing in Honduras, for the mere fact of their nationality ...." On the same day, Honduras denounced acts in violation of human rights by sectors of the population of El Salvador against Honduran nationals with the tolerance of the authorities of El Salvador. These acts occurred after a soccer game between the two countries held in El Salvador. Several Hondurans were alleged to have been injured in the melée and thousands of Hondurans attending the game suffered acts of violence against them. Both countries requested the Secretary General of the OAS to verify the fact of these violations of human rights in the territory of the other.[112] A subcommittee of the commission was formed to study the complaints on-the-spot. The governments of both countries were notified that a study of their denunciations was beginning.[113]

On July 25, 1969, a second Honduran cable was received accusing the Salvadorian army of acting against Honduran civilians in towns illegally occupied in Honduras before and after a cease fire ordered by the Provisional Organ of Consultation. The cable charged that the Salvadorian troops had indiscriminately murdered, burned homes, and sacked and destroyed private property. Honduras requested an urgent visit by the commission to verify the violations.[114] The commission gathered information on

[111] P.A.U. Inter-American Commission on Human Rights, Report on Work Accomplished During Its Eleventh Session (Special), July 21-23, 1965, at 11 (OEA/Ser.L/V II.12, doc. 10, 1965).

[112] O.A.S., Inter-American Commission on Human Rights, Report on the Work Accomplished During Its Twenty-second Session (First and Second Parts) Aug. 5-7 and Nov. 7-22, 1969, at 7-8 (OEA/Ser.L/V/II.22, doc. 15 Add. 1, 1970).

[113] *Id.* at 9.

[114] *Id.* at 11.

the alleged atrocities and notified both governments that a special meeting would be held to study violations of human rights in the two countries. El Salvador rejected the Honduran denunciation but declared that it would send proof of its innocence to the commission as rapidly as possible.

Thereafter, a confidential report issued by the commission on the first set of charges recommended that each government investigate "the responsibility of the authorities for acts of commission or omission in connection with deeds of violence" against the citizens of the other, adopt those measures necessary to make amends for such violations, and protect against future violations of human rights.

The commission continued to study the complaint filed by Honduras and other denunciations. The Honduran and El Salvadorian governments were requested to supply additional information for the preparation of the commission's report. The governments were warned that if they did not reply within the 180-day period allowed by the commission's regulations, the commission would be obliged to assume the events were true. The commission then terminated the activities of the on-the-spot subcommittee in the two countries, without prejudice to the continuation of work on the problem of human rights and to the reception of communications regarding violations of human rights there.[115]

2. Commission's Power

Under its 1960 statute, the commission was limited to discussion, study, investigation and recommendations in general. As can be gleaned from certain of the above cases, some states contended that an exercise of this power – specically through receipt of human rights complaints in an individual state and request to that state for information about the violations – amounted to intervention in its internal affairs. An acceptance of this view would, of course, have seriously curtailed the commission's power, for it would then be bound by Article 15 of the Charter of Bogotá which prohibits intervention. Ordinarily, discussion, investigation, or even recommendation would not amount to intervention.[116] Whether they are to be considered acts of intervention would depend on whether they are coercive attempts to maintain or alter existing conditions against the state's will.[117] A discussion and investigation might result in loss of international prestige

[115] *Id.* at 34-41.

[116] For discussion of intervention and its definition *see* A.V.W. Thomas and A.J. Thomas, Jr., Non-Intervention, The Law and Its Import in the Americas ch. IV (1956). For a discussion of investigation, discussion, and recommendation as intervention *see* Thomas and Thomas, *supra* note 5, at 166-68.

[117] Thomas and Thomas, Non-Intervention, *supra* note 116, at 71.

through mobilization of public opinion against a state, compelling the state to act in accord with the will of the commission even though no threat or other action was made. In such an instance, if the commission entered into a consideration, discussion, or investigation directed against a specific state with the purpose of coercing that state to follow the will of the commission, the acts would seem interventionary. The same may be said for a recommendation. A recommendation of a general nature suggesting a course or policy which all the states of the OAS should follow would clearly be within the statutory authority of the commission. But a specific censorious recommendation made against a state for the purpose of forcing that state's will would be an intervention.

Due to the controversy over the commission's interpretation of its powers and the charges of intervention, the OAS finally agreed at the Second Special Inter-American Conference in 1965 to modify the commission's statute to expand its powers and functions formally.[118] The directives of the conference were placed in the 1966 amendment of the commission's statute. Article 9(bis) [119] provided, in part, that in accordance with the wishes of the Second Special Inter-American Conference, the commission should give particular attention to observances of the human rights referred to in Articles I, II, III, IV, XVIII and XXVI of the American Declaration of the Rights of Man.

Included therein are the rights to life, liberty, and security of the person; equality before the law without distinction as to race, sex, language, creed, or other factor; freedom of religion, of speech, press, and opinion; free access to the courts to ensure respect for legal rights and equal protection of the laws; no deprivation of liberty without due process of law; speedy and public trial; no *ex post facto* laws; and no cruel and unusual punishment.

Special commission procedures were set up for the denunciations of violations of these rights, as well as for communications received threatening reprisals against signers of denunciations addressed to the commission or against any person mentioned as an injured party in such denunciation.[120] Following Article 9(bis), paragraph d, it was further provided that consideration by the commission of complaints is dependent upon verified exhaustion of the internal legal procedures and remedies of the member

[118] P.A.U., Second Special Inter-American Conference, Rio de Janeiro, Brazil, Nov. 17-30, 1965, Final Act, Resolution xxii (OCEA/Ser.C/1.13, 1965).

[119] Authorities cited note 70, *supra*.

[120] Art. 53 of the Regulations of the Inter-American Commission on Human Rights as set forth in Manual de Normas Vigentes en Materia de Derechos Humanos or 1 Revue des Droits de L'Homme-Human Rights Journal, *supra* note 70.

states involved. The denunciation must be submitted to the commission within six months of the final domestic decision after the signer of the complaints has come to realize that recourse to the domestic remedy has been hindered arbitrarily or the final domestic decision unjustly delayed.[121] If the violation is confirmed, the commission prepares a report and makes its recommendation to the government concerned. If the government does not adopt the measures recommended within a reasonable time, the commission makes such observations as it desires in its annual report to the Inter-American Conference or to the Meeting of Consultation of Ministers of Foreign Affairs. If one or the other of these organs fails to respond to the commission's recommendations and if the government concerned still has not adopted them, the commission may publish the report.[122]

Paragraph b of Article 9(bis) provides that the commission is empowered:

> "[t]o examine communications submitted to it and any other available information; to address the government of any American state for information deemed pertinent by the commission; and to make recommendations, when it deems this appropriate, with the objective of bringing about more effective observance of fundamental human rights."

Thus, the commission's broad interpretation of its powers to take cognizance of the specific denunciations of human rights becomes *de jure*. Moreover, the powers of the commission are enlarged. Although the commission had examined complaints since 1960 and had sent them to the government concerned with requests for information, it had refrained from making decisions as to the validity of the charges made.[123] With this amendment to its statute, the commission could take another step, decision on the merits, in regard to the special category of human rights.

It should be stressed that the commission's only sanctioning power has been its power of revealing information to the public. For example, in the *Haitian* and *Cuban* cases where the governments refused to permit investigation and were deficient in supplying information, the commission published reports, hopeful that the power of publicity would bring about some rectification.[124] In other instances, the commission would keep its report confidential if it thought that by so doing it could obtain cooperation from a government. At best, publication or threat thereof has been a weak sanc-

[121] Regulations, art. 55, *supra* note 120.

[122] *Id.* at art. 57.

[123] *See* Schreiber, *supra* note 70 at 53.

[124] *See* Schreiber, *supra* note 70, at 67-68; Thomas and Thomas, *The Inter-American Commission on Human Rights, supra* note 70, at 306.

tion. Dictatorial governments have suppressed the reports within the borders of their own nation and have paid little heed to the adverse comments of the commission on the laws or practices and procedures within the nation. Under the revised special procedures, if its recommendations to a government are not accepted in a reasonable time, the commission makes its observations known to the Inter-American Conference or the Meeting of Consultation. The report still can be published if no action is taken by those organs and if the state does not adopt the commission's recommendations.

The new American Convention on Human Rights continues the commission and its functions.[125] The powers of the commission are specific and detailed as are their limits. Actually, these revised provisions read like a combination of the previous statute of the commission and its regulations. The power to study and report, request governments for information, and recommend corrective measures are continued.[126] Persons, groups of persons, and legally recognized non-governmental entities may lodge petitions with the commission complaining of the violation of the human rights provisions of the convention by a state party.[127] Communications by one state party alleging violations by another state party may be received and examined if the two parties have made declarations of acceptance of the competence of the commission.[128]

If the new convention ever becomes operative through sufficient ratifications, the power of publication becomes somewhat restricted. The convention provides that if settlement is not reached concerning the violation of human rights, a report is transmitted by the commission to the concerned state, and the state is not at liberty to publish it. If, within three months, the matter has not been settled or submitted by the state or the commission to the proposed Inter-American Court of Human Rights, the commission may publish the report.[129]

THE AMERICAN CONVENTION ON HUMAN RIGHTS

The Fifth Meeting of Consultation of American Ministers of Foreign Affairs not only established the seven man Inter-American Commission on

[125] *See* note 72, *supra.*
[126] Art. 41 of the Convention, *supra* note 72.
[127] *Id.* at art. 44.
[128] *Id.* at art. 45.
[129] *Id.* at arts. 50-51.

Human Rights, but also directed the Inter-American Council of Jurists to prepare a draft convention on human rights. The Council of Jurists was also to prepare one or more conventions on the creation of an inter-American court and other appropriate organs for the protection and observance of such rights.[130] Within a short time, the Council of Jurists had prepared a draft convention, based in part on the Inter-American Declaration on the Rights and Duties of Man, which encompassed economic, social, and cultural rights, as well as political and civil rights.[131] The quick action of the Council of Jurists went for naught. The convention languished for seven years.

When the Second Special Inter-American Conference met in Rio de Janeiro in 1965, the draft was dusted off and placed on the agenda.[132] After some debate, the Council of the OAS was instructed to prepare a final version of the draft convention, taking into consideration alternative drafts which had been introduced by the Chilean and Uruguayan governments. The Council also was authorized to solicit and receive the views of the Inter-American Commission of Human Rights. The second special conference ordered the revision to be ready by November, 1966, to be submitted to members of the OAS prior to February, 1967, in preparation for an inter-American specialized conference on human rights tentatively set for March of 1967.[133] The Inter-American Commission on Human Rights, in April, 1966, began a thorough study of the three drafts and, within a few months, transmitted to the Council of the OAS its suggestions and recommendations.[134]

Despite the time table established, other events intervened to prevent fulfillment of the instructions of the second special conference. In 1967, an extensive reorganization of the inter-American system was authorized by the Protocol of Buenos Aires.[135] After this reorganization, the OAS Council finally began its consideration of the draft convention.

[130] P.A.U. Fifth Meeting of Consultation of Ministers of Foreign Affairs, Actas y Documentos, (OEA/Ser.F/III.5 pp. 308-9 1961).

[131] P.A.U., Inter-American Council of Jurists, Final Act of the Fourth Meeting of the Inter-American Council of Jurists (CIJ-43, at 48-75, 1959).

[132] P.A.U., Second Special Inter-American Conference, Rio de Janeiro, Brazil, Nov. 17-30, 1965, Final Act., xxiiv (OEA/Ser.C/I.13 (English), 1965).

[133] *Id.*

[134] P.A.U., Inter-American Commission on Human Rights, Opinion on the Draft Convention on Human Rights Approved by the Inter-American Council of Jurists (OEA/Ser.L/V/II.16, doc. 8 (English) rev.) (April 24, 1967).

[135] O.A.S., Committee on Juridical-Political Affairs, Report on a Consultation with the Member States Regarding the Draft Convention on Human Rights (Council Series, OEA/Ser.G/IV. c-i-787, at 2 (English) rev. 3, June 7, 1967). *See also,* Gros Es-

The Council, noting that the General Assembly of the United Nations in 1966 had adopted the International Covenants on Human Rights, which had been signed by a number of members of the OAS, and noting further that substantive provisions in the inter-American draft were similar to those contained in the UN covenants, decided to consult the members of the OAS before proceeding further.[136] In the desire to avoid conflicts between universal and regional rules and institutions, two questions were submitted to member states. The first queried whether the governments of the American states desired a single universal system of regulation of human rights or whether they preferred "the coexistence and coordination" of world-wide and regional conventions covering the same rights. If the latter point of view were to prevail, a second question was asked, should the inter-American treaty be limited to the establishment of an inter-American institutional and procedural system which would include the Inter-American Commission on Human Rights and eventually an inter-American court of justice?[137]

Argentina and Brazil advocated that the OAS stop work altogether on the regional convention, but most of the other responding nations were inclined to feel that there did exist a possibility for "the coexistence and coordination" of universal and regional conventions. Of these, only a few took the position that a regional convention should be limited to providing regional machinery for implementing substantive norms adopted in the United Nations Covenants.[138] The Council of the OAS instructed the Inter-American Council of Jurists to prepare a final version of the draft convention in 1968 to be submitted to the American governments for their observations,[139] and eventually for final approval at a specialized conference of the OAS to be called for that purpose in San José, Costa Rica, in November, 1969.[140]

At the conclusion of this Inter-American Conference on Human Rights, twelve members signed the American Convention on Human Rights, to

piell, *Le Processus de la Réforme de la Charte de l'Organisation des États Américains,* 14 Annuaire Français de Droit International 139 (1968).

[136] O.A.S., at 3, *supra* note 135.

[137] *Id.* at 4.

[138] *Id.*

[139] O.A.S., Observations of the Governments Regarding the Draft Convention on Human Rights (Council Series, OEA/Ser.G/V, C-d-1519 (English) Add. 2 (Sept. 13, 1967), Add. 3 (Sept. 15, 1967), Add. 6 (Oct. 3, 1967), Add. 7 (Oct. 19, 1967), Add. 8 (Nov. 17, 1967).

[140] O.A.S., Inter-American Specialized Conference on Human Rights, San José, Costa Rica, Nov. 7-22, 1969, Final Act (OEA/Ser.C/VI.18.1 (English) doc. 70, rev. 1, corr. 1).

be known as the Pact of San José.[141] As soon as eleven states have ratified (and to date only Costa Rica has deposited its ratification), it will become effective. Consequently, this treaty marks the culmination of a process of drafting that has been under way for more than a decade, and it has been hailed as a consummative endorsement of inter-American concern for the rights of the individual. Althought is was predicted that the new convention would have significant influence on future inter-American efforts to protect human rights,[142] some look upon such predictions with skepticism, pointing out that many of the basic values demanded by the convention are formulated on high levels of abstraction or are not legally precise. Furthermore, some of the standards are not acceptable to all members of the OAS.[143] Portions of the American treaty parallel the United Nations Covenant on Civil and Political Rights, while other provisions vary distinctly.

1. The Rights Analyzed

a. Equality

The OAS convention begins with a formal assertion that the ratifying states guarantee to ensure to all persons subject to their jurisdiction the free and full exercise of the rights established by the convention without discrimination for reasons of race, color, sex, language, religion, political or other opinion, national or social origin, economic status, birth or other social condition – in other words, a right of complete and all encompassing equality.[144] This is similar to Article 2 of the United Nations Covenant on Political and Civil Rights,[145] and both treaties, throughout, have provisions re-enforcing this right of equality.[146]

[141] The signatory nations are El Salvador, Colombia, Ecuador, Honduras, Paraguay, Panama, Chile, Guatemala, Nicaragua, Uruguay, Venezuela, Costa Rica.

[142] A.L. del Russo, International Protection of Human Rights 247 (1971); MacBride, *The European Court of Human Rights,* 3 N.Y.U.J. Int'l L. 1, 15 (1970); *American Convention of Human Rights,* 5 Rev. of Int'l Comm'n Jurists 1 (1970).

[143] K. Vasak, La Commission Interamericaine des Droits de l'Homme 64 ff. (1968). Bilder, *International Promotion of Human Rights: A Current Assessment,* 58 Am. J. Int'l L. 728 (1964).

[144] O.A.S., American Convention on Human Rights, art. 1, para. 1 (OEA/Ser.K/XVI/I.1, English, doc. 65, rev. 1, corr. 2, Jan. 7, 1970) (hereinafter cited O.A.S. Convention).

[145] United Nations Convenant on Civil and Political Rights, G. A. Res. 2200 A, 21 U.N.G.A.O.R. Supp. 16 at 49-60, U.N. Doc. A/6316 (1966) (hereinafter cited as U.N. Convention).

[146] O.A.S. Convention, art. 24; U.N. Convention art. 3, 26. The American convention does not include the United Nations treaty guarantees accorded to ethnic, religious, and linguistic minorities to enjoy their own culture, profess and practice their own religion and use their own language. U.N. Convention, art. 27.

Yet, of all animal species in the world, human beings are probably the least equal, differing in many ways, such as sex, intelligence, strength, ability, education, and achievement. Even the most ardent advocate of equality will recognize that there is a need for some acceptable basis for discrimination. Without reasonable or compelling classifications, serious injustice may result. These provisions have to be interpreted loosely or relatively, rather than in absolute terms, if they are to be a force in the development of international protection for the right of equality.

b. Life

The right to life, that is, the right not to be killed, is among the civil and political rights listed. The United Nations covenant makes no mention of the time for the attachment of this right,[147] but the OAS convention clearly stipulates that he right to life shall be protected by law "from the moment of conception." [148] As religious dogma, this requirement may be open to attack in nations where there is separation between church and state. Furthermore, it will encounter opposition from nations that have legalized abortion.

In addition to the time of attachment requirement, the OAS convention stipulates that no one shall be "arbitrarily" deprived of his life.[149] But the word arbitrarily is not defined, and this had led to speculation as to its exact meaning.[150] In a legal context, "arbitrarily" can signify "not in accordance with law" – "illegally" – or it can mean "unreasonably" or "unjustly." In United States legal terminology, we speak of procedural due process or substantive due process – terms which because of their peculiar common law background are unacceptable in most civil law countries. If arbitrarily means illegally – lack of procedural due process – then deprivation of life by an oppressive government in accordance with the procedures of the municipal law, no matter how unjust, would not fall within the scope of the treaty. On the other hand, if it is claimed that a life is taken unreasonably – with lack of substantive due process – an unknown subjective element is brought into the treaty. It will be up to the interpreter to decide what is unreasonable. Ratifiers of the treaties must be aware that what is reasonable to one group of people, may be highly unreasonable to another.

Although the right to life is not construed to forbid capital punishment, the inter-American convention calls for its abolition and specifies that it

[147] U.N. Convention art. 6.
[148] O.A.S. Convention, art. 4, para. 1.
[149] *Id. See also* U.N. Convention, art. 6, para. 1.
[150] Hassan, *The International Covenants on Human Rights: An Approach to Inter-*

may be imposed only for the most serious crimes, may not be imposed on persons below 18 or over 70 years of age, nor carried out on pregnant women, nor be inflicted for political offenses. Again, the vagueness of the term "political offenses" leads to possibilities of abuse.[151] Deliberate killing of law enforcement officers for political reasons may be viewed by some as murder, but by others as a political offense. In view of the debates which have ensued since heart transplants have taken place, it is surprising to find that neither treaty contains any specific stipulation as to when the right to life ends: that is, when death occurs.

c. *Humane Treatment*

The right to humane treatment established by the OAS treaty [152] involves the concept that no person shall be subjected to cruel and unusual punishment. But it goes even further by declaring that punishment shall not be extended to any person other than the criminal. This, of course, may be contra to the modern movement to impose penalties on parents for the delicts of their minor children. The treaty requires minors accused of crimes to be separated from adults and brought before specialized juvenile tribunals.[153] After the case of *In re Gault*,[154] where United States juvenile tribunal procedures were roundly condemned on the basis of legal and sociological studies, one may well wonder if such a stipulation in an international treaty may not be more detrimental than beneficial to the juvenile criminal.

d. *Slavery*

The freedom from slavery article of the OAS convention [155] goes a step beyond a similar article in the United Nations covenant [156] in that it not only forbids slavery, slave trade, and involuntary servitude, but it also forbids "traffic in women." Some female liberation movement will surely label this as male chauvinism.

pretation, 19 Buff. L. Rev. 35 (1969).

[151] 6 M. Whiteman, International Law 799-859 (1968); Evans *Reflections upon the Political Offender in International Practice*, 57 Am. J. Int'l L. 1 (1963); Green, *Political Offences, War Crimes and Extradition*, 11 Int'l and Comp. L.Q. 329 (1962).

[152] O.A.S. Convention, art. 5.

[153] *Id.* art. 3, para. 5.

[154] In re Gault, 387 U.S. 1 (1967). *See also* Paulsen, *Juvenile Courts and the Legacy of '67*, 43 Ind. L.J. 527 (1968).

[155] O.A.S. Convention, art. 6.

[156] U.N. Convention, art. 8.

e. Fair Trial

The rights conceived to be incident to a fair trial are spelled out in the OAS convention in some detail.[157] In addition to guarantees of an impartial tribunal, detailed notifications as to the charges against him, the presumption of innocence until proven guilty, adequate time and means for the preparation of his defense, and the right not to be compelled to be a witness against himself, an accused is given certain other rights. He has a right to be assisted, without charge, by a translator or interpreter if he does not understand or does not speak the language of the court.[158] He has the right to defend himself personally (which may be a dubious right under the United States attitude that only a fool would be his own lawyer) or to be assisted by legal counsel, either of his own choosing or provided by the state.[159] He is given the right to communicate freely and privately with his counsel, and the right to appeal the judgment to a higher court.[160] He also has the right to examine witnesses "present in court," a far more restricted right than the United States constitutional right of being "confronted with the witnesses against him." [161]

The UN covenant declares that the person accused of crime shall "not be compelled to testify against himself, or to confess guilt." [162] The OAS changed this language, for the worse rather than for the better, by awkwardly stating that a person accused of a crime has "the right not to be compelled to be a witness against himself or *to plead guilty*.[163]

Coerced confessions are banned, as is double jeopardy in cases where a person has been "acquitted by a non-appealable judgment." [164] Prior *conviction* apparently is no bar to subjecting the person to retrial for the same offense. If he has been acquitted in a country where the state is given the right of appeal, either on basis of law or fact, apparently he cannot plead double jeopardy.

The right of public trial is not absolute, but is circumscribed by the restriction that criminal trials need not be public if "it is necessary to protect the interests of justice." [165] This, of course, gives a great deal of discretion to the judiciary as to when the public may be banned from a criminal trial. The UN covenant is even broader, for there it is stated that:

[157] O.A.S. Convention, art. 8.
[158] *Id.* art. 8, para. 2(a).
[159] *Id.* art. 8, para. 2(d), (e).
[160] *Id.* art. 8, para. 2(h).
[161] *Id.* art. 8, para. 2(f); U.S. Const. amend. VI.
[162] U.N. Convention, art. 14, para. 3(g).
[163] O.A.S. Convention, art. 8, para. 2(g).
[164] *Id.* art. 8, para. 4.
[165] *Id.* art. 8, para. 5.

"the press and the public may be excluded from all or part of a trial for reasons of morals, public order, or national security in a democratic society, or when the interests of the private lives of the parties so requires, or to the extent strictly necessary in the opinion of the court in special circumstances where publicity would prejudice the interests of justice." [166]

It is apparent from these two treaties that the desirability of a public trial is not widely revered.

In contrast, equality before the law and equal protection of the law are emphasized and re-emphasized in both instruments,[167] and both give guarantees to establish effective, simple, and prompt recourse to a competent national court or tribunal against acts that violate the rights of the complainant.[168] Both guarantee to "develop the possibilities of judicial remedy" [169] and to ensure enforcement of such remedies when granted. Paragraph 3 of Article 2 of the UN covenant stipulates application in violation of the provisions of the covenant only, whereas Article 25 of the OAS treaty is more extensive in that it is applicable to acts that violate fundamental rights recognized by the constitution or laws of the state concerned as well as those recognized by the convention.

f. Liberty

The UN convention and the OAS convention endorse a right of personal liberty, but there are certain variations in the range of guarantees set forth by the two treaties.[170] Agreement is mutual that no one shall be subject to arbitrary arrest or imprisonment; that the accused shall enjoy a right to a speedy trial by a competent, independent and impartial tribunal; that the accused shall have the right to be informed of the nature and character of the charges against him; and that he shall have a right to a procedure closely akin to a *habeas corpus* proceeding.[171]

In their constitutions, many Latin American countries provide for preventive detention when a president declares an *estado de sitio*.[172] This

[166] U.N. Convention, art. 14, para. 1.
[167] *Id.* art. 14, par. 1; art. 2, par. 1; OAS Convention, art. 24.
[168] O.A.S. Convention, art. 7; U.N. Convention, art. 9.
[169] O.A.S. Convention, art. 25; U.N. Convention, art. 2, para. 3.
[170] O.A.S. Convention, art. 7, para. 6; U.N. Convention, art. 9, para. 4.
[171] O.A.S. Convention, art. 7, para. 6; U.N. Convention, art. 9, para. 4.
[172] Two typical examples can be found in the Constitutions of Honduras and Nicaragua. Art. 177 (ch. 7) of the 1965 Constitution of Honduras declares:

The guarantees established (in the preceding articles) may be suspended in the event of invasion of the national territory, serious disturbance of the peace, and epidemic, or other disaster, by the President of the Republic, by means of a decree...

Articles 196 and 197 of the Constitution of Nicaragua (1962) declare:

The President of the Republic, whenever in his opinion the public tranquility is threatened, may order the detention of persons presumed responsible... The would create a potential conflict between treaty law and constitutional law if it were not that the OAS treaty itself recognizes the possibility of suspension of guarantees of the treaty. Under Article 27 it is stated:

"In time of war, public danger, or other emergency that threatens the independence or security of a State Party, it may take measures derogating from its obligations under the present Convention to the extent and for the period of time strictly required by the exigencies of the situation."

In spite of all the high sounding pronouncements on personal liberty, this broad exemption permits, without incurring international responsibility, almost the same power of preventive detention existing today in the internal laws of some nations. The limitation that a state availing itself of the right of suspension shall inform all other parties via the Secretary General of the OAS of the reason given for suspension, the articles it has suspended, and the date set for the termination of such suspension would not seem to create a great deal of restraint on the right to suspend guarantees.[173]

A unique provision in the OAS treaty specifies that states which permit an individual recourse to the court if he feels his liberty about to be threatened may never restrict or abolish this right.[174] There is no similar provision in the UN covenant.

The OAS convention also abolishes imprisonment for debt, except those debts consisting of nonfulfillment of judicial orders of child or wife support.[175] This apparently was an answer to the UN convention statement that no person was to be imprisoned because of inability to fulfill a contractual obligation.[176] While the UN covenant provides that a victim of unlawful arrest or detention shall have an enforceable right to compensation,[177] the OAS document waters this down by stipulating that the victim of a miscarriage of justice has a right to be compensated thereof "in ac-

President of the Republic, in the Council of Ministers, may suspend or restrict, in all or a part of the national territory, the exercise of constitutional guarantees in any of the following cases: when the Republic becomes involved in an international or civil war; when there is danger that either of these may occur; in the case of epidemic, earthquake or other public disaster; whenever due to any other circumstances it is required for the protection, peace, or security of the nation or of its institutions or form of government.

173 O.A.S. Convention, art. 27, para. 3.

174 *Id.* art. 7, para. 6.

175 *Id.* art. 7, para. 7.

176 U.N. Convention, art. 11.

177 *Id.* art. 9, para. 5.

cordance with the law." [178] If no internal law makes provision for such compensation, apparently the victim is without remedy.

A double guarantee is established by the OAS convention against *ex post facto* laws. Article 7 Paragraph 2, states:

"No one shall be deprived of his physical liberty except for the reasons and under the conditions established beforehand by the constitution of the State Party concerned or by a law established pursuant thereto."

This is further elaborated in Article 9:

"No one shall be convicted of any act or omission that did not constitute a criminal offense, under the applicable law, at the time it was committed. A heavier penalty shall not be imposed than the one that was applicable at the time the criminal offense was committed. If subsequent to the commission of the offense, the law provides for imposition of a lighter punishment, the guilty person shall benefit therefrom."

Would this run contrary to recent Supreme Court of the United States decisions where the non-retroactivity doctrine has been accepted with reference to cases which redefine the rights of those accused or crime in the light of modern constitutional theories? [179]

g. Privacy

When it comes to the right of privacy, the OAS treaty sets forth a right which is dear to the heart of all Latin Americans, but which can best be called an ethical aspiration whose importance is less of achievement than intent: "Everyone has the right to have his honor respected and his dignity recognized." [180] Is this command addressed to governments or to private individuals? What of persons who have no honor or no dignity? Does the treaty's subsequent statement that no one may be the object of an unlawful attack on his honor or reputation modify the preceding statement? Can you really equate an unlawful attack on honor and reputation with recognition of dignity and respect for honor?

"No one may be the object of arbitrary or abusive interference with his private life, his family, his home, or his correspondence . . . everyone has the right to the protection of the law against such interference." [181] Again, one can question the meaning of the word arbitrary and here the confusion is compounded by adding the word "abusive." Are these words to be interpreted as "unlawful" or do they have a wider connotation than con-

[178] O.A.S. Convention, art. 10.

[179] Desist v. U.S., 394 U.S. 244 (1969); Johnson v. New Jersey, 348 U.S. 719 (1966).

[180] O.A.S. Convention, art. 11, para. 1.

[181] *Id.* art. 11, para. 2.

trary to law? For example, would the publication of a person's name on a list of tax delinquents (permitted in places by law) be considered an arbitrary or abusive interference with his private life? Would a listing as a bad credit risk in a merchant's retail credit association be considered an arbitrary or abusive interference with his private life?

h. Religion

The right to freedom of religion is conceded in both the UN declaration [182] and the OAS treaty,[183] but both then go on to admit this freedom may be subject to severe limitations by law necessary to protect public safety, order, health, morals, or the rights or freedoms of others.[184] The OAS broadly grants freedom to disseminate one's religion or beliefs, either individually or together with others in public or private.[185] There is no limitation on this broad grant, yet this surely must be illusory because even nations most protective of religious freedom resort to the police power of the state to regulate the dissemination of religious beliefs. One cannot, for example, disseminate one's religion in the middle of Times Square during the evening rush hour.

The apparently reasonable statement that parents have the right to provide for the religious and moral education of their children in accord with their own convictions,[186] may be a strong deterrent to the ratification of the treaty by some nations. The Government of Mexico, for example, has required all parochial schools to utilize the same text books used in Mexican public schools, in the face of parental claims that these books present religious and moral views unacceptable to them.

i. Freedom of Speech

Freedom of speech and press provisions of the OAS treaty go an astonishing step beyond those of the United Nations or of the European Convention on Human Rights. The OAS document states these freedoms shall not be subject to prior censorship but shall be subject "to subsequent imposition of liability to ensure the protection of national security, public order, public health and morals, and to ensure respect for the rights or reputation of others." [187] In other words, the ban on prior censorship is absolute.

[182] U.N. Convention, art. 18.
[183] O.A.S. Convention, art. 12.
[184] O.A.S. Convention, art. 12, para. 3; U.N. Convention, art. 18, para. 3.
[185] O.A.S. Convention, art. 12, para. 1.
[186] *Id.* art. 12, para. 4.
[187] *Id.* art. 13, para. 2.

The UN convention stipulates that freedom of the press may be restricted by law for the same reasons,[188] but does not limit this restriction to subsequent liability. In other words, prior censorship is legitimate under the UN document in some cases. The European convention, also permits prior censorship for even a wider area of information:

"The exercise of these freedoms, since it carries with it duties and responsibilities, may be subject to such formalities, conditions, restrictions or penalties as are prescribed by law and are necessary in a democratic society, in the intersts of national security, territorial integrity or public safety, for the prevention of disorder or crime, for the protection of health or morals, for the protection of the reputation or rights of others, for preventing the disclosure of information received in confidence, or for maintaining the authority and impartially of the judiciary." [189]

Unquestionably, this article places limits on free speech and the press, limits which have been accepted by many nations. The OAS treaty permits no prior measures of restriction on freedom of the press or speech to protect the rights or reputation of others (which would include libel or slander), or in order to preserve the security, public order, or the public health or morals of the nation. In the United States, obscene speech – when so determined by the Supreme Court – is not given protection, thus it could be subjected to subsequent liability and also to previous restraint.[190] Although the older United States constitutional view would permit libel to be subject to previous restraint, the new view declares that such speech cannot be subject even to subsequent liability unless the words were uttered or written with actual malice. Malice imports knowledge that the words were false or that they were uttered with reckless disregard of whether false or not.[191]

Under the OAS convention, censorship by restraint is permissible for the regulation of public entertainment which has been determined to be morally detrimental to children or adolescents.[192] The words "public entertainment" are not defined in the treaty. Apparently, they were not de-

[188] U.N. Convention, art. 19, para. 3.

[189] European Convention for the Protection of Human Rights and Fundamental Freedoms, art. 1, para. 2.

[190] Freedman v. Maryland, 380 U.S. 51 (1965), Roth v. United States, 354 U.S. 476 (1957). *See also* K. Kuh, Foolish Figleaves: Pornography In and Out of Court (1967); R. Cancel Negron, *En Torno a la Obscenidad: Un Concepto Juridico Impreciso,* 29 Revista del Colegio Abogados de Puerto Rico 169 (1969); W. F. Eich, *From Ulysses to Portnoy: A Pornographic Primer,* 53 Marquette L. Rev. 155 (1970).

[191] *See generally* N.Y. Times Co. v. Sullivan, 376 U.S. 254 (1964); Near v. Minnesota, 283 U.S. 697 (1931).

[192] O.A.S. Convention, art. 13, para. 4.

signed to extend to reading material, for such would fall within a classification of private entertainment.

Both the OAS convention [193] and the UN convention [194] permit restrictions on war propaganda and on advocacy of national, racial, or religious hatred that constitute incitements to lawless violence. The UN document would permit subsequent or previous restraint by law, while under the OAS treaty, they are offenses punishable (subsequent liability) by law. This type of restriction would probably run afoul of the United States Constitution which permits citizens to express their views freely and fully on any subject no matter how obnoxious the views may be. A government may act only where speech is associated with and threatens imminently to lead to action against which the public has a right to be protected.[195]

Query, would inciting Indians in certain South American nations to forceful illegal action against white rulers be prohibited by this portion of the treaty? Would propaganda for war among the African nations to force South Africa to change its *apartheid* policies fall within this type of ban?

Neither the OAS treaty nor the UN convention make provision for professional secrecy which is protected by the European convention.[196] Apparently, in Europe it is believed that the press should have adequate sources of information, and that a journalist may not be called upon, even in the public interest, to disclose the source of information which he has received in confidence. In many jurisdictions of the United States refusal to reveal sources to the court can amount to contempt, if there is a proven compelling interest for such information.

The American treaty includes provisions guaranteeing to a person defamed in the press or other media the right to have a correction or reply published in the same medium.[197] This right is not included in the UN instrument, probably because the UN Convention on the International Right of Correction [198] covers this.

j. Assembly

The right of peaceful assembly is recognized by both documents [199] and both contain the extensive qualifying clause that this right may be restrict-

[193] *Id.* art. 13, para. 5.

[194] U.N. Convention, art. 20.

[195] Dennis v. U.S., 341 U.S. 494 (1951). *But see* Beauharnais v. Illinois, 343 U.S. 250 (1952).

[196] *See* note 189 and accompanying text, *supra.*

[197] O.A.S. Convention, art. 14.

[198] Convention on the International Right of Correction, G.A. Res. 630, – U.N. GAOR Supp. 20, at 22, U.N. Doc. A/2361 (1959).

[199] O.A.S. Convention, art. 15; U.N. Convention, art. 21.

ed by the police power of the state. This ban is so broad that any government restraint of the right of assembly would naturally base it upon the exception. In dictatoral situations, the right could well be meaningless.

A different emphasis is placed on the right of association guaranteed by the United Nations. The UN declares that everyone shall have the right of freedom of association with others, including the right to form and join trade unions. The OAS states that everyone has the right to associate freely for ideological, religious, political, economic, labor, social, cultural, sports, or other purposes.[200] Inasmuch as some Latin American nations ban the communist party, and Argentina bans all political activities and associations, this might well be a stumbling block toward the adoption of the Pact of San José. However, both treaties add the broad limitation that the police powers may be used to proscribe this right, and it can always be argued that the right of association has been restricted in the interest of national security, public safety, or public order.

Both treaties stipulate that imposition of legal restrictions, including total deprivation of the right of association, may be placed on members of the armed forces and the police.[201] With law enforcement officers demanding the right to organize, this additional restriction may lead to strong internal opposition in some areas.

k. Family Law

Despite certain sociological claims that the family is an anachronism, and that the commune is the wave of the future, it is somewhat reassuring to find that both treaties categorically state: "The family is the natural and fundamental group unit of society and is entitled to protection by society and the state." [202]

Both treaties recognize the right of men and women of marriageable age to marry and to raise a family,[203] but the OAS convention adds the qualification: "If they meet the conditions required by domestic laws insofar as such conditions do not affect the principle of non-discrimination established in this Convention."

Under this wording, could modern homosexuals claim that denial of their right to marry one another is discriminatory, and hence illegal? Would this be upheld under the OAS treaty?

While the UN covenant states that parties to the treaty shall take "ap-

[200] O.A.S. Convention, art. 16; U.N. Convention, art. 22.
[201] O.A.S. Convention, art. 16; para. 3; U.N. Convention, art. 22.
[202] O.A.S. Convention, art. 17; U.N. Convention, art. 23.
[203] O.A.S. Convention, art. 17, para. 2; U.N. Convention, art. 23, para. 2.

propriate steps to ensure equality of rights and responsibilities of the spouses,"[204] the OAS treaty is more cautiously worded: "to ensure the equality of rights and *the adequate balancing of* responsibilities of the spouses . . ."[205] This reflects the Latin American attitude that marriage, under most Latin American legal systems, is based upon the principle of family authority resting with the husband, especially in connection with property rights. Marriage establishes a community of property between husband and wife, but it is the duty of the husband to administer this community.

In addition to spousal rights, the OAS treaty goes far beyond the universal treaty and even beyond the internal law of many western hemispheric nations when it declares that the law shall recognize equal rights for children born out of wedlock.[206]

Both treaties stipulate that a child shall have the right to a name, and to such protection as is required, from his family, society, and the state.[207] In setting forth these rights, the treaties are necessarily vague in identifying those who are responsible for assuring that the child's rights are observed.

Treatment of the right to nationality is more detailed in the OAS treaty[208] than in the UN convention, which states merely that every child has the "right to acquire a nationality."[209] The OAS instrument separates the rights of the child from the rights of nationality, by declaring that every *person* has the right to a nationality, and if he does not have a right to any other nationality, he must be given the nationality of the state in whose territory he was born. Further, no one shall be arbitrarily deprived of his nationality or of the right to change it.[210] Again, "arbitrarily" is not defined and this could lead to questioning. For example, in the *Nottebohm* case,[211] many authorities believed the International Court of Justice "arbitrarily" deprived Nottebohm of his right to change his nationality.[212]

[204] U.N. Convention, art. 23, para. 4.
[205] O.A.S. Convention, art. 17, para. 4. (emphasis added).
[206] *Id.* art. 17, para. 5.
[207] O.A.S. Convention, arts. 18, 19; U.N. Convention, art. 24.
[208] O.A.S. Convention, art. 20.
[209] U.N. Convention, art. 24, para. 3.
[210] O.A.S. Convention, art. 20.
[211] Nottebohm Case, [1955] I.C.J. 4.
[212] H. F. van Panhuys, The Role of Nationality in International Law (1959); de Visscher, *L'Affaire Nottebohm,* 60 Revue Générale de Droit International Public 238 (1956); Glazer, *Affaire Nottebohm-A Critique,* 44 Georgetown Law J. 313 (1955-56); Jones, *The Nottebohm Case,* 5 Int. and Comp. Law Quarterly 230 (1956), Loewenfield, *Der Fall Nottebohm* 5 Archiv des Völkerrechts 387 (1956).

l. Property

One right completely omitted in the universal convention is the right to property. Some societies recognize no private property rights, and others view foreign ownership of property within the nation as the result of an imposed system of exploitation.

Except for Cuba, all nations of the western hemisphere are operating under a controlled private property system, and consequently, it was thought important to include in the Pact that everyone has the right to use and enjoy his property.[213] This right is not an absolute one. The treaty not only stipulates that such use and enjoyment may be subordinated to the interests of society, but that a person may be deprived of his property for reasons of public utility or social interest, according to the forms established by law. Considering the long battle between the United States and Latin America concerning international accountability in the taking of property of aliens, it is surprising to see in the treaty that just compensation must be paid for the deprivation of property. But the OAS treaty does not go as far as the European Convention on Human Rights which provides that "no one shall be deprived of his possessions except in the public interest and subject to the conditions provided for by law and by the general principles of international law.[214] The reference to general principles of international law was made to emphasize that regardless of the attitude of a government toward property rights of its own citizens, foreign owners whose property was taken for a public purpose were entitled to just, adequate, and prompt compensation.

The OAS treaty also prohibits "usury and any other form of exploitation of man by man . . ." [215] The nature of usury varies from jurisdiction to jurisdiction, and no attempt was made to pinpoint the amount of interest considered to be usury. Nor is there a clear indication of other forms of exploitation. No government signing the treaty can be sure of the commitment it is making under this provision and the nature of implementing measures needed to fulfill it.

m. Travel

Both treaties establish a right of freedom of movement within a state, the right to leave any country freely, and the right to re-enter one's own coun-

[213] O.A.S. Convention, art. 21.

[214] European Convention for the Protection of Human Rights and Fundamental Freedoms art. 1 (Protocol No. 1, March 20, 1952).

[215] O.A.S. Convention, art. 21, para. 3.

try.[216] But these rights are again curtailed by that extensive exception relating to "prevention of crime, protection of national security, public safety, public order, public morals, public health or the rights or freedoms of others." These rights, too, can mean as much or as little as the ratifying state wishes them to mean.

The drafters of the OAS treaty are short of memory or poor historians, for it seems impossible to rationalize in a Latin American context, the stipulation that "no one can be expelled from the territory of the state of which he is a national.[217] After two incomprehensible decisions by the International Court of Justice in the Haya de La Torre asylum issue between Peru and Columbia,[218] the honor of both nations was preserved by the ingenious device of "expelling" Peruvian Haya de La Torre from Peruvian territory rather than granting him the customary safe conduct out of the country. Constitutional grants of power in certain Latin American constitutions permit expulsion or removal from the country.[219]

The treaties stipulate that aliens lawfully in the territory of a treaty member state may be expelled only pursuant to a decision reached in accordance with law. The UN treaty adds that except where compelling interests of national security control, aliens may have a full review of expulsion decisions by competent authorities.[220] The OAS treaty declares that "collective expulsion of aliens is prohibited." [221] Query: does this apply only to aliens unlawfully within a nation? One of the causes of the so-called "soccer war" [222] between Honduras and El Salvador was the collective expulsion of Salvadorans who had illegally squatted in Honduras. Does the adjective "collective" refer to *all* aliens from a certain nation, to all aliens, to a number of aliens, or to a group of aliens from a certain nation? Is

[216] O.A.S. Convention, art. 22; U.N. Convention art. 12.

[217] O.A.S. Convention, art. 22, para. 5.

[218] Colombian-Peruvian Asylum Cases, [1950] I.C.J. 266; [1951] I.C.J. 71; A. V. W. Thomas, A. J. Thomas, Jr., Non-Intervention: The Law and Its Import in the Americas 393-398 (1956).

[219] Peru Const. art. 68 provides:

> No one may be banished from the territory of the Republic, nor removed from his place of residence, except by a writ of sentence or by application of the aliens law.

See also Argentina Const. art. 23 which provides:

> But during such suspension the President of the Republic shall not convict or apply punishment upon his own authority. His power shall be limited, in such a case, with respect to persons, to arresting them, or transferring them from one point of the Nation to another, if they do not prefer to leave Argentine Territory.

[220] O.A.S. Convention, art. 22, para. 6; UN Convention, art. 13.

[221] O.A.S. Convention, art. 22, para. 9.

[222] Fenwick, *Honduras-El Salvador, Procedures under Rio Treaty of Reciprocal Assistance,* 63 Am. J. Int'l L. 769 (1969).

the weekly round-up of wet-backs in the West and Southwestern part of the United States a collective expulsion of aliens?

The OAS treaty is additionally careful of the rights of aliens when it stipulates that an alien may not be deported or returned to any country if in that country his right to life or personal freedom is in danger "because of his race, nationality, religion, social status, or political opinions." [223]

Another aspect of freedom of movement mentioned only in the OAS treaty is that relating to the right of territorial asylum in foreign nations for "political offenses or related common crimes," [224] During the San José conference, El Salvador suggested that "political offenses" should be defined in the treaty as:

> "infractions against the organization or function of the state and against the political rights of citizens. The concept of political offense shall not be considered to include a crime that gives rise to a state of terror, an attempt on the life of a chief of state, or a crime inspired by base motives." [225]

Other nations objected to the particular definition and to the inclusion in the treaty of a precise definition of political offenses, since the Inter-American Juridical Committee had prepared a study of political offenses in 1959 which had not been acted upon by the OAS [226] As a compromise, the conference requested the Council of the OAS to recommend to the Inter-American Commission on Human Rights that it prepare a study on political offenses. The commission was to consider the 1959 study, the draft presented by El Salvador, and the discussions that ensued at San José. The human rights commission was to submit its findings to a specialized conference for review and consideration.[227] Although this was probably the easiest way to skirt the issue, the exact nature of a political offense remains blurred. One might argue that, without adequate definition, it is possible to assert that war crimes, genocide, and crimes against the peace must fall within the category of "political offenses."

n. Political Activity

Except for certain restrictions in the inter-American treaty, both instruments have basically the same provision relating to the right to participate in government: every citizen has a right to take part in the conduct of public

[223] O.A.S. Convention, art. 22, para. 8.

[224] *Id.* art. 22, para. 7.

[225] O.A.S. Inter-American Specialized Conference on Human Rights, Final Act 5-7 (OEA/Ser.K/SVI/I.1 (English) doc. 70, rev. 1, corr. 1, 7, 1970).

[226] *Id.* at 6.

[227] *Id.* at 7.

affairs, directly or through freely chosen representatives; to vote and to be elected in genuine periodical elections which by secret ballot guarantee the free expression of the will of the voters; and to have access, under general conditions of equality, to public service.[228] Since single party totalitarian nations which outlaw political opposition, such as Russia and Spain, have raised no objection to these stipulations, it might well be questioned whether the phrases "freely chosen representatives," "secret ballot," and "free expression of the will of the voter" are unequivocal legal terms on the international level. In addition, this section does not measure up to the 1959 Declaration of Santiago [229] which particularly emphasized that perpetuation in power, or the exercise of power without a fixed term and with the manifest intention of perpetuation, is incompatible with the exercise of democracy in the Americas.

The restrictions on participation in government established by the inter-American threaty are those based on age, nationality, residence, language, education, civil and mental capacity, and sentencing by a competent court in criminal proceedings.[230] Age and civil or mental incapacity, standard disqualifications in most nations, probable would create little furor on the international level. But the issue of nationality contains possible elements of denial of human rights. If resident aliens can never obtain nationality, their right to eventual participation in government is foreclosed. Language and education could also raise some very fundamental human rights issues. For example, a good percentage of the Indian population of Guatemala does not speak Spanish. If the Guatemalan government requires knowledge of Spanish for voter qualification, these Indians are effectively disenfranchised. And the educational qualification is exceptionally broad – obviously more must be meant than complete illiteracy, or the word "education" would not have been used. Does it imply that a nation can set definite educational requirements for voting? For example, "no one may vote without eight years of school attendance." If so, this qualification could disenfranchise a large segment of the potential voting population of the hemisphere.

2. *Implementation*

Since a number of the Western Hemisphere nations have a federal form of government, as opposed to a unitary form, the OAS treaty declares that

[228] O.A.S. Convention, art. 23; U.N. Convention, art. 25.

[229] A.V.W. Thomas – A. J. Thomas Jr., The Organization of American States, 230-31 (1963).

[230] O.A.S. Convention, art. 23, para. 2.

in such states, the national government shall implement all the provisions of the convention over whose subject matter it exercises legislative and judicial jurisdiction. In accordance with its constitution and laws, the national government shall cooperate with its constituent units which in turn "may" adopt appropriate provisions for the fulfillment of the convention.[231] No such attempts at adjustment between federal-state relations appear in the UN convention, which flatly states the provisions of the treaty "shall extend to all parts of federal states without any limitations or exceptions." [232]

Under the guise of restrictions regarding the interpretation of the treaty, a very broad concept crept into the OAS treaty. There it is stated that no provision of the treaty shall be interpreted as permitting any "State Party, group or persons" to suppress the enjoyment or exercise of the rights and freedoms recognized in the convention.[233] Inasmuch as the treaty deals with the obligations of governments to persons within their jurisdiction and the rights of human persons as against the state, this appears to be a vast extension of the treaty to non-governmental groups and persons. If a non-governmental group or person not acting under color of law, denied one of the rights established in the treaty, would the nation be held responsible? If a newspaper editor refused to print a letter – no matter how innocuous – is he not denying to the writer freedom to express ideas in print, and thus violating freedom of expression? If a church refuses the use of its pulpit to an atheist is it not denying freedom to profess one's belief in public or in private? If a fraternal organization is selective in its membership, it is denying the right of everyone to associate freely for social or other purposes? What of a wife abusively interfering with her husband's extra-marital private life; would she be violating the treaty guarantee that no one may be the object of abusive interference with his private life?

3. Duties

The American Declaration on the Rights and Duties of Man adopted at Bogotá in 1948 concerned itself not only with the rights of individuals, but also with the duties that each individual owed to the society in which he lived. The long list of duties placed in that declaration was questioned because the theory of international protection of human rights is that the in-

[231] *Id.* art. 28.
[232] U.N. Convention, art. 50.
[233] O.A.S. Convention, art. 29.

dividual can be overwhelmed by the massive collective force of the state.[234] Consequently, in the American Convention on Human Rights is a simple statement that every person has responsibilities to his family, his community, and mankind.[235]

In 1966, the UN divided the protection of human rights into two distinct spheres by adopting the Covenant on Economic, Social and Cultural Rights, and the Covenant on Civil and Political Rights. In view of this action, the Inter-American Commission on Human Rights had suggested in 1966 that the proposed treaty should not include articles establishing binding legal obligations in the economic, cultural, and social fields. The commission had serious doubts about the appropriateness of including those rights in the future inter-American convention.[236] Instead, it suggested that the proposed convention contain a broad provision relating only to the "progressive development" of economic, social, and cultural rights in the hemisphere. This suggestion was adopted and the American treaty stipulates that the ratifying nations will undertake to adopt measures, both internally and through international cooperation with a view to achieving progressively the full realization of the rights implicit in the economic, social, educational, scientific, and cultural standards set forth in the Charter of the OAS, as amended by the Protocol of Buenos Aires.[237]

THE INTER-AMERICAN COURT OF HUMAN RIGHTS

With the growing emphasis on human rights following World War II, the inter-American system recognized that if such rights were to be protected adequately there was a need for international machinery to enforce international guarantees. The Ninth Conference in 1948 resolved that the Inter-American Council of Jurists and its permanent committee, the Inter-American Juridical Committee, should give thought to a treaty providing for an "Inter-American Court to Protect the Rights of Man." After an investigation, the Juridical Committee reported that it was not feasible to create such a court because of the lack of substantive law on human rights and because the establishment of such a court would involve a radical transformation of the constitutional systems of some of the American

[234] *See* note 22, *supra*.
[235] O.A.S. Convention, art. 32.
[236] O.A.S., Inter-American Convention on the Protection of Human Rights, Annotations 35 (OEA/Ser.L/V (English) II. 19. doc. 53, Mar. 21, 1969).
[237] O.A.S. Convention, art. 26.

states. This report was accepted and approved by the Council of Jurists and by the Council of the OAS.[238]

There the matter rested until the Fifth Meeting of Consultation in Santiago in 1959. Human rights again surfaced as a vital issue of inter-American affairs. To assure that the human rights activities of the OAS would not remain compromised at the lowest level of controversial principles – mere statements of rights without legal effect or effective implementation – some measure of enforcement was needed. The Fifth Meeting established the Inter-American Commission on Human Rights and issued orders to the Inter-American Council of Jurists to prepare draft conventions on human rights. The conventions were to include not only the human rights commission but also another supra-national mechanism to guarantee those rights – an Inter-American Court of Human Rights.[239]

This dual means of protection is continued in the present American Convention on Human Rights.

The commission on human rights is not a tribunal; its main functions are fact finding and seeking compromise. If the commission is unable to bring about a settlement, the new treaty establishes judicial machinery for implementation of the treaty, thereby attempting to remove human rights issues one step farther from the political arena and place them under the jurisdiction of an independent juridical organ. The court is to consist of seven judges elected in an individual capacity from among jurists of the highest moral authority and of recognized competence in the field of human rights.[240] The European Convention for the Protection of Human Rights and Fundamental Freedoms made no reference to possible conflict of interests between the judge's position in his home state and his position as an independent international jurist. In Europe, this oversight had to be remedied in the court's rules of procedure. No judge may be a member of a government or hold a post or practice a profession which is likely to affect public trust in his independent adjucation.[241] With this precedent, the American treaty carefully stipulated that the position of judge of the court is incompatible with any other activity that might affect the court's independence or impartiality.[242]

The judges of the court are never to be held liable for any decisions or

[238] Thomas & Thomas, *supra* note 229, at 227, 232-33, 400-401.

[239] P.A.U., Fifth Meeting of Consultation of Ministers of Foreign Affairs, *Santiago, Chile, Aug., 1959* (OEA/Ser.C/II.5).

[240] O.A.S. Convention, ch. 8.

[241] A. L. del Russo, International Protection of Human Rights 107 (1971).

[242] O.A.S. Convention, art. 71.

[243] *Id.* art. 70, para. 2.

opinions issued in the exercise of their functions.[243] Nonetheless, the treaty recognizes human frailty involving misfeasance or malfeasance in office by a judge or a member of the commission. The General Assembly of the OAS, at the request of the commission or the court, may determine sanctions against members of the commission or judges of the court when there are justifiable grounds for such action. A two-thirds majority vote of the member states of the OAS shall be required for a decision in the case of members of the commission. In the case of judges of the court, a two-thirds majority vote of the ratifying states is required.[244]

The judges of the court are to receive diplomatic immunities and diplomatic privileges and are to be paid a salary and provided with travel allowances.[245] These financial arrangements are to be determined in the budget of the OAS, which also shall include the expense of the court and its secretariat. The court is to draw up its own budget which must be submitted to the General Assembly for approval.[246]

No two judges may be nationals of the same state.[247] They are to be elected by ratifying states via a majority vote on a secret ballot. Each ratifying state may nominate three candidates, at least one of the three a national of another state.[248] Judges are to be elected for six years with the possibility of re-election for an additional six year term. A judge who is a national of a state involved in a case before the court retains his right to hear the case. Presumably, if he has a personal interest in the case or has previously acted as counsel, prosecuting attorney, or judge in the case, judicial ethics would dictate his withdrawal, although the treaty makes no such stipulation. If another state is involved in the case, it may appoint a person to serve on the court as an *ad hoc* judge. If among the judges there are no nationals of the state or states involved in a case, each state may appoint an *ad hoc* judge. Five judges constitute a quorum for transaction of the business of the court.[249]

The court is given the power to appoint its own secretary, establish its secretariat, draw up its statute to be submitted to the General Assembly for approval, and adopt its own rules of procedure.[250]

Under the heading of "Jurisdiction and Functions," [251] the court's juris-

[244] *Id.* art. 73.
[245] *Id.* art. 70, para. 1; art. 72.
[246] *Id.* art. 72.
[247] *Id.* art. 52, para. 2.
[248] *Id.* art. 53.
[249] *Id.* art. 55.
[250] *Id.* arts. 58, 59, 60.
[251] *Id.* ch. 8, § 2.

diction is limited to member states which have recognized the jurisdiction of the court as binding, *ipso facto,* on all matters relating to the interpretation or application of the convention. Such recognition may be made unconditionally, on the condition of reciprocity, for a specific period, or for a specific case.

The court also has a consultative function. Any organ of the OAS as well as any member state of the OAS (thus it is not limited to signatories of the convention) may request from the court an interpretation of the American convention or any other convention concerning the protection of human rights in the American states. This would include an interpretation of the UN covenants. A member of the OAS may also request an opinion of the court regarding the compatibility of any of its domestic laws with these international instruments.

Would such consultation fall within the concept of "jurisdiction" of the court? The jurisdictional clause declares that ratifying states will accept as binding all decisions relating to the interpretation of the convention. Yet, the treaty clearly states that the court's jurisdiction covers only states party to the convention which have acceped the court's jurisdiction. If it is argued that this consultation is merely a "function" of the court and cannot be considered jurisdictional because there is no case or controversy, the logical conclusion must be that the opinion of the court in either case must be completely non-binding on members and non-members alike. It would be contrary to international law to demand that non-ratifying states be bound by an advisory opinion; nor could the court require that the United Nations accept its interpretation of the international covenants on human rights. Only when treaty interpretation falls within the context of a case or controversy would ratifying states be bound by the Court's interpretation.

In the European Convention for the Protection of Human Rights and Fundamental Freedoms, the court established is given no consultative power.[252] Therefore, questions of treaty interpretation are always binding on the accepting parties for they must arise in the context of the court's jurisdiction.

Unlike the European treaty, the OAS treaty contains no provision stating that a dispute as to whether the court has jurisdiction shall be settled by the decision of the court.[253] In view of the role of questions relating

[252] Although Protocol No. 2, opened for signature on May 6, 1963, would amend the treaty by permitting the European Court the right to render advisory opinions at the request of the Committee of Ministers on the interpretation of treaties, insufficient ratifications have been deposited to bring this into being.

to the court's jurisdiction in cases before the International Court of Justice, such an omission is incomprehensible.

After a state has accepted the court's jurisdiction, there must be submission of the dispute to the court either by the state or states involved or by the commission on human rights and an exhaustion of the proceedings before the commission as outlined in the treaty.[254] The convention denies the individual petitioner direct access to the court; consequently, the court's decision making power is in the nature of appellate jurisdiction. The commission must first have investigated the merits of the case, made a preliminary adjudication as to the admissibility of the complaint, attempted, but failed to bring about a friendly settlement, and have drawn up a report of the commission's conclusions, proposals, and recommendations. Even if all of these prerequisites are fulfilled, apparently it is still within the commission's discretionary power to decide whether it will refer a case to the court. In this manner, the convention attempts to rebalance claims relating to the traditional sovereignty of nations against individual claims that sovereign nations are violating internationally protected human rights.

The European convention provides an alternative to judicial settlement by the European court.[255] If the case is not referred to the court, the Committee of Ministers, the highest executive and the inter-governmental organ of the Council of Europe, is given a right by two-thirds vote to determine whether or not a violation of the treaty has occurred. If it finds that a state has violated the treaty, it shall prescribe a period of time during which the defendant state must take corrective measures.[256] This additional procedure was put into the convention because it was recognized that states might well ratify the convention but refuse to recognize the jurisdiction of the court. Disputes found admissible by the European Commission on Human Rights thus could reach a final decision through the Committee of Ministers.

The American treaty copies the European convention in that it requires the regional commission on human rights to appear in all cases before the court.[257] This method was adopted in the European convention as a compromise between those who advocated and those who were opposed to direct access to the court by an individual. Although neither treaty clarifies the commission's exact role here, obviously the commission cannot

[253] European Convention for the Protection of Human Rights and Fundamental Freedoms, art. 49.

[254] O.A.S. Convention, art. 61.

[255] European Convention for the Protection of Human Rights and Fundamental Freedoms, art. 32.

[256] *Id.* art. 32, paras. 1, 2.

[257] O.A.S. Convention, art. 57.

be considered a party to the dispute. The commission suffered no injury; it was the individual concerned who was injured by state action or inaction.

It would be violative of correct judicial procedure to designate the commission as a party to the suit, because much of the evidence before the court will be contained in the report of the commission based on its preliminary proceedings which are quasi-judicial and arbitral in nature. The role of the European commission before the European court was explained in the pleadings and in the decision on preliminary objections in the *Lawless* case. In the Pleading, it was stated:

"The Commission does not pursue any interest of its own but the public interest ... in the maintenance of Human Rights and freedoms. The Commission is in no sense an antagonist of the States against which complaints are made before it. The Commission was intended to, and does act in all matters with complete impartiality, favouring neither the State nor the individual complaining against the State ... [T]he Commission, although not a party to the case, participates in the proceedings and stands in position intermediate between Government and the individual ... [W]hen it refers a case to the Court, it does so in order that the Court may give a decision as to whether or not the Convention has been violated. The Commission will, it is true, have expressed an opinion on that point ... [b]ut that opinion has the character not of a legal decision, but of an expert opinion to provide the basis for a legally binding decision ... by the Court. The function of the Commission before the Court ... is not litigious – it is ministerial." [258]

In its decision of November 14, 1960, the European court agreed that individuals are vicariously represented before the court by the commission. As a defender of public interests, the commission's main function is to assist the court by placing before it all of the elements of the case.[259] This practice is familiar through the common law concept of *amicus curiae.*

The court is required to give reasons for its judgment and judges may issue concurring or dissenting opinions.[260] If the court finds there was a breach of the convention, it shall then rule that the victim of the violation be restored to his rights by the responded state and, if appropriate, that he be paid a fair compensation for the denial of his rights. These compensatory damages may be executed in the country concerned in accor-

[258] *Lawless* Case, Hearing of Oct. 4, 1960 (Pleading, Oral Arguments, Documents) European Court of Human Rights, pp. 245, 261 (1960-61).

[259] *Lawless* Case, Judgment of Nov. 14, 1960 (Preliminary objections and questions of procedure) European Court of Human Rights, pp. 11-16 (1960-61).

[260] O.A.S. Convention, art. 66.

dance with domestic procedure governing the execution of judgments against the state.[261]

In case of a disagreement as to the meaning or scope of the court's judgment, a party may within ninety days following the judgment request an interpretation, and the court is required to hand down such an interpretation. With this exception, the judgment of the court is final and not subject to appeal.[262]

The treaty declares that "parties to the case shall be notified of the judgment of the court." [263] A person complaining of violation of his human rights obviously has the greatest interest in the case's outcome, yet is he a "party to the case?" He is not entitled to bring the case before the court and must be vicariously represented by the commission. Until the court comes into being, there is no way of determining whether he may appear before the court if the commission believes that it would be beneficial. Nor is there any indication in the treaty that he may, after the commission has brought the case to the court, make submission through an attorney of his own choice.

A major weakness in the OAS treaty is its failure to include measures for implementing the court's decision. Even though nations may agree to abide by all future judicial decisions, when the moment of truth arrives it is not unknown in the international sphere that judicial decisions are ignored. The OAS treaty provides no mandatory sanctions for the explicit purpose of enforcing the court's judgment. Coercive community measures could be used only if the failure to fulfill the judgment is such that the majority of the nations of the OAS feel it falls within the Rio Treaty's provision relating to a fact or situation that might endanger the peace of the Americas. But, even then, member-states may fail to implement such OAS decisions or fail to do so fully. Even with a judicial determination of a denial of human rights, there is no assurance that the injured party will receive reparation or that the guilty state will cease and desist.

As soon as eleven states have deposited their instruments of ratification or adherence, the Inter-American Convention shall come into force. States ratifying may not denounce the treaty for five years; thereafter, upon a year's notice in advance, the state may indicate it will no longer be bound by the instrument. The treaty points out that such denunciation will not

[261] *Id.* art. 68, para. 2.
[262] *Id.* art. 67.
[263] *Id.* art. 69.

release the state from treaty obligations with respect to any violation that took place prior to the effective date of denunciation.[264]

CONCLUSION

When it is realized that listed among the non-signatories of the American Convention on Human Rights are such states as Argentina, Brazil, Mexico, Peru, and the United States – the largest and most powerful nations in the hemisphere – the outlook for acceptance of a binding international obligation by all members of the OAS to respect human rights seems rather bleak. And even though twelve nations did sign the Pact of San José, one cannot be sanguine about a quick collection of the eleven ratifications required to bring the treaty into force.

Some will be reluctant to ratify the convention because they fear the issue of human rights may become a tool of power politics. When political animosity exists between governments, attacks based on the high plane of alleged denial of human rights have considerable propaganda effect which is often hard to overcome. On the other side of the coin, a government may wish to close its eyes to gross repressions of human rights by other nations for reasons of political expediency, particularly if such repressions occur within the territory of friendly powers.

The signing of the convention may, on the part of some, have been a cynical thing, prompted by the recognition that the propaganda effect emanating from being on the side of the angels – in the front line battling for human rights – comes at the time of signing the treaty, not at some later ratification date.

A signatory of a human rights convention may be vocal in support of the need for international protection of human rights in neighboring states. But these same nations when faced with the realization that ratification will make the proclaimed human rights available to their own citizens via international action within their own boundaries, quickly revert to that most powerful emotional appeal in the Americas, the ban on non-intervention in internal and external affairs. Ratification is thus forgotten.

An introspective study of the magnitude of human rights problems within a country may bring reluctance on the part of that country's rulers to ratify what has been signed because knowledge that their human rights problems are so interwoven into the country's political and social patterns bring with it knowledge that any solution of these problems can be obtained

[264] *Id.* art. 78.

only by a revolutionary shake up in the existing power structure. Ratification would then be the equivalent to signing one's own death warrant – something most ruling elites are reluctant to do.

Moreover, some nations of this hemisphere have experienced disruptive encounters with broad grants of civil and political rights, and the leaders have become wary. In the present stage of their political and economic development, the scales of wisdom tip in favor of internal order and peace as against extensive popular participation in the political process as demanded by the OAS human rights treaty.

Realistic statesmen find – with a tinge of regret perhaps – that on the whole, citizens of one nation are not vitally interested in the human rights problems of other nations. Only where there is a very intensive and concerted effort to arouse the populace on behalf of repressed foreigners do international human rights issues ever become imperative issues in internal affairs. Faced with such apathy, most statesmen prefer to let sleeping dogs lie.

In spite of this pessimistic outlook, one should not be completely disheartened. It may take decades before a binding agreement is widely accepted throughout the hemisphere, but the fact that the rights have been agreed upon in principle must radiate some pressure on all American governments to indulge in self-analysis. And self-analysis may bring about improvement in human rights endeavors internally.

The brightest spot in the hemispheric human rights picture is undoubtedly the American Commission on Human Rights. Its members have shown a dedication far beyond the call of duty. Their impartiality and independence is unquestioned. They have combined the innovative rationalizing legal skills of a John Marshall, the personal courage of a Simon Bolivar and the high integrity and far-sightedness of a Dom Pedro Segundo. They are undeterred by the recognition that the attainment of a reasonable protection of major human rights in every hemispheric nation is probably unachievable in their lifetime. In their unending prodding, pleading, and persuading, they may not have immediate success, but they are sowing for the future. They are creating throughout the hemisphere – particularly among its youth – an awareness of the dangers inherent in continual denial of human rights.

As this awareness spreads within the borders of each of the American nations, it may in the long run be the most productive protector of human rights. For, as has so often been reiterated, human rights protection at the international level can never be as effective as the insistent and widespread demands of citizens domestically that governmental oppression must be ended.

COMMENTARY

by

C. NEALE RONNING

With respect to the first part of the paper, it seems to me that precedents and legal instruments do exist for the taking of action of one type or another for the support of respect for human rights. And it would seem to me that even the rationale of the *fait accompli* or the self-exclusion rationale applied to Cuba might, without too large a step, be applied in the case of human rights as well; at least without a step larger than the step of the self-exclusion rationale as applied to Cuba represented vis-à-vis previous practice in the field. What seems to me more important, however, is the matter of political motivation in case of action with respect to human rights. And without being too cynical I think one could perhaps say that when the political motivation has been sufficiently strong, the legal instruments have been found, and I suppose they will be found in the future. This is particularly true, I think, in the case of the political organs of the OAS and, in particular, the meetings of consultation of the ministers of foreign affairs. And here, it seems to me, the motivation for taking action has, in one way or another, been related to the political respectability or acceptability of the state against whom charges are made.

Thus, in the Cuban Case the strongly anti-Communist attitude of the great majority of the governments certainly put Cuba at the top of the list insofar as political unrespectability of unacceptability was concerned. There was concern, nevertheless, among a number of states who later went along with the action. Or, perhaps, action, as the authors have pointed out, isn't really the corect word here, but certainly concern was shown on their part with regard to setting a precedent. Perhaps one could say here that the political unrespectability of Cuba at this time outweighed the dangers of setting precedents for the future. Now it is true that an attempt was made previous to this with respect to the Dominican Republic, which obviously was not a Communist state, but one might say here that the record of the Trujillo regime was so outrageous it could hardly be ignored and in any event, the attempt failed at this particular time. In a second round in the Dominican Republic and particularly with respect to the Inter-American peace force, this certainly was related to the future, or to the expected political or possible political respectability of a future regime, and the concern lest another Castro come to power somehow in the Dominican Republic was related, I think, to action taken there.

Looking at the record of the Inter-American Commission on Human Rights, one might suspect that the diligence with which the Commission pursues its investigation is not entirely unrelated to some of the same things, though here I would prefer to put this in the form of a question, rather than an observation, because the record is not nearly as clear. Again, it would seem that the diligence with which they have pursued certain investigations might have been related to two things: firstly, the political respectability of the regime; and secondly, the power of the state involved. Thus, again, in terms of political unrespectability, Cuba goes to the top of the list. And although Cuba didn't cooperate with the Commission (the Commission as I recall moved its headquarters to Miami and interviewed political refugees), it pursued the question very painstakingly in this case, and came up with two rather large reports, maybe more. The second most diligent manifestation of their activity was the case of Haiti and again you have a regime which by all means is not Communist but again its actions have been so outrageous that it would be very difficult to ignore it. Also, Haiti, like Cuba, fills the second qualification, the size of the regime – neither one is a very powerful state. The other investigations, which have included more than merely taking a note of what has happened, have been Guatemala, Nicaragua, the Dominican Republic, Ecuador, and Paraguay. Once more you have here, of course, small states. There have been complaints against Brazil, and reports coming all the way from bishops to the police themselves in Brazil would seem to indicate that the complaints are not entirely without foundation. The Commission, it would seem to me, has shown less diligence in these cases. There have also been complaints, as I recall, about the United States. These, of course, are very powerful regimes.

Now I am not saying this in the sence of disparaging the Commission of whose work I would make much the same evaluation as the Professors Thomas. But the importance of political factors cannot be ignored. The precedence of the legal instruments which have been outlined very well here seems to me might indeed be important in the future – more important than we think. It is not at all impossible, or even improbable, that in the future, the concept of political respectability or acceptability might very well change within the hemisphere. It is not impossible, even though it might be somewhat improbable in the immediate future, that a number of very nationalist and, if not revolutionary, at least vigorously reformist, regimes might appear and even survive for a while in the hemisphere. And it is also possible, that a coalition of such states and perhaps even a socialist state or two, joining them, would not find anti-communism very important in the test of political respectability of states and, therefore, whether or not one takes decisive action against them. They might find instead the nationalist and socialist objectives of a government more important in determining whether or not a regime is politically acceptable or desirable within the hemisphere. Now, such a coalition might not be sufficiently numerous and in all probability would not be sufficiently powerful to take any action, but it is not impossible that the number could prevent any action in the future. I would not assume that any coalition of this sort would be less politically motivated than governments which have voted for action in the past or that they would be less willing to go ahead without precedents than nations have in the past. But precedents are always useful and if you can throw them in as another argument, so much better!

One other thing that interested me was the comprehensiveness and even impressiveness of the catalogue of human rights in the hemisphere in the second part of the paper.

It is easy enough to dismiss these as idealistic documents; but I see them as more than simply that and as much more of an indication or an index of expectations within the hemisphere. They are a measure of the gap between exceptations and reality. Now, if we added to this, and went into more detail on, a number of human rights in the social and economic field, which have generally been stated much more vaguely than many of those in the political and juridical field, the gap would appear even larger, or would still, obviously, remain very large. Now, it is certainly this gap between expectations on the one hand and reality on the other that is at the bottom of a great deal of the civil strife which is occuring within the hemisphere. This represents nothing new within the hemisphere, but it is certainly on the increase all the way from the Canadian border to the southern tip of South America. (Well, I suppose Canada herself has not been free of it.)

Civil strife and the increase and bitterness of it suggests another area perhaps for consideration and concern in the area of human rights and an area that is sometimes called humanitarian laws or, in other words, attempts to ensure human rights in time of civil strife. It is interesting to note that it was in the Western Hemisphere that much pioneering activity took place in this field, in such things as codification of practices of diplomatic asylum and territorial asylum, in order to offer some measure of protection of people who had been involved, in one way or another, in the bitterness of civil strife. It is also interesting to note that in this hemisphere the matter has not really been given very much attention recently. But attempts to apply rules of war to civil strife, which have been considered by the various organs of the United Nations, seem to have been forgotten in the Western Hemisphere. The most recent conference held on the topic in Washington seemed to be concerned more with how to deal with certain extremist forms of activity during civil strife and how to prevent them than how to live humanly, if possible, with the continuing aspect of civil disorder. And, again, without disparaging the value of work on documents on human rights which implicitly are taken to apply in normal times, it may be that we are reaching a point of diminishing returns in improving and synthesizing such documents on human rights, continuing partly because we have gone a long way on it, and partly because we may not expect very much. But perhaps there may not be very many normal times, at least for a while. And one area of needed activity in the general field of human rights might very well be this problem of applying humane laws in times of civil strife or civil war.

GPSR Compliance

The European Union's (EU) General Product Safety Regulation (GPSR) is a set of rules that requires consumer products to be safe and our obligations to ensure this.

If you have any concerns about our products, you can contact us on ProductSafety@springernature.com

In case Publisher is established outside the EU, the EU authorized representative is:

Springer Nature Customer Service Center GmbH
Europaplatz 3
69115 Heidelberg, Germany

Batch number: 10830943

Printed by Printforce, the Netherlands